TAGH

SWISS AVANT-G

Grand Prix d'Horlogerie de Genève

R-50-TN-AJ

www.brm-manufacture.com

Contents

010 DIABLO GT
Last of the mad, bad pre-Audi Lambos

022 CLASSIC LAMBOS
From sublime 350 GT to ridiculous LM002

032 DIABLO 6.0 VT
Audi's influence to the fore

038 MIURA TO MURCIE
Driving four generations of Sant'Agata's finest

064 MURCIELAGO ON ICE
The Murciélago has 4wd. So we put it to the test

074 GALLARDO
First sight – and first drive – of the V10 'baby'

084 GALLARDO SPYDER
Gallardo loses its head, but none of its appeal

092 MURCIELAGO LP640
The flagship gets some extra power and attitude

102 LAMBO v FERRARI
Gallardo Spyder takes on Ferrari's 430 Spider

112 LP640 ROADSTER
Big bad Murciélago gets the open-top treatment

116 SUPERLEGGERA!
Gallardo goes hardcore

128 MIURA 'JOTA'
Driving a recreation of the 'lost Miura'

142 LAMBO SUPERTEST
Which is the greatest Lamborghini of them all?

162 REVENTON
Murciélago meets Raptor fighter plane

180 MURCIELAGO SV
Our cover star and the rawest Murci of all

186 LP560-4 SPYDER
Latest Gallardo gets the Spyder treatment

194 ESPADA SIII
A rare drive in one of the marque's unsung heroes

200 SUPERCAR EVOLUTION
Miura and Murciélago bookend the supercar story

220 EVERY LAMBO
Details and specs for every production Lamborghini

DMS AUTOMOTIVE
UNLEASHING PERFORMANCE

DMS 997 TURBO
"IT'S EPIC, HILARIOUS AND ADDICTIVE IN EVERY GEAR,
YET DOCILE WHEN CRUISING"
EVO SEPTEMBER 2008

DMS SL55 AMG
"THIS CAR IS STUPENDOUSLY FAST"
PERFORMANCE CAR MAY 2008

DMS 535D
"FROM THE WORD GO, THE DMS 535D FELT AWESOME"
AUTO EXPRESS FEB 2008

DMS 997 TURBO
"MIGHTY IMPRESSIVE. SEAMLESSLY IMPROVES THE
TURBO'S BEST ASSET"
EVO MAY '07

DMS 535D
"LAUGH-OUT-LOUD FAST"
REVIEWED EVO JUNE 2005

DMS 330CD
"NEW ECU MAKES THE CAR SO MUCH FASTER YOU
SIMPLY HAVE TO HAVE IT!"
REVIEWED AUTOCAR OCTOBER 04

DMS 996 TURBO
"STUPENDOUS EXPLOITABLE PERFORMANCE"
REVIEWED EVO AUGUST 04

DMS 996 TURBO
"NOT ONLY IS THERE STAGGERING TORQUE,
THE POWER IS UTTERLY ADDICTIVE"
REVIEWED AUTOCAR JULY 2004

PORSCHE:
997 TURBO » 600+ BHP
996 TURBO / GT2 » 600+ BHP
997 CARRERA S PDK » 400+ BHP
997 CARRERA S » 376+ BHP
997 CARRERA » 348 BHP
997 CARRERA PDK » 368 BHP
997 GT3 UP » 436 BHP
996 GT3 UP » 400 BHP
996 3.6 » 344 BHP
BOXSTER 3.4S » 313+ BHP
CAYMAN S » 317 BHP
CAYENNE GTS » 440 BHP
CAYENNE TURBO 4.5 » 522 BHP
CAYENNE TURBO 4.8 » 578 BHP
CAYENNE TURBO S 4.8 » 600+ BHP

MERCEDES-BENZ:
SL65 AMG » 650 BHP & DE-LIMIT
AMG 55 KOMPRESSOR » 580+ BHP
AMG 55 FULL DE-LIMIT
C63 AMG » 530+ BHP & DE-LIMIT
SL63 AMG » 560+ BHP, DE-LIMIT
RE-MAP & LOWER ABC SUSPENSION
CL600 BI-TURBO » 580+ BHP
S500 2008 » 411+ BHP
SLK55 AMG » 389 BHP
SLK 350 » 328 BHP
200K » 205+ BHP
VIANO CDI V6 » 266 BHP
280 CDI V6 » 257 BHP
320 CDI V6 » 274 BHP
420 CDI V8 » 358 BHP

BMW:
BMW M5 V10 » 548 BHP 205 MPH
M3 E90/92 » 445 BHP + DE-LIMIT
M3 E46 » 370 BHP + DE-LIMIT
M3 CSL » 372 BHP + DE-LIMIT
335I » 370+ BHP + DE-LIMIT
650I » 398 BHP + DE-LIMIT
330D E90 » 276+ BHP
320D E90 » 209 BHP
330D E46 » 260+ BHP
320D E92 » 210 BHP
123D » 252 BHP
X5 3.0D » 278 BHP
X6 35I » 370+ BHP
X5 / X6 SD » 334 BHP
535D / 335D » 334 BHP

EXOTIC & MISC:
FERRARI 599 » 647 BHP
FERRARI 430 » 525 BHP
FERRARI 360 » 440+ BHP
GALLARDO » 546 BHP
GALLARDO LP560 » 600+ BHP
MASERATI GRANTURISMO &
QUATTROPORTE » 438 BHP
AUDI RS6 V10 » 680+BHP & DE-LIMIT
AUDI B7 RS4/ R8 » 439 BHP & DE-LIMIT
AUDI Q7 4.2 TDI » 387 BHP
AUDI A5 30TDI » 282 BHP
RANGE ROVER TDV8 » 326 BHP
R ROVER SPORT 4.2 SC » 450 BHP
R ROVER SPORT 2.7D » 232 BHP
BENTLEY CGT / F-SPUR » 620 BHP
BENTLEY GT SPEED » 670+ BHP

ALL OTHER CARS PLEASE CALL US

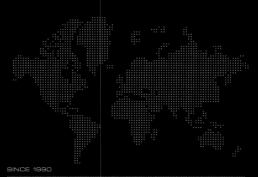

SINCE 1990

WORLDWIDE OFFICES AND INSTALLATION
UK » IRELAND » EUROPE » USA » ASIA » AUSTRALIA

+44 (0) 845 850 1845
SALES@DMSAUTOMOTIVE.COM
WWW.DMSAUTOMOTIVE.COM

Introduction

More than any other manufacturer, Lamborghini is synonymous with supercar. Its very first model, the 350 GT, combined a high-revving V12 with space-age looks. The Miura that followed was so impossibly low and beautiful that the word 'supercar' was actually coined for it. And in the early '70s the Countach set the mould for all that followed.

Fast forward almost 40 years and Lamborghini remains the world's pre-eminent supercar maker. The difference now is that whereas for so much of its history its finances teetered on the brink, now it has the benevolent arm of the Volkswagen Audi group wrapped around it.

This celebratory look back through the evo archives (with an occasional dip into the files of our sister magazine, *Octane*) begins with a visit to Sant'Agata just after Audi had taken control. As we drove the last of the old breed, the mad Diablo GT, we wondered whether the marque would be in safe hands. As the subsequent decade has shown, Lamborghini – and its many fans around the world – couldn't have hoped for a more supportive parent. Our cover car, the outrageous Murciélago LP670-4 SV, is ample proof of that. Enjoy!

Peter Tomalin, managing editor

MAGAZINE

www.evo.co.uk

EDITORIAL
Unit 5, Tower Court, Irchester Road,
Wollaston, Northants NN29 7PJ
020 7907 6310, email eds@evo.co.uk

Managing editor Peter Tomalin
Senior designer Adam Shorrock
Designers Chee-Chiu Lee, Neil Carey
Editorial director Harry Metcalfe

SUBSCRIPTIONS
0844 844 0039

ADVERTISING
30 Cleveland Street, London W1T 4JD
Email ads.evo@dennis.co.uk
Group advertising director Des Flynn
(020 7907 6742)
Advertising director Sarah Perks
(020 7907 6744)
Deputy advertising manager Tim Deeks
(020 7907 6773)

MANAGEMENT
Bookazine manager Dharmesh Mistry
Production director Robin Ryan
Digital production manager Nicky Baker
Director of advertising Julian Lloyd-Evans
Newstrade director Martin Belson
Publishing director Geoff Love
Chief operating officer Brett Reynolds
Group finance director Ian Leggett
Chief executive James Tye
Chairman Felix Dennis

MAG**BOOK**

MAGBOOK
The 'Magbook' brand is a trademark of Dennis Publishing Ltd. 30 Cleveland St, London W1T 4JD. Company registered in England. All material © Dennis Publishing Ltd, licensed by Felden 2009, and may not be reproduced in whole or part without the consent of the publishers.
Lamborghini Supercars ISBN 1-906372-90-X

LICENSING
To license this product, please contact Winnie Liesenfeld on +44 (0) 20 7907 6134 or email winnie_liesenfeld@dennis.co.uk

LIABILITY
While every care was taken during the production of this Magbook, the publishers cannot be held responsible for the accuracy of the information or any consequence arising from it. Dennis Publishing takes no responsibility for the companies advertising in this Magbook.
The paper used within this Magbook is produced from sustainable fibre, manufactured by mills with a valid chain of custody.

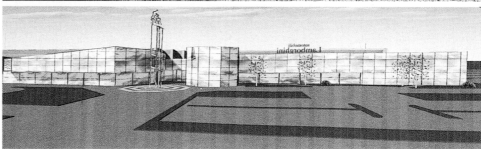

SYMPATHY FOR THE
DEVIL

The Diablo had carried Lamborghini's fortunes for a decade, but in 2000 the company had a new owner – Audi – with big plans for the marque. We performance-tested the ferocious Diablo GT and visited the factory to find out what lay in store

Heading across the flat Bolognese countryside to Lamborghini, it's always the distinctive roof of the factory you see first. As you close in, the roof's scallops look more like waves, with 'Lamborghini' spelled out in big yellow letters, riding the peaks. It's a sight that has greeted visitors since the early '60s, a constant while the company's fortunes have risen and fallen under a succession of owners. But things are changing at Sant'Agata.

Turning into the driveway, I spot the Diablo GT we've come to test, but it's not the most arresting sight – to the right is a row of neatly parked Audi saloons. It's just over a year since the German firm took a 100 per cent stake in Lamborghini. We're here to discover what effect the take-over is having, and to drive the GT, last of the pre-Audi supercars.

On the face of it, the two companies seem odd bedfellows. Lamborghini is a big name but a very small car maker. It builds a little over 200 cars per car – a tenth of the output of Ferrari. Total production since 1963 is just 8000 cars, and you don't have to be an economist to know that demand for supercars drops off whenever there's a recession.

Even the new president, Giuseppe Greco, an Italian lured away from his successful car

Below left: TV screen on console shows rear view, courtesy of videocamera mounted in aerofoil (below)

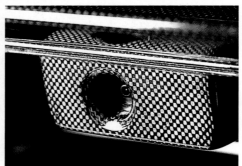

dealership in the US, isn't quite sure why Audi wants the little Italian company. Lamborghini has been starved of investment in recent years. To put that right – and produce a second, less expensive model to help provide stability – will cost many millions.

Audi is prepared to invest. It wants to make a Ferrari 360-sized junior-supercar and raise production to 600 units per year. It says it doesn't expect a return for the foreseeable future. This can't fail to warm the heart of any enthusiast – Lamborghini has found an owner that is willing and able to do what is required. Already there are signs of capital

'Even painted titanium grey, it fizzes with visual tension: wider front arches, gaping mouth and roof scoop'

injection: a fresh coat of yellow paint for the factory, new building works, new offices beside the production lines and, for the first time, a museum to show off Lamborghini's heritage.

Good signs, but the crucial question is how much influence will Audi bring to bear on the character and look of future Lamborghinis? A methodical, Germanic approach to some areas of the business will obviously be a positive thing, but no one makes supercars like the Italians. It's a rare art: the ability to turn raw emotion, drama and passion into metal.

One of Audi's first decisions on arriving was to halt the almost-complete Diablo replacement,

the 147. It has since been redesigned, though retaining the 147's running gear, and it is slated for production in early 2001. Will this new Audi-fied supercar be recognisable as a Lamborghini?

What *is* a Lamborghini? For the last decade or so that question has been easy to answer: a mid-engined V12 supercar called either Countach or Diablo. It's recorded that Lamborghini's engineers were a little disappointed that the Diablo didn't turn out to be as radical a replacement for the Countach as the Countach had been for the Miura. What did they have in mind? The wings, spoilers and wheelarch

extensions that the Countach grew to cope with ever greater power and ever wider tyres turned it from sublime, pure wedge into a visual riot. In the Diablo, those bumps and lumps were smoothed into a bigger shape, and it was aerodynamically stable enough that a rear wing the size of two snowboards wasn't necessary.

All the same, lots were ordered with it: the Diablo wasn't especially aggressive-looking, the then owner Chrysler being a restraining influence. Dynamically, the new car wasn't as polished as the final Countach, either. Only when the four-wheel-drive VT came along with power steering did it start to realise its

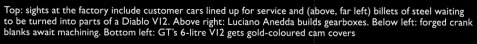

Top: sights at the factory include customer cars lined up for service and (above, far left) billets of steel waiting to be turned into parts of a Diablo V12. Above right: Luciano Anedda builds gearboxes. Below left: forged crank blanks await machining. Bottom left: GT's 6-litre V12 gets gold-coloured cam covers

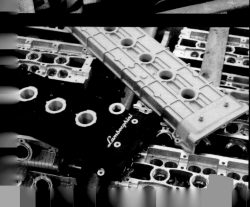

full potential; even 'real men' had to concede
that more manageable steering made it better
to drive. The stripped-out, rear-drive SV of '96
was another landmark model.

But I reckon it's the new Diablo GT that
comes closest to the vision of those engineers
as a fitting replacement for the Countach. Most
of its body is in lightweight carbonfibre, which
would have been a suitably radical material
in the late '80s. The super-light Countach
Evoluzione of 1987 (brainchild of one Horacio
Pagani) had pointed them in the direction of
carbon and impressed all who drove it.

However, the whole-tub approach, later
adopted by the McLaren F1 and most
recently by the Pagani (yes, him) Zonda, made
Lamborghini's bosses fearful. If damaged badly
enough, the entire shell would have had to
be replaced, and the ageing characteristics of
carbon weren't certain back then.

Supercars have longer production lives than
ordinary cars and once the Diablo die was
cast – tubular steel chassis, aluminium panels –
Lamborghini was committed to it for a decade.
Now in the last months of its life, the Diablo
appears to be something of a throwback. Ferrari
has returned to the front-engine, rear-drive
layout for its most potent car, and with excellent
results: the 550 Maranello is thrilling but also
wonderfully habitable. And yet…

The GT is a great argument for the mid-
engined supercar. It's also the Diablo at the top
of its game. Even painted titanium grey, its most
downbeat colour, it fizzes with visual tension:
wider front arches, gaping mouth and roof
scoop. Pop the scissor door open, snuggle down
into the Alcantara-trimmed bucket and you're
surrounded by glossy, exposed carbonfibre.
As ever, you feel you're at the pointy end of
a car designed to accommodate an enormous
engine first and everything else second. Check
the rear-view mirror and, er, there isn't one.
Glance over your shoulder and you see why: the
letterbox-sized slot that normally gives fleeting
glimpses of what's going on behind is full of the
engine's carbonfibre airbox, sitting on top of the
6-litre V12's F1 engine-style throttle trumpets.
A small camera in the rear wing relays pictures
to a navigation-style screen that pops out of the
centre console. It's over the top but that's what
the GT is all about.

A couple of tips for those of you still
pondering the specification of your GT: don't
have the air-bagged steering wheel because it
feels uncomfortably lumpen in your hands, and
go for the shortest of the three gear-sets offered,
because 186mph all-out is plenty and the
acceleration is, um, a bit nippier.

Turn the key and try to suppress the shiver
that tickles your spine. The V12 doesn't so
much as fire-up as erupt. This engine has been
around almost as long as Lamborghini, getting
more powerful (and cleaner) all the time. In the
GT it boasts 567bhp at an awesome 7300rpm
and a mammoth 465lb ft at 5500rpm. The revs
at which the peak outputs are made give you
a clue as to the nature of this engine. It sounds

'It's a rare art,
turning raw emotion,
drama and passion
into metal'

'Turn the key and try to suppress the shiver that tickles your spine'

Why did Audi buy Lamborghini? 'I'm not exactly sure,' says Dr Giuseppe Greco, with disarming honesty, then quickly adds: 'It was the last really available, properly alive company, not a dusty name. We [Lamborghini] are consistent with what Audi wants to project, at the forefront. We won't become more mellow.'

Why does he think he was chosen by Audi to be the new president of Automobili Lamborghini SpA? 'I've seen all aspects of the business, followed it from blank sheet to dealership,' he continues in his Americanised Italian accent. 'Also, whoever was chosen was required to be Italian, to get the message across that Lamborghini is not a province of the Audi empire.'

Greco has been in the industry for 30 years, starting as a graduate with Fiat, where he stayed for 25 years, rising to MD of one of its plants. He's also had short stints with Alfa and Ferrari. He gave up a multi-million dollar specialist car business in Corpus Christi, Texas, to take up the job.

The call came out of the blue from the then president, Vittorio Bi Capua, who'd been his boss at Fiat. 'It was a curved ball – I caught it quickly,' he smiles. His first job was to check the state of the company.

'Commercially, Lamborghini is not very strong but that has been taken care of. We are very strong in research and development and have some areas of excellence – carbonfibre, engine software. Technically we are getting even stronger; we're

'We'll be getting back to our roots, becoming more hardcore'

doubling R&D staff from 50 to over 100. We will borrow and adapt Audi technology.

'Previous owners weren't willing to invest and Lamborghini can't be run on creativity. Audi is good news for us – it's passionate about cars, has the money and isn't expecting a huge return in the foreseeable future. Previously, we were the lost patrol, heroic, with no one to talk to. For the first time we can go to our shareholders for advice. They may have made some mistakes that we can avoid.'

One of Audi's first decisions was to cancel the Diablo replacement, known as the 147 inside Sant'Agata and dubbed 'Canto' by the press. [Unsurprisingly, Greco brushes aside requests for a sight of anything to do with the project, though we spot a line of four Diablo-sized but not Diablo-shaped bodies shrouded in the factory.]

Reading between the lines, the Canto's outrageous air-scoops, which ballooned from its haunches like jet engine intakes, were not to Audi's taste. The design that has replaced it was 'born in Lamborghini, then Audi helped with the productionisation,' a process that Italian coachbuilder Bertone is continuing. 'It was almost complete when I came on board,' says Greco, describing the shape as 'very exciting, balanced, well proportioned'. A little too well proportioned? He said he's had some influence on it: 'It was Nicole Kidman; it needed to be turned into Sharon Stone, to be more controversial and aggressive. Lamborghinis should be controversial – we have to have people who hate Lamborghinis.'

Trying to guess Greco's taste in cars, I glance up at the portraits of the various Lamborghinis which line the walls of his office and ask him to name his favourite. He hesitates just for a second before pointing to a huge lithograph mounted behind his desk: 'The Miura.'

The Canto has bequeathed its chassis and drivetrain to the reshaped Diablo replacement. 'The 147's running gear is developed, so the car should be ready in 18 months,' says Greco. That means a 6 litre, 550bhp version of the evergreen V12 and

absurd (the notion, not the motor – that sounds utterly fantastic) but if Honda ever made such a thing as a VTEC six-litre V12, they'd find Lamborghini had beaten them to it. Except that no Honda engine would ever sound so organic, so animal, so guttural on its climb up the rev-band. At certain points there are resonances that make the whole car – and its occupants – tremble, and all the way there are hard metallic pulses and expanding and contracting howls from the tailpipes. In no time the GT is spearing up the road like a missile – and then the rev-counter needle hits 5.

KABOOM!

It's as if a nitrous oxide switch has been triggered. The GT thumps forward as though the rest was just a preamble, and the roar from over your shoulder takes on a menacing purpose that wills you to lift your foot if you've anything but a dead-straight quarter-mile ahead of you.

That's not to say the Diablo won't go around corners. Far from it. It summons up terrific grip but not even the wider tracks of the GT and the fat footprints of its Pirellis can defy physics. If you never took much interest in the subject when you were at school, don't panic, the GT is pretty friendly and communicative for a mid-engined monster. Just listen up and listen well to what it's telling you.

The steering is meaty and feelsome and lets you know that the front end is controlling only a small proportion of the Diablo's mass. The heavy rear and your right foot control the rest. Give it too much of the engine's enthusiasm

Testing the ultimate Diablo on the roads around Sant'Agata. Below: that mighty 6-litre V12

at the wrong time and you know it'll pivot around the front end faster than you can put on the opposite lock. Raw physics, see, and experienced without the aid of an electronic safety net. On the road, the margin offered is exploitable only by the most highly skilled, which is to say those who should know better.

At the track, the GT didn't quite achieve the acceleration times we'd hoped for. They might have been better had it not been so chilly and thus if the rear tyres had felt gummier but, hell, they're pretty good. Sixty in 4.1sec, 100 in 8.3 and 140 in 16.3. The first four gears are close and relatively short, fifth more long-legged, so in-gear punch in monumental; 100 to 120mph in fourth in 3.3sec and a TED (time exposed to danger) of 4sec dead. Backing this up, the brakes

probably a carbonfibre body like the Diablo GT.

And the new small Lamborghini? 'It's not going to be small, a 'baby Diablo' – that's the wrong way to think of it,' chides Greco. 'We want it to be the most powerful car in its group, to have more power than the Ferrari 360, more than 400bhp. This is significant. We also want it to feature a technological breakthrough.'

With the GT, Lamborghini was moving towards carbonfibre, but Audi's expertise is in aluminium, and four-wheel drive. How much Audi will be in the new car, and will costs be saved by borrowing heavily from the Audi group parts bins? Lamborghini won't develop its own switches if there are perfectly suitable Audi alternatives, says Greco, but they won't use Audi parts if they don't meet the engineering needs of the car. 'We need to be very careful, to more than simply *appear* to be pure Lamborghini. Our buyers are clever people, they don't want to be fooled – we have to deliver the goods.

'Ferrari now caters for an older age group. We're not going to make life difficult for them, but the form and function of our cars will appeal to people who like to be noticed. We have to make sure we *are* the niche, not going into a niche. We'll be getting back to our roots, becoming more hardcore. Let Ferrari do what they want – I don't want a moving target. We want our cars to have more horsepower and less weight, to be better value by delivering more technology at a lower price.'

PERFORMANCE

DIABLO GT

0–30	1.8
0–40	2.4
0–50	3.1
0–60	4.1
0–70	4.9
0–80	5.8
0–90	7.0
0–100	8.3
0–110	9.6
0–120	11.6
0–130	13.5
0–140	16.3
0–150	19.6
0–160	23.1

1/4 MILE

sec	11.6
mph	120

3rd/4th/5th GEAR

20–40	3.2/4.0/5.9
30–50	3.0/3.9/5.5
40–60	3.0/3.9/5.4
50–70	2.8/4.0/5.7
60–80	2.5/3.9/5.8
70–90	2.4/3.7/5.9
80–100	2.4/3.4/6.2
90–110	2.5/3.4/6.1
100–120	--/3.3/6.1
110–130	--/3.6/6.0
120–140	--/4.0/--

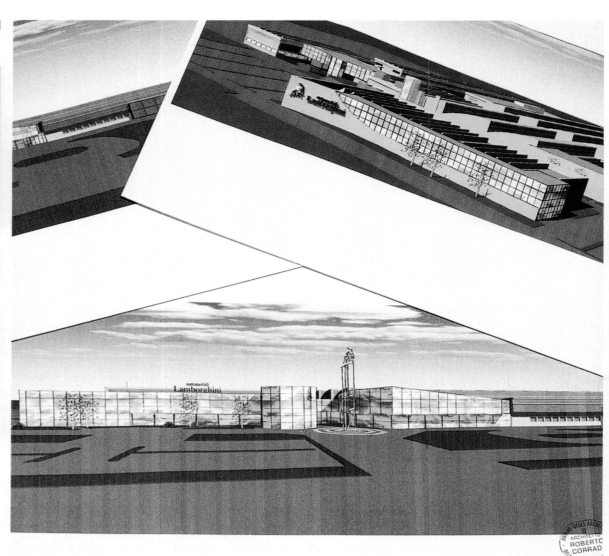

Right: plans for the impressive new frontage and, below right, new factory buildings already underway – outward signs of Audi's substantial investment

Specification

Engine	V12
Location	Mid, longitudinal
Displacement	5992cc
Cylinder head	dohc per bank, 4 valves per cyl, variable intake valve timing
Max power	567bhp @ 7300rpm
Max torque	465lb ft @ 4500rpm
Transmission	Five-speed manual, rear-wheel drive
Front suspension	Double wishbones, coil springs and electronic dampers, anti-roll bar
Rear suspension	Double wishbones, coil springs and electronic dampers, anti-roll bar
Steering	Rack-and-pinion, power-assisted
Brakes	Cross-drilled and ventilated discs ABS
Wheels	8.5 x 18in front, 13 x 18in rear, aluminium alloy
Tyres	245/35 ZR18 front, 335/30 ZR18 rear, Pirelli P Zero
Fuel tank	22gal/100 litres
Weight (kerb)	1490kg
Power to weight	386bhp/ton
0–60mph	4.1sec (claimed)
Top speed	200mph (est)
Basic price	£195,461 (2000)

evo RATING ★★★★★

are sensational, hauling the GT from 100mph to rest in just 4.4sec.

Is the mid-engined layout still a viable proposition? Perhaps only in the hands of Italians. There are, we hear, German Lamborghini owners who are concerned that Audi is now in charge. Their concern is ours: that future cars will be less passionate. To put up with the compromises in packaging, practicality and roadability, a mid-engined supercar has got to be spectacular in other areas, which the Diablo GT most certainly is.

Quite what the Audi-influenced Diablo replacement will look like is something we'll have to wait at least a year to find out.

Germany hasn't made a truly free-spirited supercar in recent history: BMW M1 – good but conservative; Porsche 959 – great but the antithesis of an Italian supercar; Mercedes-Benz CLK GTR – absurdly expensive (twice the price of the McLaren F1) and unattractive.

Audi will have much more control over the smaller Lamborghini, which is now in its embryonic stage. The company has, in the past, collaborated successfully with Porsche which is, of course, a master of making this sort of car. So perhaps we shouldn't read too much into Audi's work with a couple of other prestige names that

'The GT is a great argument for the mid-engined supercar'

have joined the VW group's portfolio in the last couple of years – Bugatti and Bentley. The concept Bugattis have been large and graceless while the mid-engined Bentley Hunaudieres proposed a new direction that the once-British firm can't ever have seriously considered.

Inside Sant'Agata, on the shop floor, the workers who put Lamborghinis together will doubtless take any changes in their stride. There are 310 employees, and since almost everything bar the engine and gearbox castings is made on site, they have a vast array of skills.

Many are long serving; veterans of two or three changes of ownership, and one, test driver Valentino Balboni, has been here for 31 years, almost since the very beginning.

'We are experiencing another big change – I think this is finally the good one,' he says. 'The company is recovering, employing a lot of young people with a lot of passion. There's a new feeling of organisation, mentality and culture: we've always been very flexible, now there are more rigid structures. I think Audi was surprised at our development potential, what we could achieve. Soon we will know what Audi thinks.'

His thoughts were echoed by Clara Simonini, who was once a hairdresser but always wanted to work at Lamborghini and currently puts V12s together. 'Things are good so far,' she says. 'People feel more confident, but everyone is waiting for the new car.'

The factory they work in was state-of-the-art in the '60s and is also set for a makeover, both inside and out. If it was in England, its landmark wave roof would probably have attracted a grade listing by now, but the old façade is set to be replaced with a cool, modern glass frontage.

Lamborghini is starting a new era. We hope that Audi holds its core values as dear as the engineers who shape them, the workers who build them and the customers that buy them.

BULL'S BLOOD

The Lamborghini bloodline began with a front-engined GT and includes some of the most extreme cars ever made

Words: Martin Buckley Pictures: Andy Morgan 023

The 350GT, and its front-engined successors, were the cars that Ferruccio Lamborghini built to suit himself. For this forty-something grey-templed tycoon, a bright yellow P400 simply didn't cut the right sort of dash, and he was rarely seen driving one. Il Cavaliere wanted something more grown-up, a mature supercar that gently raised eyebrows rather than slackened jaws as it went by: something with power and authority that could cut a swathe through traffic rather than stop it dead.

His engineering team, a bunch of frustrated young racing car designers, was eventually granted their mid-engined toy – the Miura – but Mr Lamborghini's first-born car had to be a daily business tool not a weekend trinket. Fast and glamorous certainly, but a smooth GT rather than a raw and aggressive exhibitionist's road racer.

In the rush to pay homage to the iconic Miura, Lamborghini's front-engined V12 cars, and its baby V8s, have been largely ignored. Cars that, in some respects, were the best the company ever made. And that's not just my opinion: Bob Wallace, the legendary factory development driver, has committed much the same thing to print.

Take the 350GT. Rarely was a first-time effort from a fledgling maker so technically well-rounded, a fact somewhat obscured by bug-eyed styling (by Touring) that never looked quite so effortlessly elegant as the contemporary Pininfarina-styled Ferraris. The roofline has a certain delicacy, but the squared-off rear arches look awkward and the corny pointed tail could have come off the drawing board of Gerry Anderson.

Yet this was one of the best road cars in the world, with proper race-car suspension (where Ferrari could only offer cart springs) the finest disc brakes money could buy and five speeds (where Enzo only had four) in a home-grown gearbox that even boasted synchromesh on reverse on later versions.

Its engine too, was unmatched – a four-cam V12 that blended top-end aggression with bottom-end docility like no other power unit in the world, pushing the alloy-skinned 350GT to a then sensational 155mph. And if the 350 isn't a great car to look at, then it is a wonderful car to be sat in, looking out. The slender pillars give you an almost uninterrupted 360 degrees of vision and the huge double-curvature screen sweeps well into the roofline, bathing the interior in light.

The dash, with its massive sideboard-clock dials, flick switch controls and gigantic offset Nardi wheel, is quaint. The seats are more embracing than they look. And what's that? Ah, a passenger grab handle, always a good sign. With the headlamp nacelles marking the boundary of the nose and following traffic unable to hide behind those pencil-thin pillars, this is a car that rapidly instills confidence.

Neither the clutch not steering are especially heavy and both have a silken feel to their actions that harmonises nicely with the clean, muscular pull of the engine – any revs, any gear. Once the gearbox oil is warm, you can punch the gearshift around its wide gate with wristy jabs, enjoying the power delivery that touches all exotic-car pleasure points – electric throttle response, expensive multi-cam stridency and the strong, inexorable pull of a giant electric motor that never knows when to stop. In everything but its low-geared steering and soggy brakes, the 350GT feels more '70s than '60s, striding over ripples and ridges and sweeping through curves with supple assurance.

It feels so together, so civilised, so easy to get the measure of – certainly much more so than Ferrari's 275GTB. By comparison, Ferruccio's 350 was faster, quieter, easier to drive and of higher quality. So much so, in fact, that Lamborghini is said to have lost $1000 on every one he sold.

The 350 begot the 4-litre 2+2 400 and this, in turn, sired the Islero of 1968. The Islero was the most self-effacing of Sant'Agata's front-engined cars; clean-cut and unpretentious. It was built by Marazzi, a group of employees from the defunct Touring coachbuilding factory, and was styled with a helping hand from Ferruccio himself.

The Islero is one of the most obscure Lamborghinis and one of my favourites: cool and low-key, a car for driving in your best suit,

How it all began: the 350GT, Lamborghini's first car, was also one of its best. Styling, by Touring, looks better from some angles than others, but it's undeniably exotic – and quite different from anything Ferrari was doing in the mid-'60s. It had one rear seat

350 GT

Layout	Front-engine, rear drive
Engine	V12, 3464cc, dohc
Max Power	320bhp @ 7000rpm
Transmission	Five-speed, manual
Weight	1200kg
Top speed	155mph
Years	1964-1966
Numbers Built	120

Styling details look fussy to modern eyes, but what was underneath made the 350GT truly great, including its 3.5-litre V12, forerunner of all the legendary Lamborghini V12s

'Rarely was a first-time effort from a fledgling maker so technically well-rounded'

Espada was Lamborghini's
ultimate GT – a full four-
seater with a 4-litre version
of the V12 under that
long, flat bonnet

Espada 400 GT

Layout	Front-engine, rear drive
Engine	V12, 3929cc, dohc
Max Power	325bhp @ 6500rpm
Transmission	Five-speed, manual
Weight	1480kg
Top speed	152mph
Years	1968-1978
Numbers Built	1217

Right: Espada's wonderful details are almost as
important as its extravagant shape – quad exhaust
tailpipes, numerous vents and ducts to get air into
and out of the engine bay, quad headlamps, and of
course a speedo reading to 300kph

'This was Ferruccio's 'Italian Rolls-Royce', a futuristic super-saloon'

donning wraparound drilled sunglasses and casting withering glances at drivers of lesser cars when they get in your way.

The 1968 Espada was cool too, but in a different way. This bold car took Lamborghini in a new direction, as a maker of big four-seater supercars. This was Ferruccio's 'Italian Rolls-Royce', a futuristic super-saloon that blended luxury car comforts with supercar urge and space-age Bertone styling. Some loved it, some hated it, but few were indifferent to the Espada, which had a production run second only to the Countach – a full ten years and 1200 cars.

Driving one now is a bit like piloting your own private Lear Jet, four first-class seats slung low between a massive transmission tunnel, looking out over a flat plateau of a bonnet that seems to fill the road, gutter to white line. The visual drama of the car is conveyed to the occupants as well as the onlookers. Arms stretched, legs splayed, the controls are equally matched in weight and feel and you put the Espada just where you want it, the car's tendency towards

run-wide understeer on long, fast sweepers soon fading into the neutral feel of something much smaller and lighter as you get more and more confident with the throttle.

You seem to be low-flying, not driving. There's a little road rumble, less wind noise and you appear to be pushed forward by an unseen force that treats every road with utter disdain. All you do is select the appropriate gear and squeeze the appropriate pedal, winding out the 4-litre V12 to 7 or even 8000rpm if you really want to get the sound effects flowing. It is fast, of course, but the supple ride is one of the 150mph Espada's most outstanding qualities and I love the cabin, a leather lounge that's as cool and stylised as the lair for some late-'60s Bond villain.

The early Espadas were best, the hexagonal theme of the instrument pod a throwback to the Marzal show car of '67, with its gullwing doors and silver seats. If, like me, you are a child of the '70s then you probably had a metallic pink Matchbox model of this car, Bertone's inspiration for the Espada which used half a

Miura engine (a 2-litre straight six, in other words) mounted behind the rear seats.

Like the Islero, the Jarama is another of Lamborghini's orphans. This brutal-looking 1970 coupe, based on the floorpan of the Espada, had all the power and poise of the previous front-engined cars but looks that not even its greatest admirers could call pretty: bullish, and broad-shouldered, yes – but never pretty. It was beset with quality problems and was to be the last front-engined car to emerge from Sant'Agata.

There was already a mood of expansionism in the air when the first Jaramas were being built, a desire to build a smaller, more affordable Lamborghini. A car that could take on the Dino and the 911 and give the factory greater volume – 1000-2000 cars a year was talked of but it would have to be both cheaper and easier to build than the V12 cars.

The result of this thinking was the 1970 Urraco, styled by Bertone. Here was a beautiful little car of which great things were expected,

Jalpa 350

Layout	Mid-engine, rear drive
Engine	V8, 3480cc, sohc
Max Power	255bhp @ 7000rpm
Transmission	Five-speed, manual
Weight	1510kg
Top speed	154mph
Years	1981-1991
Numbers Built	192

The bosses at Sant'Agata were convinced they could sell a smaller Lamborghini, and after the early-1970s Urraco and mid-'70s Silhouette came the Jalpa. Like its forebears, it had a mid-mounted V8, and an interior that could only have come from the '70s

but it turned out to be one of the tragedies of the Lamborghini story.

The design, codenamed P250, was besieged with problems – mostly relating to the all-new, sohc, belt-drive V8 engine and the strut suspension – and when it failed to meet production targets Lamborghini hit trouble, as it had invested heavily in the car's tooling. A four-cam, 3-litre version of the V8 appeared in 1974 and answered critics who said the Urraco wasn't fast enough, but by this time the fortunes of Lamborghini were in free-fall: Ferruccio had bailed out and Lamborghini's new Swiss owners were not showing the kind of strong leadership the company needed.

What's more, the competition was catching up, what with Maserati's cute little V6 Merak and the first of Ferrari's V8-engined baby cars, the 308GT4. When the GT4 was joined by the GTB in 1975, Lamborghini realised that it had to hit back with something more aggressive.

Enter, in 1976, the Silhouette – a more macho Urraco with fat, squared-off arches, telephone dial alloys, side scoops and a targa roof. Mechanically it shadowed the later Urraco with the 3-litre V8 sat sideways, ahead of the rear wheels and its five-speed gearbox mounted to the left of the engine in-line with the crank. The Urraco had featured tiny rear child-seats but, with the Silhouette, Lamborghini made no pretence that this was anything but a selfish two-seater.

It all looked very promising but it arrived at a time of more financial and managerial strife at Lamborghini and total production was just 52.

But the baby Lambo refused to die, and when the Mimram group injected cash into Sant'Agata in the early '80s it came back from the grave as the Jalpa, with a bigger 3.5-litre version of the V8, revamped suspension and bigger wheels. With 255bhp, Lamborghini reckoned the Jalpa was good for 160mph. Cosmetically it would be hard to tell the two apart, but the Jalpa had a new dash and a subtly different nose.

To drive, these were much better cars than they looked, among the sweetest of all Lamborghinis. Close sprint ratios and a fine spread of power make for a car that's as happy lugging as it is lunging for the redline, with a noise that's classic, full-fat, gold-top Italian. It's a fantastic engine this, smooth and cultured or raw and aggressive depending on your mood.

'To drive, these were much better than they
looked, among the sweetest of Lambos'

You savour the feel of the throttle – long in travel but wonderfully precise and progressive, and the Jalpa feels so strong and eager that you soon forget the downmarket interior with an instrument pack that looks like it was designed by Lego. Meanwhile it squeaks and rattles a bit over ripples and ridges, suggesting that the metal Bertone removed when it created the targa roof hasn't left the shell entirely rigid.

The clutch is firm and short in travel and the gearshift moves around its six-fingered gate with hefty, metallic precision, rewarding decisive, meaty inputs. The steering is more alert than the low gearing suggests, but if it lacks the ultimate feedback you'll find in a 911 then you couldn't argue with the traction: bury the throttle anywhere you like in a corner and the back end just squats down and bites, chunky P7s keying into the Tarmac as you begin to square everything up for the exit.

Although the Jalpa soldiered on until 1991, the market for the car was never really there in the face of Ferrari and Porsche opposition and only 192 were built. Few in the market for a middle-weight supercar were willing to take a gamble on a company whose fortunes were so

> ## 'Lamborghini won't build any more big, cultured front-engine GTs like the Espada'

touch and go. Buyers figured that, if they were going to have a Lambo, they might as well go the whole hog and have a Countach.

Lamborghini knows where its market is now. Under the new Audi regime there is a new Diablo replacement in the pipeline and, in the longer term, a smaller car to take on the 360 Modena. Something more raw, more aggressive, a bit less 'golf club'.

It won't build any more big, cultured front-engined GTs like the 350GT or the Espada – that's best left to the likes of BMW and Mercedes – sticking instead to the mad, bad, politically incorrect dinosaurs we know and love, cars personified by the Countach and the Diablo. Like them or not, it is these big-gun mid-engined machines that have built the mythology of Lamborghini and, for three decades, kept the company afloat as it bounced from crisis to crisis.

But it would be wrong to forget the other Lamborghinis. They represent the vision and ambition of the company's founder, they include some seriously underrated drivers' cars, and they continue to fire our imaginations. There's nothing quite like an Espada, or an LM002…

LAMBORGHINI LM002
HARRY METCALFE HITCHES THE RIDE OF HIS LIFE IN THE ULTIMATE 4WD

It must have been some lunch when the idea of this Countach-engined off-roader was hatched. Logic has no place here – the LM002 was designed primarily for military use, though the cost implications must have caused a few army generals to shuffle off and buy Land Rovers after all. Mind you, the LM was almost sensible compared with the original version, the Cheetah, with its rear-mounted Chrysler V8 and three-speed auto. This format was soon dropped when the disastrous handling became apparent (think early 911 on cross-plies) but not before the off-roader had soaked up the money which was supposed to build the M1 supercar that Lamborghini had developed for BMW.

To get a real feel for the LM002, I sit in with Valentino Balboni, Lamborghini's legendary test driver. 'We started again from scratch with this car,' he says. 'It was very different from what we had done before. I enjoyed developing it very much.' All the time he's talking he's making the car do unspeakable things. We're flying past a convoy of at least five trucks interspersed with cars whose drivers get the shock of their lives as the bow-wave of almost three tons of Lamborghini's finest beef blows them, almost literally, into the weeds.

Valentino uses plenty of revs, never dipping much below 5000rpm, regularly soaring past 7000, settling to a cruising speed of around 110mph on this equivalent of a British B-road. Some sharp-ish corners came into view and – oh, Lord – he's going to show me how to power-slide the beast. These are 70-80mph bends, not namby-pamby second-gear corners that you or I might have a go at. The LM002 stands on its nose as he sheds 40mph, he snicks it down a gear, the power is back on and immediately the rear gives up the fight as 450bhp makes a mockery of the 345/60VR17 Pirellis.

He's got an armful-and-a-bit of opposite lock applied, which is brave – I've driven this 'car' and there are no messages to be had at the wheel; it's seat-of-the-pants stuff. The car lurches straight again. What the drivers coming in the opposite direction must make of this, I can only guess. Even around the Lamborghini factory, it can't be an everyday sight.

When you start looking under the skin of the beast it soon becomes clear that the roll-centre is somewhat higher than ideal. Massive ground clearance was the priority of course, so the enormous V12 sits way above the front diff, hence the 4ft-high bonnet. The LM002 is normally rear-wheel drive but slide a lever on the side of the enormously wide centre console and all four wheels are driven. Another level puts it in a low ratio.

In fact, off-road is where this thing belongs. It's very good here, in a bull elephant sort of way. On-road is a different matter. It takes our line 'The thrill of driving' and turns it into 'The worry of driving'. The thought of filling the 230-litre tank which empties at the rate of 6-8mpg only adds to the stress. The LM002 is one Lamborghini where it's best to remain a 'tifosi' rather than an owner.

LM002

Layout	Front-engine, rear drive
Engine	V12, 5167cc, dohc
Max Power	450bhp @ 6800rpm
Transmission	Five-speed, manual
Weight	2700kg
Top speed	130mph
Years	1986-1989
Numbers Built	230

LM002 used virtually the same 5.2-litre 48-valve V12 as the Countach Quattrovalvole, then the world's fastest production car. LM002 is as massive as it looks – 8in wider than a Range Rover. Owners included Keke Rosberg and Gerhard Berger

'It soon becomes clear that the roll centre is somewhat higher than ideal…'

Max Jaffa

In 1999 the Diablo underwent the most extensive revisions in its history. David Vivian found the 6-litre VT the best ever

What you see here is the first official Lambaudi, Y2K 6-litre Diablo. On paper, a Lamborghini made-over by Audi sounds roughly as appetising as Cheesypeas. Italy's raunchiest hardcore supercar meets Teuton uber-yuppie understatement. Raw testosterone is assimilated by cool-touch techno-sheen. Passion dies in the chilly embrace of the Piech collective.

But you have to understand one thing. VW Group boss Ferdinand Piech loves this car. He counts Lambo among his proudest acquisitions. He is frequently spotted wearing a discreet charging bull lapel badge at business meetings and social functions. And he's more than happy to muck in as a development driver.

Perhaps it's because the supercars from Sant'Agata provide such a pungent contrast to his own Porsche-based car making roots. Perhaps he wants as much light and shade, as much tone and texture as possible in the VW Group's portfolio. Perhaps he's just a good old fashioned petrolhead who's supercar crazy. Whatever, he has instructed Audi to take the kid glove approach; the Diablo's heart and soul are immutable – minimal interference. The bits that have previously made it less than easy to live with, though, are another matter. Audi does some of the best car interiors in the world; the Diablo's – for all its architectural drama – was one of the least disciplined. A simple case of the complaint finds the cure.

Another thing. The Diablo, especially in GT form, had started to acquire some of the excesses that afflicted its predecessor, the Countach, in the latter stages of its evolution: scoops, ducts, macho appendages, aesthetic incongruities. For the Diablo 6.0 they're all gone. The elaboration has been skinned back. What's left is the purest, most elegant and, frankly, chin-dribblingly gorgeous Diablo shape of all, further massaged by Audi – and possibly the most beautiful set of alloy wheels ever – to purify the extraordinary dynamic and grace of Marcello Gandini's original design. Most

DIABLO 6.0 VT

obvious are the changes at the front where the softer shape of the bumper now incorporates air intakes for the brakes as well as new clear-lens headlamps and indicators. Beneath the skin, the chassis has been reinforced with carbon inserts to increase the torsional rigidity of the body structure.

Gone too, except for the US market, is rear-wheel drive. The new Diablo 6.0 is VT viscous-coupled four-wheel drive only; in America, the old rear-drive powertrain lives on in the roadster as a separate model. Sunset Boulevard wouldn't be the same without it.

'It's an image thing,' shrugs Lamborghini's director of communications, Alberto Armaroli, as we while away the time until we have access to *Quattroruote* magazine's very own test track at Viarano just outside Milan in the leaner, meaner 6.0 VT. 'On the West Coast they aren't concerned about driving fast, just looking good.' Armaroli gestures towards the Lambo being given its final checks by a posse of mechanics in the garage. 'This, however, is about driving fast…'

This is the new Diablo. Alert orange paintwork. Five-fifty horsepower (up 20), carbon body, aluminium roof and doors, engine pushed 285cc to 5992cc, torque toughened up from 450 to 457lb ft, wider front and rear tracks (by 60 and 30mm respectively), uprated ABS, reduced back-pressure exhaust system, tweaked suspension and damping, completely redesigned cabin. The biggest package of changes in the Diablo's life.

As before, the margin by which this big-boned, mid-engined V12 supercar exceeds 200mph is academic. Somewhere between 5 and 10mph seems reasonable. Double-ton capability makes it unique anyway. The claimed 0-100kmh (62mph) of 3.9secs is more readily challenged (new 911 Turbo, Esprit Sport 350, TVR Cerbera) but, in a flat sprint to 150mph, the new Diablo, like the GT before it, is out on its own. Post-Macca F1, this is the fastest car you can buy. But that, of course, will count for little if it isn't still the most thrilling.

The Audi input is easy to identify by sight and touch. Just hoist up the driver's door. The cabin is awash with blue-tinged carbonfibre cladding that usually sees service in the Audi S6. And, just as in the Audi, the dark, high-tech ambience of the carbon is offset by gleaming aluminium: most prominently the gearstick and its open-slot gate. Truly ergonomic switchgear placement simply isn't possible given that most of the available surface area is on that pommel-horse of a transmission tunnel, but the buttons themselves ooze Audi tactility and precision. Ferrari's mostly Fiat-sourced switchgear for the 550 Maranello suddenly looks and feels cheap by comparison.

The huge crescent sweep of the instrument binnacle with its seven alloy-bezelled dials is equally impressive. That you can actually read most of them through the upper portion of the small, flat-bottom steering wheel is almost unprecedented. How many is partly dependent on wheel height – the column adjusts for both reach and height (once you get past the ridiculously stiff, over-centre latching mechanism) which helps in fixing up a comfortable driving position.

This is now more achievable because the driver's seat has been moved towards the centre axis of the car to reduce the wheel and pedal offset and distance your bonce from the A pillar. There are longer seat runners, too, and decent lumbar and rake adjustment for the all-new leather seats.

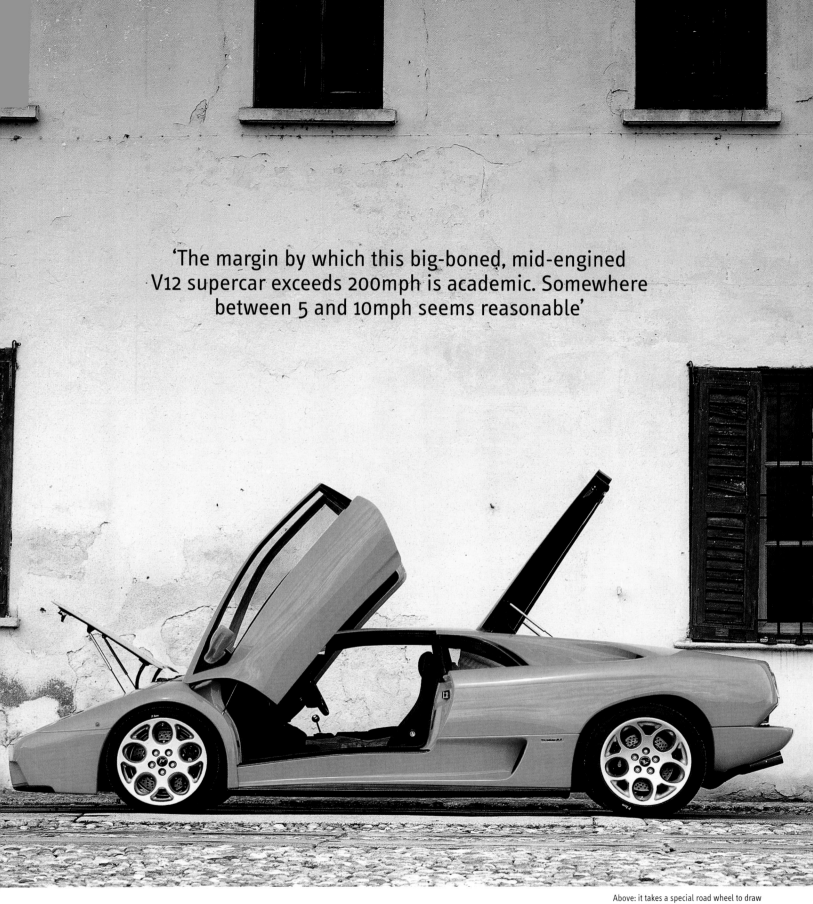

'The margin by which this big-boned, mid-engined V12 supercar exceeds 200mph is academic. Somewhere between 5 and 10mph seems reasonable'

Above: it takes a special road wheel to draw your eyes from the Diablo's plunging lines. A reminder of the Countach's 'telephone dial' alloys perhaps? Opposite: V12 expanded to 6 litres; power is slightly down on limited-edition GT, but 550bhp isn't too shabby. Cabin is transformed – that's the Audi effect

DIABLO 6.0 VT

Airbags for driver and passenger are standard and the wiper has been redesigned to improve visibility at high speed.

Not much chance of that at Viarano today. The 2.5km circuit's twists are appropriately devilish but there isn't much of a straight to speak off. Certainly nothing long enough to get a handle on what a 6-litre V12 with titanium con-rods, a lighter crankshaft and 550bhp might ultimately be capable of. Fortunately there are other things to consider. The new 32-bit management system is claimed to improve driveability at low speed and the latest exhaust noise control system (ENCS) has been designed to keep the lid on the Diablo's considerable potential for volume without compromising performance.

And, come my 2pm track slot, it starts to rain – a test for the wider track, recalibrated suspension and VT four-wheel drive if not the high-speed water clearing capacity of the single wiper. In fact, the wiper isn't much good at moderate speeds; it leaves a border that obscures your view in acute left-handers and there are plenty of those at Viarano. But it hardly matters because the car handles so beautifully. Yes, it understeers in tighter turns and, yes, the tail will flick out if you kill the power on the edge in faster sweeps. Yet the feel and collectability of it all borders on the astonishing when you consider what an exacting and unforgiving animal the GT was. Between the extremes there's a broad band of behaviour that rewards commitment and flatters mistakes. And, with all that grunt in the wet, perhaps you wouldn't want it any other way. On a greasy, twisty little circuit more suited to an MR2 than the world's most ferocious supercar, the Diablo is anything but a handful. I'm amazed.

It even pootles like a Fiesta; no transmission snatch, no induction coughs or sneezes. Fine gearchange, too. And it isn't very noisy – not by Diablo standards. Almost hate to say this, but your granny could drive it. Has Audi slugged the Diablo's savagery after all, then? Maybe some. But when a car looks as good and goes so hard and sounds as special as the Diablo, a little behaviour coaching probably doesn't count as major reform. We'll have to wait for a sunny day in the mountains to know if Audi really is the best thing that's ever happened to the Diablo. ∎

>> specification
Lamborghini Diablo

Engine	V12, mid-mounted, longitudinal, 5992cc
Cylinder block	Aluminium
Cylinder heads	Aluminium alloy, twin cams per bank, 4 valves per cylinder
Fuel and ignition	Lamborghini multi-point fuel injection and electronic ignition
Max power	550bhp @ 7100rpm
Max torque	457lb ft @ 5500rpm
Transmission	Five-speed manual, four-wheel drive
Suspension	Double wishbones, coil springs, electronic dampers, anti-roll bar front and rear
Steering	Rack and pinion, power-assisted
Brakes	Ventilated, cross-drilled discs, front and rear, ABS
Wheels	8.5x18in front, 13x18 rear, alloy
Tyres	235/35 ZR18 front, 335/30 ZR18 rear
Power to weight	314bhp/ton
0-62mph	3.9secs (claimed)
Top speed	200mph-plus
Price	£155,000

>> **EVO** Rating ★★★★★

Above: new nose features clear light lenses and bigger air intakes. Opposite page: shape of VT is the cleanest since the Diablo was launched ten years ago; gone are the macho spoilers and roof-scoops. Interior features a compelling mix of carbonfibre and gleaming aluminium

FAB FOUR

To mark the launch of the Murciélago in 2001, we brought together four generations of Lamborghini supercars

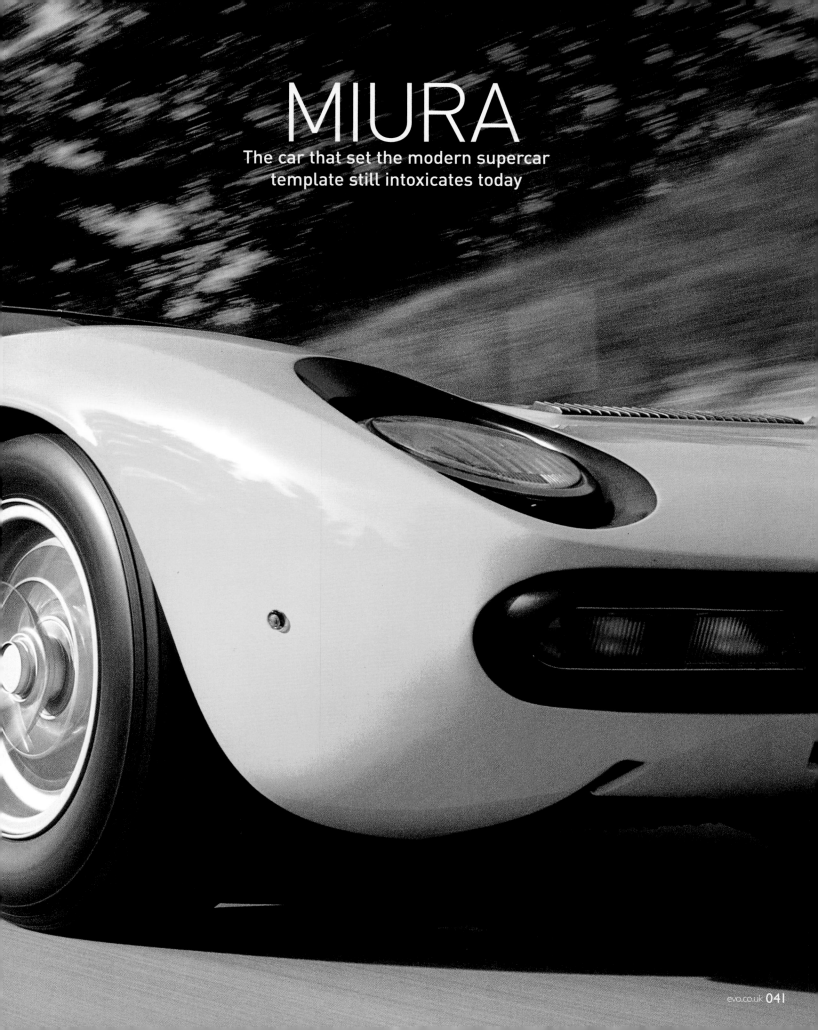

MIURA

The car that set the modern supercar
template still intoxicates today

Miura. Not Lamborghini's first car, but without doubt the model that shot the Sant' Agata concern into the supercar stratosphere. Forefather of the Countach, Diablo and Murciélago, the Miura still epitomises all that's great about Lamborghini, nearly 30 years after it went out of production.

In short it is the reason I'm here, at 9am sharp on a bright October morning, anxiously sipping a cappuccino in the Lamborghini staff canteen. My anxiety is well founded: Lamborghini's reputation as a masterful supercar maker is matched by its equally notorious talent for keeping journalists waiting for cars. It's nothing personal you understand, just the way things are.

True to form, after 15 minutes or so a mildly flustered PR man arrives to confirm that we really *do* want a Miura for Mr Meaden and a Countach for Mr Bovingdon, along with the services of test drivers Valentino Balboni and Moreno Conti, if you'd be so kind.

In time-honoured fashion he announces that the cars will be ready in ten minutes and we slump into our seats, taking long slugs of coffee in readiness for a much longer wait.

In the end I'm not sure what stuns us more: the distant sight of a bright yellow Miura SV being fitted with its *prova* plate, or the fact that it has appeared within ten British minutes, rather than ten Italian ones – which often last several hours.

However long the wait, very little prepares you for seeing a Miura up close. It's so low, so small and so incredibly, aggressively beautiful that it simply defies description. As a motoring writer this is, frankly, a bit of a bummer.

Undeterred, photographer Shepherd and I mill around it oohing and ahhing like schoolboys, looking but not daring to touch, as though we'll get told off for leaving fingerprints on something so precious. It strikes me that I'll stand a better chance of thinking up something profound once I've managed to roll up my tongue and put it back in my mouth. Fat chance.

Valentino waits patiently for us to regain our composure before politely suggesting that we get going. I've already bagged the Miura's passenger seat, ruthlessly relegating photographer Dave Shepherd and fellow scribbler Martin Buckley (he's driving a Diablo tomorrow) to our Renault Megane rental car. Life's a bitch and all that.

Getting into a Miura is much more straight-

forward than with its scissor-doored descendants. The low, narrow sill is easily negotiated and you fall naturally into the steeply reclined, fixed-back seat. Once inside you notice how tight the packaging is, and how the transverse-mounted V12 all but touches the glass partition that

'These fabulous roads could have been made for the Miura'

separates the open, airy cockpit from the claustrophobic engine bay.

Clunky but cool-looking rocker switches in a roof-mounted pod and an exposed metal gearshift gate set the Seventies supercar tone. Around us the Bertone bodywork shrink-wraps the chassis as if made from lycra, those magnificent curves rolling and merging into one another like well-toned muscle. Only one word comes close to describing the Miura's stance and proportions: perfection.

Valentino slips behind the wheel, fires the 4-litre, 385bhp V12 into life, slots first and drives smoothly through the Sant' Agata suburbs.

A lifetime spent behind the wheel of cars like the Miura and Countach, not to mention the Diablo and Murciélago, means he's immediately in the groove. This has to be the ultimate introduction to this most exotic of supercars, safe in the knowledge that my turn behind the wheel will come soon enough. Time then to sit back, relax, and discover what Lamborghini's most famous employee thinks of the Miura SV.

'The Miura is my first love. It was the first car Bob Wallace [Lamborghini's legendary development driver and Balboni's tutor] allowed me to road-test on my own. It was early 1973, and the car was a black Miura SV built for the Innocenti family. I left the factory early and headed for the Ferrara-Padova autostrada, a quiet stretch with little traffic to make sure I had the best time in the car.'

It's a romantic image. Watery sunshine, diffused though the wintry mist that clings to the Emilian plains at that time of year. Balboni, on his first solo drive, painfully conscious of the trust and

faith put in him, bursting with excitement and apprehension as he gently strokes the black SV towards the autostrada. A quick check of the temperatures, a glance in the mirror and then down the slip road onto the ribbon of pale concrete. So how fast did the young Balboni go?

'Ah, not more than 220km/h or so, I think', he smiles, 'but remember, I was a young guy on my own in a Miura for the first time. It was such a special moment the speed was not important. Even now it is a special feeling to drive one. A special car. So very special…'

And with that, the normally animated Balboni falls silent for a brief but poignant moment, his

'One word describes the Miura's
stance and proportions:
perfection'

Time hasn't dimmed the
beauty of the Miura's lithe,
sinuous Bertone body.
Interior (below, left) a typical
piece of '70s design but kind of
cool with it. Detailing (below)
including side vents and
wheels is perfectly executed.
Get 7000rpm on that rev-
counter and the SV flies

mind swimming in the memories brought flooding back by this most special of supercars. It's a happy coincidence that this is my first time in a Miura, and the serendipity isn't lost on either of us. For a few kilometres we sit in silence as the characteristic transmission whine and busy V12 chatter flow around us like warm water. Judging by the smiles creasing our faces, the Miura can still work its magic.

Our destination is the Umbria-Tuscany border, where the Futa and Raticosa passes writhe their way over the Apennine mountains. After the busy monotony of the motorway, these fabulous roads could have been made for the Miura. Better still, it's now my turn to drive the machine that changed the face of supercar design forever.

The driving position isn't perfect, but it's far from the impossibly awkward affair I expected. The steering wheel could do with being a little more upright to counter the laid-back seat, but the pedals don't demand too much leg splaying nor does the clutch need a steely calf muscle. There's plenty of weight to the controls, sure, but the Miura is a surprisingly delicate machine that demands deft rather than heft.

The most striking thing about the Miura is its throttle response. With four big Weber carburettors feeding the V12, each prod of the throttle brings the kind of clean, instantaneous response you simply don't get with a modern engine. There's plenty of grunt from low revs, but the way the power builds and builds as the revs rise feels unusually pure. No clever electronic massaging of the power and torque curves here. Drive it like a modern car and the motor coughs its displeasure. You soon learn to s-q-u-e-e-z-e the throttle from low revs rather than simply flooring it. That way you can feel when it's ready for maximum fuelling, feed it accordingly and delight as the engine comes to life, delivering the most organic, enthralling 385bhp you will ever experience.

The noise is busier than a Diablo's V12, but the origins of that thunderous voice are clearly audible whenever you tread the Miura's throttle. What it loses in big-capacity bass it gains in the brittle snap, crackle and pop of the overrun.

It's not just about a satisfying soundtrack, however, because the SV still cuts it in sheer performance terms. Use 7000rpm in the first three gears and it's still genuinely quick. We don't have the chance nor the inclination to push towards the outer limits of the SV's straight-line ability, but it feels as capable of hitting 170mph as a modern 911 Carrera. Whether its front wheels would be on the ground at the time is something we'd probably rather not consider.

On the sinuous Futa and Raticosa roads, the Miura feels supple and all of a piece. The balance is surprisingly neutral – more forgiving than a Ferrari Boxer and without the pendulous feel of a Diablo. As a result you have more confidence to push harder and later into the corners. That's just as well because the lack of stopping power means you sometimes arrive at your turn-in point a bit faster than you intended. The steering isn't super quick, so you need to feed in a bit more lock than perhaps you might expect, but the net result is a car that flows cleanly from curve to curve in a manner not dissimilar to an E30 M3. Despite all this it's slightly depressing to discover that a Renault Mégane (albeit a mercilessly driven hire car) can

Miura's glorious 4-litre V12 (top) still sounds superb, snorting air through four big Weber carburettors which give it throttle response to shame more modern machines. The SV (above) can still show most cars a clean pair of heels on the straights. Along twisty roads the car flows from turn to turn, especially with legendary Lambo test driver Valentino at the wheel

keep pace with it on these twisty roads. That's three decades of progress, I suppose.

Fittingly, it's Valentino who restores the Miura's honour on a 60-mile dash back to the factory. I'm in the 'chase car' now, and in a virtuoso demonstration of point-blank overtaking and extensive use of the SV's peak power he comprehensively blows us away. The sight and sound of Lamborghini's finest powering into the distance, stabs of flame popping from the exhausts, is a memory I will cherish forever. And one from which I suspect a certain Mégane rental car will never fully recover.

Specification

LAMBORGHINI Miura SV

○ Engine	V12, mid, transverse
○ Displacement	3929cc
○ Cylinder head	Aluminium alloy, dohc per bank, two valves per cyl
○ Fuel and ignition	Four Weber 40 IDL carburettors, two coils and two distributors
● Max power	385bhp @ 7850rpm
● Max torque	295lb ft @ 5750rpm
○ Transmission	Five-speed manual, rear drive
○ Weight	1245kg
● Power to weight	314bhp/ton
○ 0-60mph	6.0sec
○ Top speed	175mph

COUNTACH

Nothing can match a Countach for sheer drama. We drive the very last of the line

f you could travel back in time, where would you go? Maybe the late-'50s, to watch Fangio conquering the 'Ring in '57 or see Moss dicing with death on the glorious Mille Miglia. Or maybe 1966 to witness England winning the World Cup. You can probably think of a dozen more. And even though you know it isn't possible, I bet you occasionally look at black and white images of heroic drivers drifting impossibly unwieldy machines inches from buildings, armco and massive crowds and try to imagine what it must have been like to be there.

I bet 1990 doesn't figure on your fantasy time-travel wish list. It certainly didn't on mine, but I can assure you that it's well worth the visit. The term 'politically correct' didn't exist, abysmal '80s haircuts were a distant memory and the ultimate supercar was coming to the end of its production life. Never a shrinking violet, the Lamborghini Countach grew old disgracefully and went out with a suitably flame-spitting bang.

By 1990 the Countach's image was as much a caricature as the various scoops, spoilers and ducts that adorned its stunning lines. Everyone agreed that it was a pig to drive and impossible to see out of – even those who'd never clapped eyes on one. It was seen as an embarrassing relic of the '70s and '80s; painfully flamboyant in a time of recession, brutally fast but essentially unusable, and way, way past its sell-by date. Even now the Countach is much maligned by those who proclaim to be in the know.

The Anniversary model was the swan song for the Countach. It shared all the mechanicals of the qv but ditched the rear spoiler and added

'Throttle response
is electric and the
power just keeps
on coming'

huge air intakes over the engine. The profile was meant to be 'cleaner', in homage to the pure design of the original and much lauded LP400. The Anniversary went on sale in 1988, 25 years after Ferruccio Lamborghini launched his first car. Production ended on May 7, 1990.

The last Countach ever produced remains at Sant' Agata. Between appearances in the factory museum it's been trundled around the building at walking pace. In the 11 years since it was built it has covered a grand total of 130km. That was until **evo** decided to revisit the legendary mid-engined Lamborghinis…

We've come to Sant' Agata to discover what lies behind the hype. Are these cars actually any good to drive, and how do they compare to modern supercars? The bottom line is, would we have raved about them if **evo** had been around back then? We are about to find out. The completely original, ultra-low-mileage, last-of-the-line Countach is about to get the first meaningful drive of its otherwise quiet life.

Purists always bemoan the Countach's evolution from stunning minimalism to '80s

excess. Poring over the first LP400 in the Lamborghini museum, I can sympathise with them. Lithe, focussed and wonderfully chiselled, the LP400 is the RS of the Countach family.

Weighing only 1100kg and producing a claimed 375bhp from its 3929cc four-cam V12, the original doesn't lose much in the way of performance either. But when test driver Moreno Conti sweeps round in front of the factory in 'my' Countach it's clear that this model beats the LP400 hands-down in at least one respect: for sheer road presence the brutal and faintly ridiculous Anniversary has no rivals.

A Diablo seems insipid by comparison. As a kid I remember clutching magazines with bewinged Countachs on their covers. Pitted against the Ferrari Testarossa there was never any contest, for me at least. Angry, fiercely functional and downright intimidating, it's what supercars are supposed to be about.

Clambering over the wide sill, the time-warp feeling re-emerges. There's not a single curve to be found. The instrument binnacle looks like a hide-covered shoebox, the huge transmission

tunnel dominates the cabin and the dull grey leather is unpleasantly oppressive. Of-its-time is probably the politest way to describe it. Despite this, the 320kph speedo and a rev counter marked to 9000rpm give a hint that the performance is going to be timeless.

Pump the accelerator, twist the key and six cylinders splutter into life. Another prod on the power and the full orchestra wakes up. I laugh at the thought of piloting this 185mph museum piece, whilst Moreno just smiles quietly. It's going to be a special day.

The Countach is pretty claustrophobic at the best of times but the Anniversary's electric seats rob the cabin of what little headroom it had in the first place. Sitting on top of the various motors controlling the seats – which still work perfectly – I almost have to tilt my head to get comfortable. At least the pedals aren't as severely offset as legend has it. Moreno says the optional racing items were far better. Still, I'm not going to let anything spoil this experience.

The metal-gated gearlever is perfectly positioned and runs straight into the 'box below;

the Countach gearbox is mounted ahead of the engine, which means no complicated linkages to diminish feel or impair accuracy. Even so, it's not a delicate movement and you'll need all your strength to engage gears cleanly. Yet if you're forceful without rushing, the change is fantastically rewarding – and gives you access to one of the greatest engines in the world.

Despite having its origins in the 350GT of 1964, Lamborghini's V12 is still spectacular. With the introduction of the Countach qv in 1985, capacity grew to 5167cc and power was up to a dizzying 455bhp at 7000rpm. And despite this car's lack of use, I can feel every one of them kicking and screaming behind me.

Every aspect of driving the Countach requires full attention and maximum effort. The clutch needs a hefty shove – though it engages cleanly near the top of its travel – the unassisted steering is horrendously heavy at parking speeds and visibility is always an issue. And yet town driving is not the nightmare you might expect. The suspension takes the edge off all but the worst surfaces whilst the engine is happy to potter along on small throttle openings. And if you need to reverse simply open the door, perch on the sill and try to look cool. Believe me, you'll feel it. But the Countach isn't designed for traffic jams. Fast, wide, sweeping roads are this car's natural habitat and Moreno knows just the place to exercise that ever-willing engine.

When I finally get the chance to hit the throttle stop, the results are astonishing. With anything over 3000rpm dialled-up, the Countach simply flies. Throttle response is electric and as the revs rise the power just keeps on coming. Such is the acceleration and the mechanical pandemonium gnashing and snarling behind

you, it takes grim determination to ring out every last rev in second, third and into fourth. In the right conditions this car could live with anything. Before you catch your breath, 200 clicks come and go, proving that time hasn't diminished the impact of the Anniversary's storming performance.

Moreno grins as I gain the confidence to push a little harder and brake deeper into the bends. He says the Countach will do 300kph (185mph), but the look on his face suggests you wouldn't want to confirm it. Apparently at that sort of speed it will change lanes of its own accord with the merest hint of cross-wind. Moreno wipes his brow and feigns relief – the sign of a man who has maxed a Countach and lived to tell the tale.

If top-drawer performance was expected, the chassis is a real surprise. Through fast bends the Countach is utterly stable and never deflected off line. The steering feel is excellent, although when cornering forces build up you'll need all your strength to kiss an apex. At first this can

fool you into thinking that it's not eager to change direction when in fact this couldn't be further from the truth. Its reactions are go-kart like – steering is ultra-quick, there's no discernible roll and grip levels are so high that you're never likely to breach them on the road. Check out the rear tyres – 345/35 ZR15s, wider than those fitted to the Murciélago – and you start to realise how hard you'd have to push to get the Countach out of shape.

For the truly brave, Moreno confirms that the Countach isn't easy to recover when it does let go. He mimes armfuls of opposite lock and grimaces. In truth you don't need to play the hero in the Countach to make ludicrously quick progress. Driven smoothly and with confidence, Lamborghini's craziest supercar is still devastating. The nose turns-in with the merest whiff of lock, feeling as if it's nailed to the tarmac; the ABS-less brakes are heavy but reassuring; the thrust out of corners is, of course, phenomenal.

Time hasn't diminished the impact of the Countach's looks, even in heavily adorned Anniversary guise. Car still draws crowds wherever it goes

Photographer Andy Morgan later likens following the wrung-out Anniversary to watching speeded-up film footage. On testing British black-top there's no doubt the Lambo would be on a knife-edge, but in this Italian playground it feels ready and able to take on the world all over again.

Even now, 11 years later, the Countach shape still defines the word 'supercar' more than any other. The first prototype, the LP500, was shown at the Geneva show in 1971, where its rakish styling caused a sensation. Demand for the car was enormous and that design study became the basis for the Miura replacement, finally entering production in 1974. A radical departure from the curvaceous Miura, the production Countach – called LP400 – matched the show car's clean lines with compact dimensions and low weight to create an incredibly fast and fabulously futuristic work of art.

It seems unbelievable that what is basically a 30-year-old design can still drop jaws and stop traffic. But it does. As we pull up in the centre of Bologna we might as well be in a spaceship. The Italians aren't shy when it comes to admiring cars, but this is something else entirely – within seconds a throng of people is poring over every inch of the bodywork, laughing and pointing at the air intakes and the scissor-style doors. Moreno is bombarded with questions and cameras are thrust into my hands so people can have a souvenir picture of the day they saw a Countach.

This isn't the kind of reaction you get with other 'classic' cars. There's no patronising smile, no 'ah, isn't it nice'; the appearance of a Countach anywhere in the world still shocks. Nobody asks how old it is, that's not important. Aggressive, outrageous and truly dramatic, the Countach oozes charisma from every taut line

and razor-sharp angle. It is the epitome of Lamborghini design and many people still struggle to get their head around its anarchic lines. No other car, before or since, captures the imagination quite like the Countach.

To drive the closest thing to a brand new Lamborghini Countach on the very roads that shaped its character is a great privilege. To realise that, even in the 21st century, it exhilarates like few others is a welcome surprise.

By the end of this long day I'm physically tired from the exertion required to get the best from a Countach. Mentally tired too, because of the weight of responsibility attendant with driving the last of a breed that existed for 16 years as the fastest and most exciting car in the world.

Most of all I'm stunned that the Countach came to be viewed as an anachronism. Sure it's got heavy steering, a recalcitrant clutch and terrible rearward visibility. But find a good stretch of road and you'll forget all of that. When traffic dissolves and that tireless engine screams to 8000rpm on a wide-open ribbon of smooth tarmac, 1990 seems like somewhere we should all visit at least one more time. ■

Specification

LAMBORGHINI Countach

○ Engine	V12, mid, longitudinal
○ Displacement	5167cc
○ Cylinder head	Aluminium alloy, dohc per bank, four valves per cyl
○ Fuel and ignition	Six Weber 44 DCNF carburettors, Marelli electronic ignition
○ Max power	455bhp @ 7000rpm
○ Max torque	369lb ft @ 5200rpm
○ Transmission	Five-speed manual, rear drive
○ Weight	1490kg
○ Power to weight	282bhp/ton
○ 0-60mph	5.0sec
○ Top speed	185mph

LAMBORGHINI GENERATIONS: DIABLO 6.0 VT

Never known for its subtlety, the low-nosed, high-drama Diablo still attracts affectionate attention, even in Lambo country around Sant' Agata. Buckley (inset, far right) revels in the relentless thrust of that monster V12, now grown to 6 litres. This car is one of the last off the line before the factory is given over to the new Murciélago

DIABLO

The Diablo was the first Lamborghini to crack 200mph. Even now, it's shockingly fast

Words: Martin Buckley Photography: Andy Morgan

My girlfriend tells a story about the day she went to see *Star Wars* back in 1977. It was her second date with a lad called Carl Varney. All was going well until, as they walked hand-in-hand out of the cinema, the lad gave his verdict on this exciting new era in blockbuster sci-fi movies: 'A bit far-fetched.'

Poor Carl. So earth-bound, so tedious he had totally missed the point and, at the same time, sealed his fate as a potential suitor. He would probably have said much the same thing about a Diablo if he ever encountered one (which is very unlikely given that he probably ended up as a supermarket manager in Leicester).

Certainly this car is 'far fetched', or at least slightly unreal, but that, as we know, is the very point of a true mid-engined supercar. To qualify for the title it must surrender itself totally to visceral excitement above all other considerations. Practicality is an optional extra.

Like the Miura and Countach before it, the Diablo is an end in itself, the antithesis of humdrum and mundane, pure and uncompromised in its ability to thrill. This is not a supercar dressed like a hatch, a boring-looking Japanese coupe nor any other exercise in subtlety. If you don't like the Athena poster dynamism of its rising wedge profile, the latent intent of its wide-hipped stance, then you'd probably be better off with the drug dealer chic of an AMG Mercedes or a tricked-up 3-series.

The Diablo's development wasn't always completely straightforward but Valentino Balboni, Lamborghini's chief test driver and purveyor of easy charm, remembers it well.

'It was a beautiful experience,' he says wistfully as we admire the now static Diablo 6.0 in the fading October light. 'We started in 1986 and kept developing for four years. We did the first road test at two o'clock in the morning because nobody was supposed to see the car.'

Back then the Diablo ran a mechanical four-wheel-drive set-up, rather than the viscous system it eventually received. 'The gearbox was a

mess, with everything upside down, back to front,' says Valentino. 'It was very crude.' He recalls blowing engines and gearboxes testing at Nardo. 'We had many problems. Oil and water temperatures were very high because the car's aerodynamics were wrong.' That early four-wheel-drive system was soon cancelled because 'it was both noisy and unreliable'.

The Diablo was designed to cure all the Countach's weaknesses, accommodating a more

Diablo still looks incredible; the broad hipped, wedgy stance shouting supercar from every angle. Carbonfibre trim (above) already starting to look dated, but the seats are good and the major controls are all well-weighted

powerful engine and stronger brakes in a stiffer frame. With 492bhp it was the world's fastest production car, hitting a verified top speed of 202mph. 'Nothing was taken over from the Countach,' says Valentino. 'We developed the car from a white piece of paper.'

Lamborghini was bought by Chrysler during the Diablo's development and it was American money that paid for its completion. 'They supplied not only money but technology,' Valentino remembers. 'Chrysler was a good owner of the company, they made a lot of things better. Iacocca was an Italian supporting Italian products. He was the one who wanted to buy Lamborghini. A very nice guy. He owns a lot of property in Tuscany so he was coming to the factory a lot. It was a nice partnership.'

Sadly the partnership wasn't to last and Lamborghini was sold to a new, Indonesian owner. This period was a 'big disaster' according to Valentino: 'They had no love, no passion for the cars. It was only a hobby for them.'

Now Audi is at the helm in Sant' Agata and we're here to drive one of the last Diablos to be built before the factory gives itself over to the Murciélago in a few days' time. In its home town, where you'd think people have seen the odd Lamborghini before, the VT Diablo still turns heads and raises smiles. Even a granny, towering above us in a Punto, grins benignly at the gold car and lets us out into the traffic.

Styled, like the Countach, by Gandini, the Diablo must look to others as if it's been artificially superimposed onto this humdrum scene. It's low and vast, the cabin piled forward into the snub nose as if to liberate more space for the 6-litre, 550bhp V12 – perhaps the world's greatest production engine – that whines and bristles behind you. The design shows its age in the lack of sixth gear which wasn't considered essential back in 1990, even for a supercar. The change itself – other than the ponderous dogleg first-to-second movement – is precise and meaty, the hefty polished steel knob adding welcome inertia to the lever's click-clack progress around the six-fingered alloy gate.

The sombre cabin isn't especially impressive with its passé carbonfibre trim (most of the Diablo's body, other than the doors and roof, is made of the stuff), lumpy facia and Fiat parts-bin detailing. But the Diablo still offers adequate visibility and, once you've popped open the scissor door, tumbled over the deep sill and fallen into their embrace, exceptionally good seats. Wieldy power steering and a friendly, medium-weight clutch mean that initial intimidation quickly turns to confidence, any frustration with heavy, processional mid-morning traffic caressed away by the air-con.

As the road opens up a little we spear through a roundabout and a couple of curves, the Diablo sitting perfectly square, its rear wheels biting as the fronts pull you through in a seamless action that defies any notion of understeer or roll. Suddenly you're travelling rather faster than you might think, holding the thick-rimmed wheel in a firm grip as you turn it against well-judged feel and soft-focus feedback, the front of the car moving in obedient proportion to each precise degree you twirl in.

Not that I'm really pushing the car yet. To drive truly quickly demands a level of concentration and co-ordination many drivers

'At 150mph it's still pulling hard and the sound is intense, shuddering through the cockpit'

might be unwilling – or unable – to give. But if you've got the time and bottle, the sensory rewards are undeniable. The gearbox whines and chatters on the over-run but it's swamped by the engine which whoop-whoops with instant response when you blip to change down.

Gaps in the traffic are there to be exploited as the VT sweeps forward and slots in almost before the thought has fully formed in your brain. Half a dozen mortal tin-boxes are dispatched in an instant of buttock-clenching pick-up using only two thirds of the revs.

That was just a taster. When the traffic melts away on an anonymous stretch of road, 40 minutes drive from the factory, I can level the throttle at a clear horizon. The P-Zeros' grip is such that the clutch slips before the tyres do and the Diablo lunges forward, winding out to something over 7000rpm in second, third and fourth. I'm pinned in my seat at 100mph even before I've made my first gearchange, smacking the lever through with a slickness that wasn't there at lower speeds. At 150mph it's still pulling hard and the sound is intense, shuddering through the cockpit: base and visceral in the way it moves you on some unspoken emotional level yet also speaking of sophistication and

complexity, the nobility of the hardware.

The view out is a rush of grey. I'm paralysed with adrenalin, eyes fixed on the horizon for a Fiat that might trundle out of a side road, fighting every sweaty-palmed survival instinct to lift off. I finally come off the throttle at 175mph in fifth, just as the acceleration is beginning to tail off – although it's claimed there's another 30mph yet to be realised. A good jab on the brakes and the massive cross-drilled discs wipe off speed so quickly that you feel your breakfast rise in your throat and your internal organs bang against your rib cage.

There's nothing much wrong with the Diablo now. It's come a long way from the rough and ready original of a decade ago. It shamelessly flaunts its credentials as a high-fat, non-filter-tipped V12 fantasy car from an era before video games and shaven-headed geeks in Impreza turbos. If we're talking cars and haircuts, then Diablo man would definitely wear his mullet with pride. But to me there's something quite refreshing about this last-of-the-line Diablo's honesty of purpose.

It is to Lamborghini's credit that it has stayed loyal to this type of car, no matter how unfashionable such machinery might have

become. The Peter Stringfellow Factor has not swayed the company from its calling, and neither should it. Cars like this – whether you think they're in terrible taste or not – make the world a more wondrous place.

Unless your name is Carl Varney. ■

Specification

LAMBORGHINI Diablo 6.0

○ Engine	V12, mid, longitudinal
○ Displacement	5992cc
○ Cylinder head	Aluminium alloy, dohc per bank, four valves per cyl
○ Fuel and ignition	Lamborghini electronic injection, electronic ignition with individual coils
○ Max power	550bhp @ 7100rpm
○ Max torque	457lb ft @ 5500rpm
○ Transmission	Five-speed manual, four-wheel drive
○ Weight	1625kg
○ Power to weight	343bhp/ton
○ 0-60mph	3.8sec (claimed)
○ Top speed	200mph+

MURCIÉLAGO

John Barker samples the first new Lamborghini for over a decade

Photography: Andy Morgan

Spawn of the devil: Murciélago's dramatic styling has Diablo and Countach cues plus Miura-like slatted rear (opposite). Attention-grabbing detailing (opposite, below) includes Maglite-look lights, huge drilled brake discs and 'active' air intakes which extend at speed to force more air into the engine bay

The small card on the bedside table confidently predicted that Milan would be bathed in autumnal sunshine this morning. The small card was wrong because the sky outside is dark grey with rain. I don't care though, because today I'm driving a new Lamborghini, the first in a decade and the first that will reflect the influence of new owner Audi. Only hail, snow or ice could seriously dent my mood. Andy Morgan, evo's staff photographer, is less happy. 'I'm jinxed,' he groans as we make our way to the test track. 'Every time I come to Italy to shoot a supercar it rains.' I consider telling him it could be worse but think better of it.

Lamborghini has decided to give us our first experience of the new Murciélago at Vairano, the test track near Milan where we first drove the final iteration of its predecessor, the Diablo 6.0 VT. Andy came here then, and it chucked it down. I've never been to the place before and, having driven through the underpass onto the infield, I find myself standing in front of the Lamborghini awning, in the drizzle, unable to make out a circuit. There aren't any Murciélagos here either, so we step inside in search of a warming coffee.

That's when we hear the unmistakable growl of not one but two Lamborghini V12s. We move to one of the vinyl windows and see a pair of Murciélagos, one black, one sky-blue, approaching the tunnel. Coffee forgotten, we step briskly outside to listen as they thunder through the tunnel and park up in front of us. Instinctively I'm drawn to the black one, even though I know that the light blue car will make the photos easier. I'm just formulating a futile argument for it when the sound of a third V12 resonates through the tunnel and a glowing orange Murciélago bursts into view. Very Sant' Agata. Very us. Andy smiles.

My snap reaction is that the Murciélago looks like an evolution of the Diablo. Tidied up, slightly fuller around the middle (a characteristic it shares with its up-coming cousin, the Bugatti Veyron) and definitely Lamborghini. The slatted engine cover shouts Miura, the shape of the bonnet is pure Countach and there's a very mild, vestigial wedge to its rear wheelarch.

I'm not surprised to find that the Murciélago is more impressive in the flesh than any photo I've seen. Like the Diablo, it's a sculpture you admire as you walk around it, watching the way the surfaces interplay, enjoying the details. You could lose a small dog in the sill scoops, and there's a shoulder along the base of the side windows that channels more air towards the 'active' air intakes. The projector headlamps look like the business end of a pair of very large Maglite torches, while the body's bevelled edges around the rear and the flattened arches give it a suitably substantial look. There's a touch of Audi, too; check out the rear corner in the side profile shot.

Opening the trademark scissor door is made easier by Fiat Barchetta-style handles that flip up when you press them, giving you something to grab hold of. The cockpit seems rather plain in photos, but once you're settled into the firm grip of the Alcantara/leather seat, it looks stylish and neat. The instruments are now clustered into one very clear pack and the facia has a mild wrap-around feel, putting you at the centre of things. The aluminium embellished pedals are still fractionally offset to the right (in this lhd car) but it's easy to get comfortable behind the rake and reach-adjustable wheel.

Amongst the scattering of switches is one that we haven't seen in a Lamborghini before

and which I suspect might go unpressed today on this damp and narrow track. It's the button that deactivates TCS, or traction control. The Murciélago is four-wheel-drive of course but, as in the Diablo, the front wheels don't get a huge amount of the drive so the car will feel rear-drive most of the time.

Test driver Giorgio Sanna kneels by the door sill: 'I like this car because it is comfortable and fast. The Diablo was hard and fast,' he explains. 'When the Murciélago oversteers it is much easier. The Diablo…' he searches for the words and resorts to a hand gesture that describes the tail rocking. 'With the engine five centimetres lower, the Murciélago is also much better going left then right. You will see. Try it with traction control for a few laps first.' Sure thing, Giorgio.

The door comes down, I twist the key, the high-pitched starter motor whirrs and the V12 growls into life, same as it ever was: complex, rich, guttural, bloody marvellous. It's now hooked up to a six-speed gearbox whose shiny ball-topped lever is taller than the Diablo's,

'The V12 growls into life – complex, rich, guttural, bloody marvellous'

presumably to give more leverage and lessen the shift weight. The clutch action is considerably lighter and it's a doddle to manoeuvre the Murciélago, feeding in the clutch against the V12's high idle.

I can appreciate Lamborghini's desire to let us get our first taste of the Murciélago in a controlled environment but, as David Vivian discovered when he drove the Diablo 6.0 here, Vairano is really too narrow for such a big, heavy car. Despite being carbonfibre-bodied (steel doors and roof excepted) the tubular steel-framed Murciélago weighs a hefty 1650kg. That's a fraction more than the Diablo 6.0, although with its 6.2-litre, 570bhp development of the V12, the Murciélago manages 351bhp per ton to the Diablo's 343. It easily out-muscles the heavier 485bhp Ferrari 550 but has no answer to the Pagani Zonda S, which conjures up 441bhp per ton from 542bhp and a mere 1250kg.

Any one of them would be a handful on this thin, rain-lashed track, which I'm trying to learn as I get to know the Murciélago. There

aren't many landmarks but there seems to be plenty of scope for making one — an expensive, crumpled orange landmark just off one of the third-gear sweeps.

Initial impressions are that the Murciélago is easier to handle than the Diablo, thanks to its lighter clutch and the smoother throttle action. The throttle linkage is now drive-by-wire instead of a series of friction-inducing rods and couplings — and that makes traction control a simple addition. Giorgio has advised me that the TCS is 'very firm', meaning that very little slip is allowed before the ignition and fuelling are knocked back. There's plenty of weight to the steering, which seems to match the general feel of the Murciélago, while the gearshift is typically supercar-notchy until the gearbox oil has warmed through. Even then it's at its most co-operative when you shift positively and double de-clutch on downshifts. Very tactile, very rewarding.

Not that you need to stir the lever much if you don't want to. There's so much low-down urge so cleanly delivered that you can stay in

Above: Murciélago looks neater and is easier to drive than its predecessors, but the bellowing V12 is still at the heart of it

third for the whole lap and still go very quickly. The V12 simply digs in and hauls out from what feels like walking pace without a murmur of protest. For me, this is when the engine sounds at its menacing best, though the heavy beat as it overcomes the body's mass doesn't last long. As soon as the rev-counter

That fabulous Lambo V12 (above, left) has now grown to 6.2 litres, while its output has swollen to 570bhp. Interior (above) looks plain in pictures but it's well-made, comfortable and easy to use. Thanks to you, Mr Audi

Specification

LAMBORGHINI Murciélago

○ **Engine**	V12
○ **Location**	Mid, longitudinal
○ **Displacement**	6192cc
○ **Bore x stroke**	87mm x 86.8mm
○ **Compression ratio**	10.7 to one
○ **Cylinder block**	Aluminium alloy
○ **Cylinder head**	Aluminium alloy, dohc per bank, four valves per cylinder, variable valve timing
○ **Fuel and ignition**	Lamborghini LIE electronic ignition and fuel injection. Variable intake geometry
○ **Max power**	570bhp @ 7500rpm
○ **Max torque**	479lb ft @ 5400rpm
○ **Transmission**	Six-speed manual, four-wheel drive
○ **Front suspension**	Double wishbones, coil springs gas dampers, anti-roll bar
○ **Rear suspension**	Double wishbones, coil springs, gas dampers, anti-roll bar
○ **Steering**	Rack and pinion, power-assisted
○ **Brakes**	Ventilated discs, 355mm front, 335mm rear, ABS
○ **Wheels**	8.5 x 18in front, 13 x 18in rear, alloy
○ **Tyres**	245/35 ZR18 front, 335/30 ZR18 rear Pirelli P-Zero Rosso
○ **Fuel tank capacity**	22 gal/100 litres
○ **Weight (kerb)**	1650kg
○ **Power-to-weight**	351bhp/ton
○ **0-60mph**	4.0sec (estimated)
○ **Max speed**	205 mph plus (claimed, dependent on aero configuration)
○ **Fuel cons (EC combined)**	not quoted
○ **Insurance group**	20
○ **Basic price**	£160,000 (2001)
○ **On sale (UK)**	2001-06

evo RATING ★★★★ 1/2

needle gets to 2000rpm it takes on a nape-prickling urgency and the Lambo thumps forward with a strength that, even in a straight line, makes you grateful for traction control.

As you'd expect after clocking the massive front discs crammed inside those gorgeous alloys, stopping power is phenomenal. It's as hard to activate the anti-lock as it is to trigger TCS on the drying track, and the nose seems to hold up better under heavy braking, as if there's less weight transfer than in the Diablo. If you need reminding that you're at the pointy end of a V12 wedge, a glance in the mirrors, showing those massive scoops raised hungrily into the air stream, does the trick.

Out of the tightest corner I finally succeed in activating TCS. As Giorgio described, it reacts very quickly, catching the tail before it has the chance to swing more than a few degrees, the engine dropping onto what feels and sounds like six cylinders until there's enough grip again. Given that it keeps the tail on such a short leash, there's a surprising amount of low-speed understeer built into the Murciélago's balance. It's impossible to judge the dynamics definitively, of course – the Diablo 6.0 proved much more impressive on real roads, with bumps, cambers and the circumspection that comes with them, than it did here.

Still, later in the day I was able to confirm Giorgio's assertion that the Murciélago is indeed more stable thanks to its engine's lower centre of gravity. It could be sensed through the left-right-left at one end of the track but more so once TCS was disabled and the tail was allowed to edge out under power. You still need to be committed and steady with the throttle but the Murciélago slides and recovers much more cleanly than any Diablo I've driven. A front-engined car like the 550 Maranello still feels less likely to bite your bum if you do have to get off the gas in a hurry, but the fact that you can even consider

bringing the tail into play around such a narrow track is impressive.

The Murciélago is still very much a Diablo at heart. Easier to handle, more dynamically poised but still a challenge to drive well. It's loaded with character too, a large proportion of which is provided by that glorious V12. The engine's nature is slightly changed so that it delivers more mid-range thrust and a little less top-end vigour, but this will only make it more exploitable and enjoyable on the road. A brief sortie away from the track alongside Giorgio proved that its ride is firm yet supple, and that it's solidly built, too. So Audi hasn't radically changed the script, but that's pretty much what Diablo fans would have hoped for. Only a full road test will show if it has changed enough to keep Lamborghini at the forefront of supercar design. We look forward to bringing you the definitive answer very soon. ∎

FIRE
AND ICE

The original Murciélago came with a 570bhp 6.2-litre V12.
And four-wheel drive. In 2003, Harry Metcalfe decided to put it to
the test on some snow-covered mountain passes

It's three hours since we pointed the nose of our Tango Lambo north out of mid-morning Milan and aimed for the little town of Tirano, just to the south of the Swiss border and the start of our Alpine adventure; as we arrive at the border post it looks like the fun could be over before it's even started. We're headed for the Bernina pass, 2344 metres high up in the Alps. First, though, we've got to get past the Swiss border police. Who apparently had their sense of humour removed at birth.

I'm beginning to wonder if they're going to allow the Lambo in at all. Passports are handed over, swiftly followed by the car's papers. Just as I'm rehearsing my explanation as to exactly why I'm in an orange Murciélago, which isn't mine, and about to drive up a snowy Swiss mountain

pass, an unsmiling policeman marches up to the car and demands I turn it off. This, I can't help thinking, is a bad sign. I think it's safe to say they're not Lamborghini fans. But then, in the few minutes it's been standing here ticking over, the Murciélago has probably dumped more pollution into Switzerland than residents are allowed to do in a lifetime.

Including noise pollution. The 6.2-litre V12 isn't exactly the shy, retiring type. In fact it reminds me of Dom Joly, the way it booms out its intentions to anyone in the vicinity. Twist the key all the way and the starter motor whirls for a few seconds before, *blam*, the V12 erupts with a wall of noise as if you've left a brick on the accelerator, hitting an instant 2500rpm before falling back just as quickly to idle. Subtle it isn't.

The police finally succumb to the pleas of

Moreno Conti (one of Lamborghini's elite group of test drivers and my companion for these three days) and we're allowed to continue. First, though, they give us a stern lecture on the icy conditions to be found up ahead, before turning to our bright orange Murciélago and, well, *laughing*. I point to our very special tyres and the fact that I'm English and therefore slightly barmy by way of some inherited birthright (though I doubt this icy adventure would give Ranulph Fiennes any sleepless nights). Actually, thinking about it, they may have a point.

We're heading up the pass now, aiming for St Moritz, and whereas there was just the odd slippery patch hiding in the shade of the trees as we left the border crossing, we're now above the tree line and there's enough snow up here to paralyse the UK for months. So much has fallen recently they're having to measure it in metres (later we learn there's a full 2.5m of the stuff at the top of the pass, enough to prevent access to most of the villages for miles around).

Inside the cosy Murciélago cabin it's gone ominously quiet between me and Moreno. The trouble is there's a very healthy 570bhp behind me but, right now, that's probably at least 500 horses too many as I desperately try to keep the revs from flaring out of sight as the wheels spin effortlessly on the snow and ice. As spindly road-markers guide us across the snowfield, I know the last thing I must do is lose momentum, but even on a whiff of throttle the Lamborghini is gently

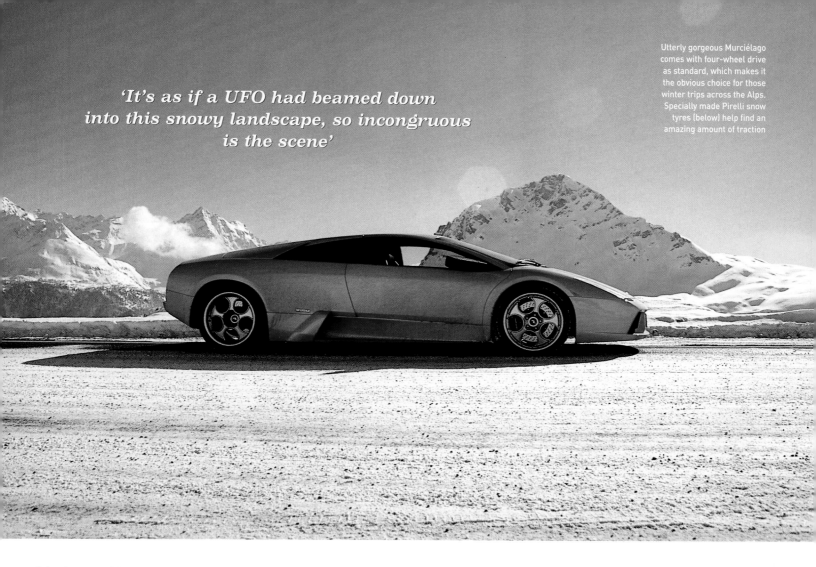

'It's as if a UFO had beamed down into this snowy landscape, so incongruous is the scene'

fishtailing out of the sweeping corners and up the short straights, the tyres sniffing out whatever grip is on offer.

That addictive mixture of fear and aggression is pumping through my body. The last time I felt like this was during my first race, many years ago. Outside the conditions worsen as the narrowing pass disappears under yet more snow. Ooh er.

It's so beautiful outside we decide to pull over into a non-existent lay-by, partly to admire the view but mainly to have a pee. The dash readout is indicating an outside temperature of -9C but there's no wind about and the sun has a hint of heat to it, so coats aren't needed. What we do need though are some spikes in our shoes; both of us are on our backsides within seconds. Looking like two drunks at closing time, we giggle helplessly as we circle the Lambo, both hands

gripping its extremities in an effort to keep upright. It's so slippery out here, how those tyres are finding any grip at all I've no idea.

A couple of four-wheel-drive vans appear above us, the first vehicles we've seen since we started the pass. They clank by, snow chains on all four wheels, their drivers looking utterly and understandably amazed at the sight of the Murciélago. It's as if a UFO had beamed into this snowy landscape, so incongruous is the scene.

LAMBORGHINI HAD barely batted an eyelid when I requested a Murciélago for our rather unconventional road trip. It's four-wheel drive, of course, with a central viscous coupling directing up to 25 per cent of the power to the front wheels when the rears start to slip, but 'our' car would also come equipped with a set of handmade

Pirelli snow tyres. Not your average snow tyres either, but a one-off set specially made for Lamborghini and in standard Murciélago sizes too, namely 245/35x18 at the front and a ridiculous 335/30x18 for the monster rears. And when things get particularly tricky, I've a button on the centre console to raise the front suspension by 50mm for added ground clearance.

There's no getting away from it though; we're still on the edge of what's 'do-able' in a Murciélago. While Lamborghini is rumoured to be working on a proper all-road all-weather vehicle, this isn't it.

As we blast down from the summit towards St Moritz I'm tempted to make a detour to the Cresta run, which seems an appropriate thing to do, but our map-reading fails us and time's pressing. Still, it's been quite a day. Tomorrow

'We continue to climb...
Tunnels burst open onto snow banks that tower
above us some two metres deep'

Lambo crew didn't meet much
traffic – just a few mad bikers, snow
ploughs and the odd skidoo.
Unfortunately the Col de la Bonette,
the highest of the Alpine passes,
was closed, but there was good
sport to be had on the Bernina pass
(right), once past the over-zealous
Swiss border police. Tunnels on
Splugenpass (above) get extremely
tight in places. Driving is pure
pleasure – though gearshift can be
stiff until oil warms through

we're meeting photographer Charlie Magee and his hire car in the French Alps some 200km away. The plan is to find the 2802m Col de la Bonette, officially the highest pass in the Alps, though the French added an otherwise useless loop-road at the top of the pass to wrest the title away from Italy's 2758m Stelvio pass.

First we have to head back south and negotiate the rush hour around Milan. I'm happy to let Moreno take the wheel. It's a good call; Milan is its usual knot of traffic as thousands of Italian jostle for position across four clogged lanes. After nearly an hour and a half crawling we finally break clear and head for Turin.

Moreno has been a Lamborghini test driver for 20 years. He adopts a relaxed, go-kart-style driving position, tiny steering wheel set quite close, legs bent, seat almost upright. He looks as if he's ready to go racing and in a way he is. As we power down the three-lane, he proceeds to give me a masterclass in the finer points of Italian autostrada driving.

Nothing is allowed to get in the way of the Lamborghini. If anyone baulks the outside lane the Murciélago charges up behind them until it feels as though our front number plate must be nuzzling their exhaust. From my super-low position in the passenger seat I devise an impromptu league table based on the elegance of rear suspension set-ups. Ugliest has to be a Chrysler Grand Cherokee; if a potential owner ever saw how tractor-like they were from where I'm sitting right now, he'd think twice before

buying one. Other shockers include a prolapsed Honda CRV and the crude, iron-age beam of a Renault van. Top of the table is an Alfa 147, each rear wheel suspended from superbly elegant aluminium wishbones that, thanks to relatively soft springing, get to move about a lot as the 147 drifts through the corners and over bumps, the Lamborghini hounding its every move.

Every car and lorry we fly past gets a double dose of Xenon headlights to warn of our approach. The snow tyres limit our speed to just over 200kph (125mph) but even so it doesn't take long to reach our hotel, tucked away in Pinerolo, 30-odd miles west of Turin.

After a dismal bed in an equally dismal hotel, the only redeeming feature of Pinerolo turns out to be the excellent hand car wash to be had on the way out of town. Four guys get to work in the freezing conditions and, one espresso later and 6.5 euros lighter, we're back on the road to Cuneo.

I'm back behind the wheel and finding the gearbox typically obstructive from cold; the low temperature has turned the oil to treacle and gummed up the synchromesh, so selecting second requires a mighty shove. Once it's warmed up, though, the Murciélago explodes past lines of trucks as we travel down the B589 to our meeting point with Charlie. It simply storms through this nondescript part of Italy, the road a mix of long straights and sharp corners, punctuated by easily forgettable towns. Soon we're crossing the bridge high above the Gesso river and heading out to the

first pass of the day, the 1948m Col de Larche.

Blissfully traffic-free, the road grips the side of the valley as it heads towards the summit. After a relatively tame approach, it starts to twist through the trees, and there's a flourish of hairpins to finish off the climb. These are magnificent roads on which to exercise a Lamborghini, and I'm struck again by just how much Lambo handling has improved since early Diablo days. The traction control can be a nuisance though, getting too easily upset by bumps and cutting the power crudely; it remains permanently switched off after this climb.

We drop through Larche, packed with skiers today; just what they make of the Lamborghini crunching past on the crisp snow I can only imagine, but we need to get to Jausiers, the start of the Col de la Bonette. As we drop down the valley the snow quickly disappears from the road; we're on the southerly side of the mountain now, so the sun's heat is stronger than before, especially this far south. The landscape here isn't as dramatic either, but the roads are good and, with very little

'Familiarity has done nothing to dull its truly stunning looks, surely the pinnacle of supercar design'

in the way of industry around this corner of France, there are fewer of the lumbering trucks we encountered yesterday.

I'm growing rather fond of the Murciélago's cockpit. There's a pleasingly meaty feeling to all the major controls; the steering wheel is VX220-small and needs heft to move lock to lock. Same with the gearstick, a beautifully crafted alloy stick that heats up as you drive, the temperature dependent on how hard you're working the mighty engine. Thankfully the clutch is of a more manageable weight these days; there are plenty of gearchanges on these roads and the heavy old Diablo clutch would have become very tedious by now. The brakes feel perfectly weighted too, grumbling slightly from high speeds but always feeling up to the job, the pedal perfectly placed to make heel-and-toe second nature. The only glitch is a piece of trim around the hinge of the throttle pedal that gets in the way during those fleeting moments of flat-out acceleration, as if some cabin flotsam has become wedged under the pedal. At least the intrusive engine vibration that afflicted earlier Murciélagos appears to have been cured.

EVENTUALLY WE FIND the start of the pass, snow-covered and newly snow-ploughed. There's a series of bumpy hairpins through the chalets before it opens out and heads up the ravine. It's a pretty innocent start to what is, in terms of height if nothing else, the daddy of alpine passes. And then, after a few kilometres, we drift through a right-hander to find our way blocked by a locked metal barrier across the road. Arse. The surface beyond seems perfect but the French authorities obviously don't want us to continue; perhaps the Swiss are happier to let the risk lie with the driver. Whatever, this is one pass we'll have to save for another day.

We try the 2109m Col de Vars, highly recommended by the bikers who come out here, but there are only sporadic patches of snow on it today. Driving on snow-covered roads is what this trip is all about, and snow-covered roads are what we need, not least for photographer Magee, who's starting to look a little anxious. I park next to the skidoos while we peruse the map. While there are

some terrific driving roads around here, few, we conclude, will be covered in snow today. It seems strange to leave such a lovely area, especially after driving down a tiny mountain road to a cross-country piste near Chianale and stumbling across the local husky station, but we decide it's best to decamp and head north again towards yesterday's gloriously snowy roads.

As we leave I watch Moreno approach and descend into the Lambo's cockpit. It's like witnessing a well-rehearsed dance routine – a reverse shuffle at right-angles to the open door before dipping at the last moment and entering bum first and flicking his legs into the footwell in one fluid move. How is it that Italians have this innate sense of style in everything they do? My attempt at the manoeuvre either ends with me missing the seat and ending up perched on the wide sill covered in slushy snow or with the seatbelt stalk on the outside of the seat getting intimate with the Metcalfe nether regions in eye-widening fashion.

Next morning, after a comfortable night at Lecco on lake Como, we head for Chiavenna and the 2113m Splugenpass. It starts gently enough as it sweeps through the lower valley and over numerous rivers, but soon you arrive at the most

extraordinary set of hairpins I know. They're not really suited to the Murciélago – some of them are so tight that there's nothing for it but to shuffle round using reverse – but they look so amazing we just have to give it a go. It's as if the whole road has tumbled down the mountainside and ended up in this tangled heap of tarmac.

There are tunnels too, some so narrow the Lambo only just squeezes through (the limited headroom is less of a problem). Behind us is a Citroën C5 Estate driven by a smart-suited Italian gent who had stopped earlier to take a closer look at the Murciélago. The Lambo had developed its only fault of the 1850km trip when the wipers packed up after I'd tried to wash the screen while they were still frozen to the glass. It should have been an easy fix, though finding the blown fuse proved rather tricky.

But boy do the Italians love their supercars. Whatever business our C5 man was supposed to be conducting today has been cancelled so he can trail us for the next hour or so as, wipers fixed, we blast up the mountain. Later, while I'm doing some passes for the camera in a remote village, pupils and teachers from the tiny village school suspend lessons and rush out to watch the Lambo rumble past. Can't imagine this happening in the

UK these days, but in Italy the love of the motorcar runs very deep.

Photography finished, we continue our climb, passing through a succession of partly enclosed tunnels that burst open onto snow banks that tower above us some two metres deep. It's exhilarating stuff. The Lambo always behaves as if it's rear-drive rather than four-wheel drive in these conditions; a squirt of throttle soon boots the tail out, but this sort of indulgence needs careful planning – on the icy surface there's nothing to 'lean' against if you try to add any extra power and ride the slide through the corner onto the straight. If only I knew the road ahead was clear I could be a real hooligan, but the consequences of getting it wrong would be rather embarrassing to explain.

Near the top of the pass we look down on a frozen lake trapped behind a dam, skidoos racing across the surface. I'd love to join them on the open expanse of snow-covered ice but we can't find a way down. Never mind; we've a Lamborghini and a deserted road. Charlie's much happier now that we're back in such beautiful and, crucially, snowy surroundings. And after three days of constant gearchanges and short, sharp blasts up some of the most challenging roads ever created, I'm exhausted and elated in equal measure.

THESE THREE DAYS have reminded me what a very special car the Lamborghini Murciélago is. Familiarity has done nothing to dull its truly stunning looks, surely the pinnacle of supercar design. Luc Donckerwolke has created an instant classic with this car, simple surfaces harmonising into one beautifully fluid shape, as if formed by a master in origami.

On the day I return from this trip, waiting at the office is a Mercedes CL600: 5.5-litre V12, 493bhp, 590 lb ft and utterly accomplished. Rather than making the Lambo seem a complete nonsense, it proves to me just how much we should value cars like the Murciélago. Yes they're hard work, but the rewards are so much greater than the soulless performance offered by the likes of the CL, which might cover the ground every bit as fast but offers so little in the way of feedback. Lamborghini's philosophy is as refreshing as the icy mountain air. The whole company is stuffed full of people who you feel would probably work there for free if it meant that could continue to produce objects of such inordinate beauty and flare.

After three days in the Murciélago I may even have become a better driver; heeling and toeing is easy and so pleasurable when you get it right, the gearchange requires firmness and precision but it's so much nicer to interact with a mechanical change than a Playstation-style paddleshift. Then there's the noise; words really don't do justice to the sonic rewards to be reaped from hammering that 6.2-litre V12 engine to the red line. It adds so much pleasure to the driving experience, yet it's a sensation that's totally absent in the Mercedes. The one area the Murciélago isn't so hot on is the steering feel, which is where the rival Pagani Zonda is so much better, but then the Zonda is almost twice as expensive as the Lambo so it should be a damn sight better. In fact the Zonda makes the Lamborghini seem like a bit of a bargain. Especially if you get a set of snow tyres thrown in. The all-road all-weather supercar. Who wants a Cayenne anyway? ■

Specification

LAMBORGHINI Murciélago

Engine	V12
Location	Mid, longitudinal
Displacement	6192cc
Bore x stroke	87mm x 86.8mm
Compression ratio	10.7 to one
Cylinder block	Aluminium alloy
Cylinder head	Aluminium alloy, dohc per bank, four valves per cyl
Fuel and ignition	Lamborghini LIE electronic ignition and fuel injection. Variable intake geometry
Max power	570bhp @ 7500rpm
Max torque	479lb ft @ 5400rpm
Transmission	Six-speed manual, four-wheel drive
Front suspension	Double wishbones, coil springs gas dampers, anti-roll bar
Rear suspension	Double wishbones, coil springs, gas dampers, anti-roll bar
Steering	Rack and pinion, power-assisted
Brakes	Ventilated discs, 355mm front, 335mm rear, ABS
Wheels	8.5 x 18in front, 13 x 18in rear, alloy
Tyres	245/35 ZR18 front, 335/30 ZR18 rear Pirelli snow tyres
Fuel tank capacity	22 gal/100 litres
Weight (kerb)	1650kg
Power-to-weight	351bhp/ton
0-60mph	4.0sec (estimated)
Max speed	205mph (claimed, dependent on aero configuration)
Fuel cons (EC combined)	not quoted
Insurance group	20
Basic price	£160,000 (2003)
On sale (UK)	2001-06

EVO RATING ★★★★★

Simply sublime: Murciélago makes us remember why we fell in love with supercars in the first place. Left: lurking under the engine cover is the 6.2-litre version of Lamborghini's immortal V12, now apparently cured of the resonance that was so intrusive on earlier cars

PREDATOR

The Gallardo was Lamborghini's long-awaited baby supercar, eager to prey on Porsche and Ferrari. Back in summer 2003, this was our first encounter

Unlike other Lamborghinis, the Gallardo (pronounced ga-yardo, in case you're struggling) doesn't intimidate, but like its big brother Murciélago, the savagery of its full-throttle performance is still awesome

You know you're in the presence of a genuine supercar when just the sight of it triggers an uncontrollable surge of adrenalin, a tingly, hollow-feeling hormonal rush that ties your guts in knots and makes your head feel fizzy. It's a sensation just a handful of cars can provoke. Cars like the Lamborghini Gallardo.

No other manufacturer in the world boasts an all-wheel-drive, V10-engined, 192mph entry-level model, but then no other manufacturer in the world has Lamborghini's unrivalled reputation for building jaw-dropping supercars. Consequently, absurd as it may seem, Gallardo is Lamborghini's baby. All 1440kg, 500bhp and £120,000-worth of it.

It's been an elephantine gestation period and a troubled labour, but the birth of Gallardo heralds a bold new era for Sant'Agata. Such rejuvenation wouldn't have been possible without significant investment from parent company Audi. But although this has inevitably brought some cultural changes to this most Italian of marques, Gallardo is proof that the talented minds working at Lamborghini remain as fertile as the agricultural region in which the factory has its foundations.

We're waiting, as we always do, in the Lamborghini factory café just a stone's throw across a courtyard from the factory floor itself. As we stand at the window, sipping slugs of coffee so strong our eyelids begin to sweat, tantalising glimpses of part-constructed supercars can be seen above the rims of our espresso cups. Then, with a bark and rumble that makes the window pane tremor in its frame,

a yellow Gallardo nudges out of the shadows, scruffy 'Prova' trade plate gaffer-taped casually onto the otherwise immaculate tail in time-honoured fashion.

Unmistakably Lamborghini, yet uncharacteristically trim and compact of form, the Gallardo manages to pack a quart's-worth of presence into a pint-sized supercar pot. At first glance there's much to link it with big brother Murciélago. Gaping, angular intakes and slash-cut headlights are exaggerations of the V12 flagship's familiar facial cues, but the minimal front and rear overhangs, snake-hips and gill-like vents that slice into the rear haunches hint at a tightly-focused design that trades gratuitous stylistic extravagance for bullet-like singularity of purpose.

That's not to say the Gallardo is a barren exercise in heartless form-follows-function styling, for thanks to the combined efforts of Italdesign and Luc Donckerwolke, memorable detail flourishes abound. Just take the door

mirrors. Beautiful, abstract, functional sculptures that jut defiantly forward into the airstream, they are a directional contradiction that perfectly emphasises the Gallardo's otherwise tensed, ready-to-pounce stance. The tail-lights are also a highpoint; exposed, enticingly integrated bricks of ruby red that extend into the upper surface of the rear wings. The more you look, the more you see. Like a great work of art, you could spend hours poring over the fine detail of this thing.

Surprisingly, given they've become a Lamborghini trademark, the most ordinary aspect of Gallardo is its doors. No flamboyant, crowd-pleasing scissors here. Only the range-topping Lambo warrants that particular eccentricity. Instead, driver and passenger gain access via conventionally hinged portals. Disappointing? A little, yes, but whether you swing the driver's door up or out, climbing into this newest Lamborghini is nothing less than momentous.

You sit low in the Gallardo, backside just inches off the ground, windscreen arcing off into the distance, stubby nose diving out of sight, view ahead dominated by a neat, bubble-shaped instrument binnacle. Glance in the door mirrors and you'll catch the leading edge of each rear wing scribing a long, looping trajectory before being cut off in their prime by the ruthlessly abbreviated tail. It's an extreme driving environment: thick A-pillars partially obscuring your diagonal sight-lines, letterbox rear window and worrying over-the-shoulder blindspot. Though falling short of the Diablo's levels of sensory deprivation, it's more confined than the light, airy ambience of a 360 Modena. The result is an authentic shrink-to-fit supercar interior that effortlessly overshadows the humdrum environs of a Porsche 911, while retaining a semblance of everyday usability.

Though initially a little daunting, you soon feel at home in the Gallardo. There's less intimidation, less of the paranoia that is part and parcel of sitting at the pointy end of a seven-foot-wide monster like the Murciélago. You might not be able to see the Gallardo's farthest flung extremities, but you can certainly sense where they are with some confidence. It feels comfortable, tailored for the purpose of driving fast (and slow) on real roads. In this respect it combines the instinctive, go-for-the-gap 911 wieldiness with a genuine sense of occasion. Perhaps uniquely for a Lamborghini, you feel like you can really drive the thing before you've so much as started the engine.

Ah, the engine. Displacing 5 litres and delivering 493bhp and 376lb ft of torque, the

Lamborghini's Viscous Traction four-wheel-drive system, a limited-slip diff and electronic traction control ensure that the Gallardo squanders little of its 493bhp on the exit from even very tight corners. However, it will respond entertainingly to a heavy right foot...

'Perhaps uniquely for a Lamborghini, you feel like you can really drive the thing before you've so much as started the engine'

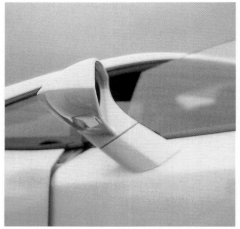

Gallardo's dry-sumped, all-alloy V10 is one of the world's most potent production motors.

One of the most sophisticated, too, thanks to a variable-length inlet manifold, variable valve timing on both inlet and exhaust valves, drive-by-wire throttle and emissions levels that satisfy the toughest global legislation. It's also set in a wider 'V' angle, opened out from the 72degrees adopted in the V12 engines to 90degrees to keep the centre of gravity as low as possible.

Like the Murciélago, the Gallardo employs Lamborghini's Viscous Traction all-wheel-drive transmission. Although set to direct 70 per cent of the V10's output to the rear wheels in steady-state driving, when accelerating hard, or travelling uphill on a high-grip surface, the bias will increase further towards the rear. However,

when the rear wheels begin to lose traction, the viscous coupling within the transmission can direct as much as 50 per cent of the load to the front wheels.

Traction is further enhanced thanks to a limited-slip rear differential at the back, while wheelspin is contained at the front via the ESP system, which can brake individual front wheels to regain traction. It's a neat system.

In a first for Lamborghini, there's also the choice of a conventional stick-shift six-speed manual or F1-style sequential-manual paddle shift gearbox. Developed specifically for Lamborghini by Magnetti Marelli, the paddle-shift 'box employs the same basic concept as that of Ferrari and Aston Martin. Operated via a pair of paddles fixed to the steering column, it's this

version we'll be driving today.

Turn the key, watch as the LCD portion of the dash illuminates, depress the brake pedal, pull back on both paddles to select neutral, twist the key against its spring loading and wait for the bang. It takes a while to come: a second or so of piercing starter motor wail penetrating the cockpit before all ten cylinders kick into life. It's a big, bruising sound, busy at idle, satisfyingly sonorous when you give it a juvenile blip-blip on the throttle. Pull back on the right-hand paddle, squeeze the throttle and away we go.

I find it somewhat galling that thanks to the programming expertise of some sad computer nerd, a total novice could quite happily jump in a car like the Gallardo and change gear with all the hard-earned, decade-and-a-half learned

Gallardo's 5-litre V10 (left) develops a 360-humbling 493bhp though it doesn't really have a discernable power 'peak', which means you sometimes change up too early. We're nitpicking, though; in all other respects it's marvellous. Friendly chassis encourages you to switch off traction control. Cabin (top left) is accessed via conventional doors; it's well appointed and easy to live with, for a supercar

smoothness of a sad car nerd like me. Still, the adoption of such new-fangled technology does make for an uncannily refined low-speed Lambo. No calf-busting clutch pedal to pump, no recalcitrant gearlever to stir around until the gearbox oil is warm. Just slick, finger-flippin' short-shifts, perfect for creaming that awkward getting-to-know-you phase, which invariably takes place on traffic-clogged, stop-start roads.

Part-throttle and steady-state noise levels are pretty subdued, which seems at odds with the hardcore, animalistic Lamborghini ethos of old. But modern times demand a certain level of civility, even in a thoroughbred Italian supercar.

The damping is tolerant of urban lumps and bumps, soaking up road shocks with a minimum of fuss and demonstrating how well isolated the extruded aluminium space-frame chassis structure is from what punishment the double-wishbone suspension is going though. What's obvious from the outset is that the Gallardo is built to be used regularly, not just for high days and holidays. So has Lamborghini gone soft? Not exactly…

Having cleared Sant'Agata and skirted around Modena, we find ourselves on familiar **evo** testing territory, high in the hills above Maranello. In the five years since **evo** was launched, I've been fortunate enough to drive some momentous cars on these roads: Maserati 3200GT, Ferrari 360 Modena, Spider and 575M, the very first Pagani Zonda C12 and C12S. They are roads I know as well as my journey home from work. This is going to be fun.

The first opportunity to floor the throttle is one to savour, for the noise is unlike that of any other road car in production. The response is instant, hardening from a mellow, slightly distant warble to a sharp-edged, no-nonsense bellow. Once on song, the noise is like two Group B Audi quattros singing slightly out of sync.

Finger the 'Sport' button on the transmission tunnel and the upshifts become snappier, downshifts accompanied by sickeningly sweet throttle blips and a barrage of spits, pops and bangs. It's a riot of mechanical music.

It might be the baby of the Lamborghini range, but the Gallardo has grown-up muscle, the gearing true supercar reach. The numerous hairpins that pepper our test route are tight but not excessively so, but it still feels right to hook first gear when you're going for it. As you'd expect, there's immense traction, even with this much power, and it's not long before the ESP system is switched out, such is the confidence you gain from the front end's faithful feel and the innate balance of the chassis.

In fact the front feels ever-so-slightly reluctant for the first part of any given turn. But where a Ferrari 360 is all initial bite and response, quickly followed by a mild but significant sense of under-tyred understeer, the Gallardo settles into the subtlest whiff of understeer before finding its feet and remaining resolutely on-line. You can hear it working each tyre in turn, first the fronts, then as you begin to feed in the power, so the rears begin to chirrup in unison. In terms of tangible, reliable feedback and sheer chuckability, the Gallardo has the Modena licked and gives the 911 a run for its money.

Play with the throttle mid-turn, or even chance a lift on the entry to the tighter corners and you can provoke a delightfully exploitable shift from safe 'warning shot' understeer to holdable power-oversteer. It's a car you can grab by the scruff of the neck and drive. The power delivery helps – all that low and mid-range muscle to keep the Pirelli PZero Rossos lit up. Its beefy, sustained shove is reminiscent of big hitters like the Maranello and Murciélago. What it lacks, or rather what you'll miss if you're a fan of the 360 Modena's savage top-end race to the redline, is a perceptible power peak, a point at which the V10 is giving its all.

The best way I can describe it is that, when driving purely by ear, it feels natural to pull for a higher gear 1000-2000rpm short of the 8000rpm redline. It's not that the engine gets rough, tails off or runs out of puff (maximum power is reached at 7800rpm). Tellingly, though, its torque peak is reached at 4500rpm, and it's this threshold that makes the biggest impression. Yet in raw accelerative terms the Gallardo is never less than mighty.

Equally awesome are the Gallardo's brakes. Monster 365mm front and 335mm rear discs shimmer behind glorious 19in alloys and are gripped by fist-sized eight-piston front and four-piston rear Brembo callipers. They work sensationally well. Braking extremely late into the bumpiest corner entry we can find, the ABS refuses to be wrongfooted, with just the slightest pulse underfoot hinting at the battle being fought between tyres and tarmac. Pedal feel remains firm and consistent, even at the end of a prolonged and committed hill descent peppered with hairpins and punchy first-second-third straights. This is one bull that charges and stops with equal conviction.

Diehards were quick to pour scorn on Audi's involvement with Lamborghini, but far from diluting the essential appeal of this most charismatic of supercar builders, Audi's commitment to the long haul has provided Lamborghini with the stability, security and continuity it has been crying out for since the Countach days.

Ironically, just as the breed of fighting bulls from which the Gallardo takes its name were made stronger and more courageous through selective breeding, so the union between Lamborghini and Audi has developed a new and formidable supercar. Be in no doubt, the Gallardo will send shock waves through the heart of Maranello, Stuttgart and beyond. ■

'The union between Lamborghini and Audi has developed a new and formidable supercar'

Stance and proportions of Gallardo are spot-on. With short overhangs and lack of body add-ons, it has a sense of purity akin to a McLaren F1, especially in side profile. Amazingly it's no bigger than a 911 or 360

Specification

LAMBORGHINI GALLARDO

○ Engine	90deg V10
○ Location	Mid, longitudinal
○ Displacement	4961cc
○ Bore x stroke	82.5mm x 92.8mm
○ Cylinder block	Aluminium alloy, dry sumped
○ Cylinder head	Aluminium alloy, dohc per bank, four valves per cylinder, variable inlet and valve timing
○ Fuel and ignition	Lamborghini LIE electronic engine management, sequential multi-point fuel injection
○ Max power	493bhp @ 7800rpm
○ Max torque	376lb ft @ 4500rpm
○ Transmission	Six-speed manual or 'e.gear' paddle shift gearbox, four-wheel drive, lsd
○ Front suspension	Double wishbones, coils springs, dampers, anti-roll bar
○ Rear suspension	Double wishbones, coil springs, dampers, anti-roll bar
○ Steering	Rack and pinion, power-assisted
○ Brakes	Ventilated discs, 365mm front, 335mm rear, ABS, EBD, ESP, ASR
○ Wheels	8.5 x19in fr, 11 x 19in rr, al alloy
○ Tyres	235/45 ZR19 fr, 290/30 ZR19 rr, Pirelli PZero
○ Weight (kerb)	1520kg
○ Power-to-weight	330bhp/ton
○ 0-62mph	4.2sec (claimed)
○ Max speed	192mph (claimed)
○ Insurance group	20
○ Basic price	£120,000 (2003)
○ On sale (UK)	2003-05

EVO RATING ★★★★★

Converti**bull**

191mph with the roof down – in 2006 came the
Gallardo Spyder, Lambo's first full convertible

Lamborghini is a creator of the outrageous. A company that has never grown out of its boisterous, fearless youth, and one that, despite a history littered with financial woes, has never run short of inspiration. Miura, Countach, Diablo, each one a defining chapter in the history of the supercar.

Of course other manufacturers have built wild-looking, low-slung supercars. But Lamborghinis are different. Their extrovert shapes and rude power are almost a by-product of that boundless, fearless enthusiasm. There's nothing calculated about the shock factor. Lamborghini doesn't try to build the maddest cars in the world, they just sort of happen.

I love that, and even with Audi's continued involvement in Lamborghini, the products still feel authentic. The same spirit of gleeful abandonment that created cars like the Miura and Countach still infects every scoop, duct and outrageous curve of a Murciélago or Gallardo. They're still the real deal, still happiest at full cry and driven in anger.

So why are we in Miami? To be honest I'm not sure. It's a week before Christmas and it's 85 degrees, which is nice, but if Lamborghini wanted guaranteed sunshine then southern Spain would have been a more appropriate

Open-top Gallardo loses little of the coupe's visual aggression. Opposite: canvas roof takes just over 20 seconds to emerge from beneath the huge one-piece carbonfibre engine cover. It's all done electrically, of course

location. Instead we've just been thrown the keys to the jaw-dropping new Gallardo Spyder and have the free run of the city and all its heavily policed, pathetically speed-limited roads. Great.

In a plush hotel lobby, chunky Audified key in hand, I can't help wondering if it's all gone wrong. I want a mad Italian test driver running me through the controls, gesturing to me to make sure I use every last millimetre of throttle travel, and marking a map with the most demanding roads he knows to make sure we get the undiluted Lambo experience. Maybe I'm just an old romantic, or maybe Lamborghini has finally sold its soul…

It couldn't be orchestrated better, though. As photographer Andy Morgan and I step through the huge, ornate doors, a crowd of valet parking attendants screen the Spyder from view. One looks up and moves aside and we get a tantalising glimpse of the Gallardo's razor sharp headlight. The rest of the attendants quickly peel to the right and it's like a human sheet has just been pulled from the Spyder's tiny, radically sculpted profile.

The flat grey sky may not be what Lamborghini had been hoping for, but it does nothing to detract from the car's stunning profile. The Gallardo, now close to three years old, combines cutting-edge precision with timeless aggression better than any other car on the planet. Perhaps by losing its roof it's lost its very sharpest teeth, but even hood-down the Gallardo always looks ready to take a chunk out of anything that dares get too close. And the colour is just perfect. Lamborghini calls it Celeste Phoebe, but to you and me it's just Miura baby blue. They haven't forgotten after all. The Spyder is a proper Lamborghini all right. Now we just need to find somewhere to drive it…

Of course, in reality most Spyders will spend their lives prowling around cities like Miami and LA. Which is a waste, but the sense of occasion when you drop behind the Alcantara-rimmed steering wheel, twist the 5-litre V10 into life and drop the roof means that even at 5mph the Spyder is a uniquely thrilling car to be in.

Like its coupe sister, the Spyder benefits from the recent upgrades that have sharpened-up the Gallardo considerably. The steering is more direct than before and, combined with retuned springs and dampers, the chassis retains its incredibly pliant ride and ease of use but is tangibly more responsive and transmits more feel both to your hands and through the beautifully trimmed seats.

Shorter gearing – by 27 per cent in first, a useful 13 per cent in second, and lesser amounts in later gears – makes the most of the modest power hike to 513bhp (up from 493bhp), and in the tight confines of urban streets the Gallardo literally leaps forward with every brush of the throttle.

And the noise is just incredible. The old Gallardo was always surprisingly timid, aurally at least, but with a new exhaust system borrowed from the flame-spitting limited edition SE, the V10 booms and shrieks with an F430-humbling rage. Like the F430, it has a bypass valve that opens above certain revs, but as far as I can ascertain the magic moment is one revolution above idle. Very Lamborghini and, with the roof down, very addictive. To be honest I can't imagine how it's legal, but Lamborghini assures me that it passes noise regulations, even in the US. Maybe the drive-by test is conducted in Italy but measured on the West Coast of America…

Miami's nipped, tucked and silicone-stuffed residents are used to exotic metal drifting around

the city, but the Spyder renders every pearl-white Phantom and chrome-plated Hummer invisible. Even Ferraris slip past unnoticed when the Gallardo is stalking the streets. And we bump into more than one Gallardo coupe owner who looks a little crestfallen to see the Spyder making their pride and joy look like yesterday's news.

For people who care more about rigidity and clenched-fist dynamics, though, an open-topped supercar is always going to be viewed with suspicion. Lamborghini has gone to great lengths to ensure the Gallardo doesn't lose its composure

in this, its first ever full convertible. There are heavily reinforced A-pillars and added bracing in the side sills of the aluminium spaceframe chassis to eradicate any nasty scuttle-shake and allow the suspension to retain its superb control.

The broken surfaces, speed humps and generally shoddy nature of Miami's road network certainly test the Spyder's resistance to the wobbles, and in the main it copes admirably. There's little noticeable shake in the vast windscreen, and only over the very worst ruts does the steering column shimmy in your hands. For a weight penalty of just 50kg,

the Spyder really does feel almost exactly like the coupe for much of the time.

With the roof down you're pretty well protected from the elements, too. A gentle breeze permeates the cabin, but with the electric rear wind-deflector and side windows left up it's perfectly easy to conduct a normal conversation at motorway speeds – the Spyder is capable of 191mph with the roof down, increasing to 195mph with the canvas up. Despite the modest weight penalty, Lamborghini's 4.3sec claim for the 0-62mph sprint is 0.3sec slower than the coupe.

Much of the morning is spent covering every inch of Miami's diverse districts in search of photo locations, and I'm glad to report that the e-gear automated manual gearbox is finally acceptable in everyday low-speed situations. The paddle shift has always worked with an incisive thump at high engine speeds, but in the past its propensity to lurch clumsily and with the expensive whiff of hot clutch through towns or whilst manoeuvring always made the system feel agricultural, especially compared with the excellent F1 system in the Ferrari F430. It's still not quite as polished as Ferrari's effort, but it's vastly improved since early e-gear-equipped Gallardos.

It's lunchtime and we're perched on a stool on a

Closed section of old Grand Prix circuit provides rare opportunity for Gallardo to stretch its legs in otherwise restrictive Miami

street corner in Little Havana, Cuban fare in hand and slightly disturbed that so far we've probably failed to top 70mph. South Beach, Downtown, the Dockyard… all explored but hardly a corner in sight. And then the guys who look after VW's press fleet in Miami mention that the closed section of the old Miami Grand Prix circuit is easily accessible, and if we don't mind dodging the construction workers who are dismantling fences and grandstands from the music festival that's just finished they'll happily take us there. Erm, okay then…

It doesn't look too promising as we turn off Biscayne Boulevard, a busy six-lane artery that used to make up the main straight, then slowly pick our way past dozens of workers and trucks loaded with fence panels. But just 100 yards or so from the busy Downtown Miami hustle we find five or six medium-speed corners, complete with yellow marker kerbs and only the odd stationary

truck on the straights that link them together. It seems highly illegal (and I'm sure it is), but Andy gets his camera out and we decide to do some gentle cornering shots. Well, I say gentle…

We've got a bit of an audience (there's only so many fences you can pull down without a break), but the stretch of ugly, rippled tarmac/concrete mix is empty. The e-gear system is locked in Sport, quickening the shifts, and the ESP is off. The tight right-hander we choose is taken in second and has a very bumpy approach. The Spyder skits momentarily on the surface, steering slightly corrupted, but the tyres are still coping easily with the braking effort. I lift-off in an exaggerated style as the nose snaps towards the apex kerb and then

click the throttle all the way open.

It sounds brutal, but Gallardos respond best when really grabbed by the scruff of the neck. Keep it neat and the four-wheel-drive system is devastatingly effective, but it is deliberately tuned for mild turn-in understeer (they even mention it in the press pack). Deliberately provoke the rear, however, and the heavily rearward-biased Viscous Traction system (30:70 in normal circumstances) comes into its own, allowing pleasingly lurid slides and always shuffling power to help the car pull cleanly back onto the straight and narrow; 513bhp has never felt so exploitable.

Well, that's usually the story, but this time the tail snaps hard left and I find myself with armfuls of

'The engine is so angry, and the shortened ratios add a ferocious edge to its bite'

Above right: rear-biased four-wheel-drive system permits lurid slides provided you keep your nerve – and your boot in. Right: clean roof-down lines helped by rear window that can be fully lowered if you don't want to protect your hairdo. Integrated roll-hoops deploy in a split second should things start to go pear-shaped

opposite lock wound on well before the corner has really started. This could be embarrassing…

If in doubt, keep you foot in, or so I'm told. So I do and the Gallardo drifts around the corner perfectly. Plenty of drama, but no fuss. Well, maybe a bit, but the four-wheel-drive system and limited-slip diffs on both front and rear axles conspire to save my blushes. Phew.

With my heartbeat returning to normal and my 'practice' run complete, we keep on going. Each time the Spyder feels much more tail-happy than the SE we drove just a couple of months ago at eCoty (086). There's a bit of understeer to overcome, but as soon as you're into the meat of the powerband the Spyder seems determined to kick loose and show you a good time.

The dusty surface isn't helping, but somehow this car feels slightly heavier at the rear and keener to adopt an oversteery angle than I'd expected. It's running on PZero Rosso rubber (as opposed to stickier PZero Corsas), so outright grip is down on the SE, but the balance definitely feels more

pendulous. Having said that, the owner of a Ferrari F430 Spyder would find it positively benign and rather less intimidating to drive in a committed fashion.

Linking the corners together is slightly riskier, but the workers seem pretty relaxed and we've already made friends with one traffic cop today, so it'd be crazy to ignore the only meaningful curves in Miami. With something to really get its teeth into, the Spyder feels awesome. The engine is so angry, and the shortened ratios add a ferocious edge to its bite, snapping the Gallardo forward in sharp but still sustained lunges.

Traction is unimpeachable in a straight line, and despite the ragged surface the damping feels utterly controlled. There's no float and no crashing, just consistent, nuggety accuracy. The coupe would feel better still, of that I'm sure, but not by the margin that you might expect. Only the occasional wobble and inconsistency through the beefy steering betray the Spyder's sacrifices in rigidity. As we recently found with the F430 Spyder, a chopped

roof doesn't always mean a mortally compromised supercar.

Playtime is over and we've managed to avoid the wrath of any police (funny, they always seem so much scarier with a huge gun within convenient reach), so it's back to the urban crawl. The rich exhaust note smashes into the endless high-rise buildings, and although the Spyder might look incongruous trapped within the confines of a big city, it feels positively at home. Comfortable, supple and perfectly happy to trickle around on light throttle openings.

The locals will love it, and I'm sure the next time we're in Miami there'll be at least one Spyder replete with chrome wheels and nasty spoilers. Okay, so they don't get it, don't deserve a Gallardo to trundle around in. But you can rest assured that Lamborghini is still producing cars that can deliver the goods in the cut-and-thrust of real supercar country. We've had a taste of what the Spyder is all about, and as soon as the opportunity arises we'll be back in the hills above Modena… ■

'Even with the hood down
the Gallardo looks ready
to take a chunk out of
anything that gets too close'

Return to the
WILD

Faced with ever-faster
supercar competitors,
in 2006 Lamborghini hit
back with the ferocious
Murciélago LP640

When you twist the key back to kill the LP640's 6.5-litre V12, and the rich, complex, beautiful cacophony is gone, it's like the world has stopped spinning. The silence is empty, the colours that before punched through the panoramic windscreen seem to have faded; everything is greyer, less exciting. The LP640's intensity and exuberance put you in a world of the super-real. And when you climb out, dizzy from adrenalin and spent from the effort of keeping all 631bhp in check, you know that the real world will never be enough. You need an LP640. Believe me, everyone needs an LP640…

I'm not sure everyone could handle it, though. Lamborghini's newest, most powerful Murciélago might retain four-wheel drive, traction control and, should you tick the appropriate box, some of the best carbon-ceramic brakes we've ever tried, but with its huge, mid-mounted V12 putting out well over 600bhp, it has the potential to ask some very serious questions of whoever is sitting behind the wheel. The LP640 demands respect, and you'd better give it

its due if you want to stay sticky side down…

The Murciélago as we've always known it is one of the most exploitable supercars of all time. Massive grip, gently understeery-to-neutral balance, enormous traction. But the LP640 is different. The grip is undiminished, but with another 61bhp delivered in an intense lunge towards 8000rpm, the LP640 will easily spin-up its huge 335/30 ZR18 Pirelli rear rubber and spit you sideways in the blink of an eye. Understeer? Not that you'd notice…

Even as you approach the LP640, key in hand and heart thumping a little harder than usual, there's a tangible sense that this is a new sort of Murciélago. It's in the details: the sharper front splitter, the wider intakes ahead of the rear wheels and that huge missile-launcher exhaust. The tension in the shape and the sheer scale of the Murciélago have always marked it out as an archetypal supercar; the new car's styling tweaks simply add to the already epic drama of Lamborghini's biggest hitter.

Under the carbon and aluminium skin of the LP640 beats the latest evolution of Lamborghini's iconic V12. The basic architecture of the engine has served Miura, Countach, Diablo and

V12 (opposite page, top) stretched to 6.5 litres, resulting in 631bhp. Huge exhaust (above) ensures it sounds as good as it goes

Murciélago, and over the years its capacity has grown from 3.9 to 6.2 litres. To be honest, when we first tried the 6.2-litre version, back when the Murciélago was introduced in 2001, we wondered if it was a stretch too far. The formerly sweet-spinning V12 felt a little strained, a touch harsh. But it improved month-on-month and matured into a bellowing, rev-hungry masterpiece. Quite an act to follow.

Clearly this hasn't been lost on Lamborghini. In an effort to draw every last ounce of performance from the V12, over 90 per cent of the components

in this latest version are completely new or thoroughly revised. Capacity has been increased to 6496cc, and new cylinder heads and a variable inlet manifold help it to breathe better at high revs. And it really revs. That 631bhp is produced at 8000rpm, and even the torque peak – 487lb ft – arrives high, at 6000rpm.

The big numbers add up to a very small 0-62mph time of 3.4sec, according to Lamborghini. Keep the throttle hard against the bulkhead for long enough and the LP640 will finally Vmax at 211mph. That's faster than Porsche's Carrera GT

The Factory

From the smiles on the workers' faces and the row-upon-row of cars waiting to be shipped all over the world, you know that Lamborghini is a pretty good place to be right now. Gallardos dominate – they're everywhere, in every conceivable colour – and the baby-Lambo production line is buzzing with activity: V10s being lowered into sparkling engine bays, muted howls emanating from the soundproofed rolling road (the last station before a Gallardo is ready for its new owner), bare aluminium chassis stacked and waiting to continue the process. It's a fantastic sight.

But the other side of the factory, where the LP640 is lovingly crafted, is where you'd want your car to be born. This is old-school supercar construction. Men with huge hammers and huge experience piecing together engines; men and women working alongside each other cutting and then hand-stitching intricate leather patterns; beautiful components lying on pallets waiting to create yet another epic V12.

And in amongst the timeless craftsmanship and seemingly ancient engine-machining facilities, there's the odd flash of state-of-the-art tech – the woman with an endoscope camera checking each block for imperfections, the open box filled with a dozen or so massive carbon-ceramic brake discs, the superb engine dyno

facilities. Lamborghini has melded tradition and tech to perfection, and the LP640 is perhaps the ultimate fruition of this wonderful, unique amalgamation.

When you see a Murciélago's crude tubular-steel chassis completely bare it looks like a throwback, like it couldn't possibly underpin anything remotely relevant for the 21st century. But the LP640 isn't

Above and right: various Murciélago components waiting to play their part in the supercar's relatively labour-intensive build process

some quaint oddity, it's a fully-fledged supercar capable of delivering frightening pace and all the thrills that you could ever want. When the Murciélago is finally replaced, no doubt they'll ship-in an aluminium spaceframe chassis from Germany, use a modular V12 version of the Gallardo's V10, and cut down many of the labour-intensive processes. I'm sure it will be a great car, but maybe just a little of that Lamborghini magic will be lost. The LP640 is the last stand. What a way to go out.

LP640's rear-end is much keener to get involved in the action than previous Murciélagos', but requires quick, measured responses

'The LP640 loves being grabbed by the scruff and really driven'

and not too far behind Ferrari's Enzo. Not bad for a car with its roots firmly in the last century.

Okay, enough of the foreplay. Press your thumb into the indent on the door handle and the other end flicks up above the top edge of the door. Grab it, pull up and the door arcs upwards with a slow, damped action. Swing your legs in and then drop into the seat. Reach up and pull the door down until it clicks home (it takes quite an effort) and you're in. The instruments themselves feel a long way away, but the chunky three-spoke wheel telescopes right out so you can sit with bent arms but straight legs. Perfect.

The speedometer catches your attention first, with bold graphics going all the way up to 360kph. Beside it, the rev-counter's digits stop at a big red 9, though that's a bit of artistic licence – the engine actually clatters into the limiter at 8000rpm, but if any car should be granted leeway for dramatic effect it's this one.

The size of the numbers roll around your mind as you slot the big key into the ignition

and almost think twice about actually firing the LP640 into life. It's a fleeting reticence, though, and with a twist of the key the high-pitched starter zizzes for a second or so before the big V12 wakes in a defiant, triumphant *whhaaaahhhhh!* The noise is hard, constant and seems to wrap around your shoulders and push you deeper into the seat's embrace. It sounds *big*, but when you give in to the urge to blip the throttle, the rev-counter needle flicks around the dial so fast that it looks like it's got an electrical glitch. Only the immense, inertia-free bark just behind your head verifies that this 6.5-litre motor really does rev like a demented four-pot racer.

Perhaps surprisingly, this car, the first LP640 to roll off the production line, is not fitted with Lamborghini's e-gear paddle-shift system but with a conventional six-speed manual. The gated gearchange is fantastically evocative, and when I dip the heavy clutch, grab the cool sphere of aluminium and click the lever into first, it's a relief and a surprise to feel just how light and

positive the shift action is. Certainly, the e-gear system gets better every time we try it, but by the time I've slotted second, enjoying the sweet, precise movement and the clichéd but irresistible *clack-clack* of metal on metal, I've already decided that should I ever have the opportunity, my LP640 would come with a clutch pedal.

The ride feels taut, perhaps a shade firmer than in previous Murciélagos, but the wheel control is superb. The structure feels stiff, too, and combined with the tight damping, the LP640 seems impervious to even the crumbliest tarmac.

The V12's effortless torque makes town driving a cinch (the high figure at which peak torque arrives misrepresents the flexibility of the huge-capacity engine). Only the wide hips cause the odd sharp intake of breath. Well, that and the random manoeuvring of other traffic as drivers and passengers strain for a closer look or a better position from which to capture the LP640's form on their camera phones.

You need a sensitive right foot to meter out

Styling changes include larger air intakes (right) and a new wheel design (bottom left). Optional carbon-ceramic discs, as fitted to this car, are 380mm in diameter front and rear, with six-pot calipers at both ends

the V12's thunderous power, though, the throttle feeling a little too responsive to tiny requests. Fortunately the delivery smooths out when you want to really open the taps – once you're past that first centimetre of accelerator travel you can play the engine to whatever tune you choose.

Pent-up anger of the engine and deft damping aside, it's the steering that stands out in your first few miles in the LP640. It still requires a firm grip and a bit of muscling at low speeds, but as you pick up the pace there's more subtlety and less weight about the rack. The road surface seems to stream back through the thick leather steering-wheel rim with more clarity, and because you aren't steering with your shoulders you're more alert to what it's telling you. Even before you've tasted the full fury of that V12 or tested the grip of the broad Pirellis, the LP640 feels lighter on its toes, more responsive and less likely to coddle you when you're at maximum attack.

With the congested roads of Bologna and the roadwork-crippled A1 dissolving in the LP640's widescreen wing mirrors, a spike of adrenalin surges into my blood. I've driven lots of miles in

Murciélagos, some of them chasing a wrung-out Ferrari 575M HGTC, others staring down the multiple-barrel exhaust of a flame-spitting Zonda S. Awesome experiences, but I can't remember feeling so wired, so alert as I am now. The LP640 is sending out a new, edgy vibe, and somehow I just know I'm in for a serious workout.

The Raticosa and Futa passes are a size too small for the Murciélago, narrow and tree-lined, visibility hampered. Even so, the big Lamborghini devours whole sections with no fuss and without even needing to change gear. At low revs the V12 occasionally stutters momentarily, like it's clearing its throat, but by 3500rpm the forces are really building. It means that even tight turns can be negotiated in third, and as they open out you can enjoy the V12's ever-changing voice right up to the far side of 100mph.

That first kick at 3500rpm is followed by a more intense jump in effort at 4500rpm. Now you sense that there really is 631bhp nestled behind your shoulders. Despite the typically long gearing, the revs are piling on here. At around 6500rpm – just when you're fighting the instinct to change

'The engine just never stops giving, the brakes show no sign of fade'

up – the engine hits hard again and howls up to 8000rpm. The brick-wall limiter shocks you into an upshift, and with barely a pause to gather your faculties, the ride starts all over again. It's an assault on the senses, your neck pushing against the g-forces, your eyes working hard to process how quickly the scenery is rushing towards you, the V12's pure scream ringing in your ears.

The LP640's other trump card is played when you hit the middle pedal and the six-pot callipers bite into the (optional) carbon-ceramic discs. There's no dead play in the brake pedal, so the deceleration hits you hard as the seatbelt cuts into your shoulder, but the LP640 stays composed. Punch some lock into the steering wheel and the front tyres key into the road as the nose slots in towards the apex. Steady the throttle and a bit of understeer does initially build – but it's here that the LP640 departs from lesser Murciélagos.

Stay committed and the understeer stabilises, and as you prepare for the corner exit and start

to work the throttle, the car pivots around its gearstick, tightening your line before whipping into a flourish of oversteer as the road straightens. You need to be quick to catch it, flicking on a stab of opposite lock before you can really fill the V12's lungs again. Admittedly it only occurs with the (very intrusive) TCS turned off, but even so, the first time it happens it's a bit of a shock. You could always poke the Murciélago's tail wide, but it took brutality and never felt like its natural stance (at least at road speeds). The LP640, however, is happier to adopt oversteer, but demands you stay on top of it where a standard Murciélago would be covering your mistakes.

Of course, when that tiny amount of understeer first appears you can just back off and keep it neutral, right? Well, you could back off, but then you've got a new problem. Instead of power oversteer, the rear unloads as you come off the gas and the car rolls into momentum oversteer. It's still controllable, but the slip angle

tends to be bigger and you need to be careful not to overcorrect. And even with a measured correction, a sideways Murciélago takes up an awful lot of road…

With time you can actively promote the LP640's adjustability, pitching it into clear-sighted corners on a trailing throttle, catching the tail and then unleashing the V12 to overwhelm the rear tyres and ride-out a big, scary and intensely satisfying slide. It sounds more terrifying than it is, as the LP640's four-wheel-drive system does its best to assist you by shuffling power to the front wheels as soon as the rears start to spin. Just beware that final injection of power from 6500rpm – when that V12 starts to sing it has a habit of stabbing the tail even wider.

On the wide and deserted roads that fork away from the Raticosa, the LP640 is immense. The engine just never stops giving, the brakes show no sign of fade, and when you're comfortable with the chassis set-up you can make it flow like you

Pared-back, pumped-up and positively bursting with energy, the Diablo SV embodies everything that makes Lamborghini special. Back in the mid-'90s when Mr Barker had his first taste of an SV, his conclusion was simple: 'the best drivers' car Lamborghini has ever made'.

Today, the SV still makes a vivid impression. The car pictured here, currently for sale at TopGear Specialist Cars, Bath (01501 763800), is one of the first batch of SVs. It might not have the bold SV script across its flanks, but under the engine cover there's a 510bhp 5.7-litre V12, and every scrap of power is channelled rearwards to its 335/30 ZR18 Pirelli P Zeros. There's no traction control, no ABS. And it's raining.

The SV still looks fabulous, and although there are sharp lines where the Murciélago has smooth curves, the basic proportions and sheer scale of the Diablo are broadly similar. It even wears

might an M3. The epic tussle between 631bhp and four sticky contact patches plays out to a soundtrack of shrieking V12 and the howls of expensive vaporising rubber.

I can't remember driving a mid-engined supercar with such abandon. The LP640 loves being grabbed by the scruff and really driven, and when you're getting all the messages that there's yet more to exploit, its size and value are forgotten. You're committed, the LP640 is reacting to your every input, and soon you're completely absorbed, delving deep into your own abilities and the car's awesome potential. It's one of the motoring world's great challenges.

Perhaps this first example is a little more edgy than later production cars will be, but I suspect that all LP640s will remain a bigger challenge than the old car. It has to stand comparison with the new generation of supercars, after all – Lamborghini's heritage and pride demands nothing less. Now isn't the time to go for the soft option.

And the LP640 is anything but soft. When you've worked that wonderful gearbox hard, headbutted the 8000rpm limiter and extracted every last scrap of power, breached the limits of the tyres and pushed uncomfortably close to your own, the LP640 has got you. You need another hit. And when you've cut the engine dead and you sit in that weird, enveloping silence, you can only hope it's not the last time you get to experience the LP640's super-reality. In those few moments all I could think was 'I want one, I really want one'. And so should you.

SPECIFICATION

MURCIELAGO LP640

■ **Engine**	V12
■ **Location**	Mid, longitudinal
■ **Displacement**	6496cc
■ **Cylinder block**	Aluminium alloy
■ **Cylinder head**	Aluminium alloy, dohc, four valves per cylinder, variable valve timing
■ **Fuel and ignition**	Lamborghini LIE ignition and fuel injection, variable intake geometry
■ **Max power**	631bhp @ 8000rpm
■ **Max torque**	487lb ft @ 6000rpm
■ **Transmission**	Six-speed manual or e-gear paddle-shift gearbox, four-wheel drive
■ **Front suspension**	Double wishbones, coil springs, gas dampers, anti-roll bar
■ **Rear suspension**	Double wishbones, coil springs, gas dampers, anti-roll bar
■ **Brakes**	Ventilated discs, 380mm diameter front, 355mm rear, ABS
■ **Wheels**	8.5 x 18in front, 13 x 18in rear
■ **Tyres**	245/35x18 front, 335/30x18 rear, Pirelli P Zero Rosso
■ **Weight (kerb)**	1665kg
■ **Power-to-weight**	385bhp/ton
■ **0-62mph**	3.4sec (claimed)
■ **Top speed**	211mph (claimed)
■ **Basic price**	c£180,000 (2006)
■ **On sale**	Summer 2006 – present

evo RATING ★★★★★

the same-size rear rubber.

If anything, it looks more aggressive than the LP640, the twin roof-intakes and rear wing screaming its intent. Swing the door up and drop into the seats and the SV's minimalist, roughly finished interior is very un-Audi. But it really makes you smile. The slim-hipped, barely-padded seats are fantastic, too. Despite pedals offset to the left (although no worse than in right-hand-drive Murciélagos) you feel instantly comfortable, at ease.

Only when you pull down the door and check the view in the wing mirrors do you feel suddenly on edge. The broad hips fill the mirrors completely, and when you flick your eyes up to the internal rear-view mirror you see the engine imprisoned behind a thick black mesh. Bloody hell. It's so mad they had to lock it in a cage...

The engine wakes with less exuberance than the LP640's, and in fact the 48-valve V12 sounds very subdued (this car doesn't have the sports exhaust option). Hook the gearlever across and back to engage first gear. The shift action is heavy – much heavier than the LP640's – but it feels very deliberate and precise. The clutch requires some effort too. The

SV is not a car you pussy-foot in.

Having said that, the ride quality is remarkable. Better than the LP640's at low speed, although it lacks the newer car's control over rapid-fire bumps, the front wheels occasionally hopping instead of sticking to the road. Despite the heavy gearchange, the SV is incredibly easy to stroke around town. This DNA survives to the LP640 today, but I have to say it's a surprise to find that the hardcore SV is so docile.

The lighter, more delicate and quicker steering is perhaps the one area where the SV really departs from the LP640, and it feels all the better for it. There's more feel, more enthusiasm to change direction (the lower weight – 1576kg vs 1665kg – helps here too) and it makes the huge Diablo feel nimble, light on its feet. Sometimes too light on its feet...

On these wet roads that V12 will kick the tail loose if you provoke it, and unlike the LP640 there's no clever electronic brain there to help you out. It's just you and that pendulous engine fighting it out for supremacy. Fortunately the precise, weighty throttle and quick steering give you plenty of options, and although you wouldn't relish a thrash in sodden conditions, the SV can be driven quickly and securely even when the heavens open. In fact, traction is very impressive, and because the smaller-displacement V12 doesn't have the instant massive torque delivery of the LP640, the rear tyres rarely fizz into wheelspin without provocation.

When it's dry, the SV is fabulous. The V12 has solid, insistent grunt in the mid-range and a strong top-end. It's not crazy, LP640-fast, but when you've got it wound up on the right road, I can't imagine you'd often crave more horsepower. And the chassis allows you to carry so much speed, turning in crisply with hardly any understeer and little roll, then really digging-in and letting you jump on the power.

Rear-drive, when it's done this well, needn't be scary. The LP640 is faster, has more grip, more pure uncut speed, but you have to work just as hard to unlock its potential as you do the SV's. Which is cause for celebration in my eyes – Lamborghinis are meant to really engage you. But an LP640 SV, now that really would be something...

Specification

Engine	V12, 5707cc, 48v
Max power	510bhp @ 7100rpm
Max torque	428lb ft @ 5200rpm
0-60mph	3.9sec
Top speed	187mph

First SV (short for 'Sport Veloce') arrived in '96, a stripped-back, more powerful version of rear-drive Diablo. This car is later, slightly more civilised version; interior (top) swathed in Alcantara

S O L A R P O W E R

In 2006 we chased the
sun in two of the most
desirable convertibles
around: Lamborghini's
Gallardo Spyder and
Ferrari's F430 Spider

Gallardo's wedgy shape loses none of its aggression in decapitated form, helped by a profile that, with the roof folded away, is uninterrupted by protrusions, from wing-mirror to tail light

The Touareg driver never saw it coming. Mesmerised by the receding sight and sound of the slate-grey Gallardo Spyder burbling through the bustling Highland town of Glen Coe, his eyes are glued to his rear-view mirror rather than the road ahead.

Watching incredulous from the Ferrari, it's clear that the Corsa innocently parked in his path doesn't stand a chance. Nailed by two and a half tons of wayward SUV with a grimace-inducing *crump-thump-skrrsssch*, the hapless Vauxhall hatchback buckles under the force of the collision, while the distracted Touareg driver wears the expression of a man who's just swallowed his own tongue, snapped from blissful daydream to waking nightmare in one sickening thud.

It's an unexpectedly dramatic end to a fabulous two days in which we've enjoyed these Modenese roadsters to the full amongst the towering peaks and tranquil lochs of the Scottish Highlands. It's also a timely reminder of just what a spectacle these cars make amongst ordinary traffic. They certainly made an impression on the Corsa…

Rewind 48 hours, and John Hayman and I have just emerged from the Gallardo after a five-hour haul from Northamptonshire to Livingston, on the outskirts of Edinburgh. We've not lowered the roof once, which feels a bit fraudulent, especially when

the sun's out, but when you've got big miles to cover you stick to the motorways, at which point the appeal of open-top driving is torn to shreds in the conversation-killing slipstream. Better, we think, to keep our powder dry until tomorrow, when we're due to collect the Ferrari F430 Spider and make for the roads that lie between Fort William and Mallaig, on the west coast. Not only are they a fittingly epic stage on which to drive these two towering supercars, but the endless Highland days see the sun rise at just after 4am and darkness held at bay until almost 11pm. Short of driving to Scandinavia, nowhere packs more sunshine into a summer's day. Let's just hope Mother Nature doesn't rain on our parade.

We arrive bright and early at Rio Prestige (the

supercar hire company) to collect the Ferrari which they have kindly made available to us for this test. It's finished in the classic combination of Rosso Corsa paint and Crema leather, and looks quite a sight. More of a surprise is that it's also fitted with an equally 'classic' manual gearbox and steel brakes, rather than the optional F1 paddle-shift transmission and carbon stoppers that the vast majority of F430 customers are reported to select. It's fortunate in a way, because the Gallardo has three pedals and a stick, too, so we'll be comparing old-school like with like.

For the most part, the drive up to Fort William isn't a memorable one, thanks largely to a satnav system that seems determined to take us through every unremarkable, traffic-choked town between

Edinburgh and the Highlands. Things pick up once we get to Crianlarich, from which point the roads open, the traffic abates and Hayman decides to stretch the Lambo's legs.

It's quite something to follow, even when you're chasing it in a Ferrari. Emitting a ground-shaking soundtrack, the chiselled Gallardo, with its broad, square shoulders, looks just as cohesive as the coupe from which it's derived, and is more convincingly sculpted and pleasingly proportioned than the slightly awkward-looking Ferrari.

The reason becomes apparent when we decide to drop the roofs. The complexity on show in both is jaw-dropping, even if the assorted whirring, clunking and straining of electric motors is ultimately a bit of a palaver compared with the simplicity of, say, a BMW Z4. But while the entire engine deck of the Lambo tilts skywards to allow the tightly folded hood to contort itself into the small rectangular compartment close to the rear scuttle, the Ferrari's mechanism is confined to the small humps that surround each roll-hoop, thereby preserving the beautiful 'display case' engine cover.

While it's wonderful to see the red crackle-finish of the Ferrari's 4.3-litre V8 on show, the roll-hoops, roof cover and humps interrupt the F430's sharp lines. The Lamborghini's design is tidier and less disruptive, even if it does deny you any glimpse of the equally impressive V10. The flat, vented deck runs in one unbroken line from cockpit to tail lights, creating a beautifully clean, lean profile. It also incorporates a brilliant glass anti-buffeting screen, which raises and lowers like an electric window from the bulkhead behind the seats. It's a very neat touch.

With our pace increasing and the road punctuated by some wicked crests, dips and smooth sequences of corners, both cars are finding a fast rhythm. The F430 has that distinctive, pointy-steering feel of the Berlinetta, with very keen front-end responses, and it's an easy,

'The F430 is a sharp, dashing blade, quick-witted and hungry for revs'

satisfying car to thread along these unfamiliar roads at a brisk pace.

I have to confess to inadvertently pulling at the indicator stalk a few times and wondering why the transmission wasn't delivering a punchy shift, before remembering, somewhat embarrassed, that I should be stirring that quaint alloy stick down by my left knee. It feels odd in a car I normally associate with fingertip immediacy, but the action of the clutch and lever are light and positive, and the evocative ball-topped stick is soon clacking between the fingers of the hallowed open gate in satisfying style.

We power through the humbling beauty of Glen Coe, two raucous wedges of aluminium darting through the holiday traffic, in pursuit of possibly the only car and driver combination capable of upstaging us: a Hertz rental Focus driven by photographer Andy Morgan. By the time we pass Fort William and find the roads we enjoyed so much back on eCoty 2003 (evo 063), it's well into the afternoon, and Morgan's shutter finger is clearly getting itchy.

While he and Hayman busy themselves with

some shots of the Lambo, I make off with the Ferrari for a solo drive. It's a sharp, dashing blade, the F430. Quick-witted and hungry for revs, it thrives on the fast, flowing roads that characterise this remote region of Scotland. You need to work at it, though, for although tractable, the V8 really hits its stride, and finds its voice, above 5000rpm. Below this the engine emits an intrusive but not especially pleasant blare. Stay above it, though, and the Spider builds to a shrieking crescendo that ricochets off the craggy outcrops at the road's edge, filling the open cockpit with echoes of Fiorano.

There's tremendous feel to the brakes, and excellent stopping power too. In fact, for all but the most extreme road and track use they feel plenty strong enough, even if they do look a bit weedy behind the five-spoke alloys. It's delightful to brake hard into a corner, roll your ankle across to execute a heel-and-toe downshift and find the brake and throttle pedals perfectly placed.

Less satisfying is the scuttle-shake that shivers through the structure over major road imperfections. It's not catastrophic, but it is

noticeable, and it does diminish the sense of precision you feel compared with the Berlinetta. Worse is the pronounced kick-back through the steering wheel when you hit a mid-corner drain-cover or pot hole with the inside front wheel. It really does jar, especially when the flow of information is otherwise detailed and delicate. The impact wrong-foots the car for a moment or two. If you've experienced the rock-solid integrity of the Berlinetta, it comes as quite a shock.

Inherently, though, the F430 Spider's chassis balance remains exciting, exploitable and minutely adjustable. Entering one of the countless tightening corners a shade too fast, I'm forced to brake deeper than ideal, and wind-on another quarter-turn of lock. It's one of those moments that makes you catch your breath, but the Ferrari is with me all the way, tightening its line without complaint, the mildest hint of understeer the only outward sign of my misjudgement. For an agile, prickly mid-engined car, it's impressively forgiving.

By the time I return to Morgan's photographic base on the shores of Loch Shiel, he's done with the Gallardo. Having got really dialled-in to the

'The Gallardo is astonishingly sure-footed and surreally rapid'

F430's responses, the contrast between it and the Lamborghini is immediate and startling: where the Ferrari is all about lightness of touch, the Gallardo is a chunky heavyweight that demands a more muscular approach.

The clutch, gearbox and steering are all significantly weightier than the Ferrari's. The engine brims with bombast from the moment you fire it up, and the chassis feels beefier, all four tyres planted squarely on their treadblocks where the Ferrari always feels light on its feet. It's a more physical, all-encompassing car. You drive it with your forearms rather than your wrists, and while you don't have to bully it, you do have to assert yourself before the Gallardo gels.

If there's one element that dominates the Gallardo experience, it's the engine. Moments when the Ferrari can be caught off the boil simply don't exist in the Gallardo, for the big-capacity V10 has grunt to spare. It pulls with conviction from nothing and even manages an inspiring second wind between 7000 and 8000rpm, it's note hardening, the sense of acceleration intensifying just when you think things are about to tail off. Full-revs with the roof down is a cataclysmic experience, the brutal, tortured howl surely ranking as the most visceral cry since Chewbacca did his flies up too quickly.

The Lambo's gearshift isn't as quick as the Ferrari's, thanks to the extra effort required and also because of a slight gristly feel as the lever passes the neutral plane of the gate. It's not obstructive, in fact if you like to get stuck in, the shift's meaty quality can be particularly satisfying. However, for sheer speed and purity, the Ferrari 'box is best, although I can't help thinking that the superb F1 system better suits the F430's character. Heresy I know, but…

Wearing Pirelli P Zero Corsas, the Gallardo is a gripfest on these smooth, well-surfaced roads, long swooping corners highlighting its high-g abilities to perfection. Coupled with weighty steering that increases in effort and feel as you pile on the speed and cornering force, it's astonishingly sure-footed and surreally rapid. The one fly (or should that

be midge?) in the ointment is a pronounced self-centre effect which tries to pull the car straight when you relax your grip on the suede-rimmed wheel as you see a corner begin to open out. You can drive around the trait, but you're forced to steer the car straight rather than let the wheel flow through your hands, which compounds the physicality of hustling the Gallardo.

As ever with the Gallardo, the brakes come in for some criticism. Not for their lack of staying power, as the roads here are fast and flowing rather than tight and twisty, but for the initial lack of feel and pedal travel, making smooth driving, not to mention effective heel-and-toeing, less than intuitive. Again, you do learn to compensate with time and familiarity, but it could be better.

It's been a memorable day's driving, but it's not over yet, for we have an appointment with a sunset on the shores of the Sound of Arisaig. Keen to get prepared in plenty of time, Andy leads us back to our hotel, the amusingly named Cnoc-na-Faire in the equally chucklesome Back of Keppoch. The plan is to check-in, dump our bags and head back out, but as we assemble outside at just after 7pm the sun's still beating down as though it's mid-afternoon. As photographers are as fickle as farmers when it comes to the prevailing weather conditions, we go back indoors 'to let the light soften', whatever that means…

Quiet, open roads of
the Highlands provide
the perfect territory for
enjoying cars with this level
of performance. An 11pm
sunset is an added bonus.
Gallardo's raucous exhaust
note emphasised when you
have the top down (and a
towering rockface close by)

Three fine courses and two hours later, it's still broad daylight, but with Hayman twitching every time a resident orders a pint of lager, we decide to head back out, finally running out of light at 11pm. The nights really are short this far north.

Next morning we have a few more shots to do before heading back to Edinburgh. It's an opportunity to let thoughts and feelings crystallise, and hopefully find a way of picking a winner. But it won't be easy…

As we've established, faults are few and far between. The Ferrari's biggest failing is the mild but noticeable scuttle-shake and serious steering kick-back, while the Lambo suffers from clumsy brake feel and a certain lack of delicacy. Neither, it has to be said, are as pure or precise as their tin-roofed relatives, but hasn't that always been the case?

After many memorable miles, deciding between them is almost impossible. Both deliver a rare sense of occasion and connect you with the world you're driving through like few other cars, their speed, sound and involvement all top-drawer. In all honesty, when two cars are this closely matched, aesthetics are as good an arbiter as any.

Forced with making a choice, we'd go for the Lamborghini. While annoying, with time you learn to drive around its ham-fisted brake response and the steering's over-keenness to self-centre, but the Ferrari's steering grates more. Perhaps the surgical precision of the Berlinetta means the F430 has more to lose in the transition to Spider. That to our eyes the Gallardo also gets the styling nod seals the win for Sant'Agata, but by the slimmest of margins.

Ferrari has ensured that the Spider's hood arrangement doesn't interfere with the view of the V8, with its trademark red, crackle-finish cam covers, through the glass engine cover (above)

SPECIFICATION

	F430 SPIDER	GALLARDO SPYDER
■ Engine	V8	V10
■ Location	Mid, longitudinal	Mid, longitudinal
■ Displacement	4308cc	4961cc
■ Bore x stroke	92 x 81mm	82.5 x 92.8mm
■ Cylinder block	Aluminium alloy, dry sumped	Aluminium alloy, dry sumped
■ Cylinder head	Aluminium alloy, dohc per bank, four valves per cylinder	Aluminium alloy, dohc per bank, four valves per cylinder
■ Fuel and ignition	Bosch engine management, sequential multipoint fuel injection	Lamborghini LIE engine management, sequential multipoint fuel injection
■ Max power	483bhp @ 8500rpm	513bhp @ 8000rpm
■ Max torque	343lb ft @ 5250rpm	376lb ft @ 4500rpm
■ Transmission	Six-speed manual, rear-wheel drive, E-Diff, CST	Six-speed manual, four-wheel drive, rear lsd, ESP, ASR
■ Front suspension	Double wishbones, coil springs, 'Skyhook' adaptive damping, arb	Double wishbones, coil springs, gas dampers, anti-roll bar
■ Rear suspension	Double wishbones, coil springs, 'Skyhook' adaptive damping, arb	Double wishbones, coil springs, gas dampers, anti-roll bar
■ Brakes	Ventilated and cross-drilled discs, 330mm front and rear, ABS, EBD	Ventilated discs, 365mm front, 335mm rear, ABS, EBD
■ Wheels	7.5 x 19in front, 10 x 19in rear	8.5 x 19in front, 11 x 19in rear
■ Weight (kerb)	1505kg	1570kg
■ Power-to-weight	326bhp/ton	332bhp/ton
■ 0-62mph	4.1sec (claimed)	4.3sec (claimed)
■ Max speed	193mph+ (claimed)	195mph (claimed)
■ Basic price	£127,050 (2006)	£131,000 (2006)
evo RATING	★★★★★	★★★★★

'After many memorable miles, deciding between them is almost impossible'

MURCIÉLAGO LP640
ROADSTER

Pictures: David Shepherd

LP640's more aggressive styling works well on the Roadster, while the open top is all the better for enjoying Lamborghini's mighty 631bhp V12. Hairdressers need not apply

Lambo LP640 Roadster

Open-top Murciélago boosted by 631bhp, 6.5-litre V12

I can't tell you what a roofless 205mph feels like because I lost my bottle at just over 170. At this rarefied velocity, wind turbulence has enough power to drown out the wild shriek of a wrung-out Lamborghini V12 pumping out 631bhp just a few inches from your ears, while the storm whipping around your scalp becomes so violent it threatens to suck your head off your shoulders. An experience that was thrilling just a few seconds ago grows increasingly hostile with each additional mile-per-hour, to the point where it's just too uncomfortable to go on.

In the same vein as the Veyron, the buzz from the monumental v-max of the Lamborghini Murciélago LP640 Roadster comes not from terrifying yourself attempting to verify those top-speed boasts, but just from the knowledge that it's theoretically possible.

Undoubtedly the best bits all happen between zero and 150mph. Aurally they happen at just over a ton, with your right foot buried deep into the carpet and the soaring revs climbing towards the business end of fourth gear. The swirling air has yet to distort the purity of the exuberantly aggressive soundtrack. In fact, here it adds to the intensity, blowing the epic 12-cylinder cacophony around the cabin, enveloping you in the outrageous wail as though filtered by the latest Dolby 5.1 surround-sound system. And then, just when you think life can't get any better, you find a tunnel...

The LP640 looked a likely candidate for Roadsterisation as soon as the 6.5-litre evolution of the iconic V12 proved to be significantly superior to the 6.2 installed in the original Murcie rag-top. Smoother, sweeter, more sonorous and endowed with an almighty kick from 4000rpm all the way to the 8000rpm limiter, it is arguably the finest powerplant ever to have come out of the Sant'Agata factory. Where the 6.2 would send vibrations through the chassis at high revs, the 6.5 just pours on the power.

'Each pull of the right-hand e-gear paddle unleashes another savage burst of thrust'

Mixing the LP640's hard-edged, muscular styling with the Roadster look has created probably the most visually arresting Lambo since the Anniversary Countach. The wide windscreen combined with the cut-down side-screens gives it the appearance of a supercar wearing Oakleys. Be in no doubt, the Roadster is seriously cool.

Unless, that is, you fit the roof. As the Roadster is designed to be a barchetta rather than a full convertible, the canvas cover is to roofs what a space-saver is to tyres – only to be used in an absolute emergency. The mix of rods, poppers and

bracing struts will have your head spinning and thumbs aching, and erecting the contraption takes at least five minutes. You're even speed-limited with it up (160kph or 99mph) to prevent it blowing away like a tent in a gale. Probably best to do what we did – leave it behind.

Flick up and pull on the handle, and the door arcs skywards in the same slickly damped manner of the coupe. With both doors up, the centre section appears surprisingly exposed and vulnerable to torsional twisting; without the fixed roof, you wonder whether the floorpan alone can provide enough

strength to contain the might of all that power and torque. The Roadster, however, benefits from a revised backbone structure that uses both steel and carbonfibre, bonded and riveted, along with an engine bay covered by a comprehensive web of bracing struts (either made from steel or, as seen here, in carbonfibre for a £3000 premium).

The result is remarkably impressive. The steering column occasionally shimmies over sharp potholes, but regular bumps and cambers are soaked up easily enough, while overall composure remains surprisingly comparable to the fixed-head car. Most of the strength in the coupe structure must also be in the floor then, because the weight penalty for choosing an open car is a negligible 25kg.

We take the Roadster to the same roads where we tested the coupe LP640 six months ago (093). The Raticosa and Futa passes south of Bologna are narrow, winding and riddled with tightening turns and testing, bumpy apexes to catch out the unwary. As a supercar test route it's as tough as they come; if there are any weakness with the Roadster's chassis, we'll discover them here.

The steering requires a firm hand, particularly through hairpins, but, as before, it lightens at speed, feeding a high level of confidence-inspiring detail back through the thick suede wheel and allowing accurate placement – vital in such a wide machine.

The springs and dampers have been revised from those fitted to the coupe LP640, however the

resulting handling characteristics remain very like those of the coupe we drove on eCoty (evo 099), suggesting there was something wrong with the first coupe which we drove here. That car was a nightmare – very edgy in corners, permanently on the tips of its toes. The Roadster feels much more benign, much more settled and driveable. Its set-up allows for a mid-turn rethink should it prove necessary. Need to tighten your line? No problem. Push hard and the nose eventually begins to scrub wide – and if you leave the traction control switched on, this is as far as things will develop, the electronics neatly keeping everything on the curved and narrow.

Switch the system out and initially the results are the same, with the gentle understeer building further and the nose running wider still. Back off now and the Pirelli P Zeros recover their hold on the tarmac without fuss. Stay on the power, however, and things rapidly become very exciting indeed. The 13in-wide rear tyres are finally overwhelmed by the onslaught of power and flick wide, and when it happens you'd better be ready to deal out some rapid and decisive corrective action, for there's a whole lot of mass on the move. Don't panic and jump off the power, though – the sudden weight transfer will accentuate the slide to dramatic, road-filling proportions. Instead, balance the throttle and the LP640's four-wheel-drive system will divert more motive energy forwards, giving the front added bite and pulling the Roadster clear from the slide.

Drive just under this rather hairy zone and the alfresco Lambo flows over these near-deserted mountain roads, each pull of the right-hand (optional) e-gear paddle unleashing another savage burst of inexorable thrust. The (again optional) carbon-ceramic brakes with six-pot callipers perform tirelessly all day, repeatedly hauling off speed with a firm and consistent feel, allowing you to develop a rhythm similar to that in the coupe and cover the ground at a similarly scorching pace.

Out here, when you're wrapped up the drama of it all, the small degradation in structural rigidity and the tiny weight penalty count for nothing. Coupe or Roadster? It all boils down to whether you like driving occasionally in the rain.

Roger Green

Specification

Engine	V12, 6496cc, 48v
Max power	631bhp @ 8000rpm
Max torque	487lb ft @ 6000rpm
Top speed	205mph (claimed)
0-62mph	3.4sec (claimed)
Basic price	£200,000
On sale	Summer 2007

evo RATING

★★★★☆

+ Performance to match the looks
− Don't bother with the roof

Words: Richard Meaden Pictures: Gus Gregory

Incredi*bull!*

Lighter
and more
powerful, the
Superleggera
was launched
in 2007 as
the ultimate
Gallardo. We
drove it on road
and track

Left: interior swathed in Alcantara, with carbon visible everywhere from the seat backs to the door panels. Carbon brakes (above) an option

How

special is the Gallardo Superleggera? Special enough to grab a key and go for a night-time drive immediately after a ten-and-a-half-hour flight from Heathrow to Phoenix. Special enough for Gus Gregory to want to take pictures of it in the dark. Special enough for the good people of Scottsdale to be drawn from their homes like zombie nightwalkers to cup their hands at the side windows.

Hot on the heels of the gob-smacking Murciélago LP640, the Gallardo Superleggera isn't just special, it's spectacular. It's also continued proof that Lamborghini is a genuine force to be reckoned with. Not just as a maker of supercar pin-ups – Sant'Agata has been doing that since 1963 – but as a manufacturer fit to stand alongside Ferrari and Porsche, both for the standard of its engineering and the robust state of its business.

With sales up 30 per cent, turnover up 43 per cent and pre-tax profits up by a staggering 311 per cent (thanks in part to a burgeoning clothing and accessories range), Lamborghini is well on course to achieve its goal of being the most

profitable supercar manufacturer in the world. Total production for 2006 was just 2087 cars (compared with 5000-plus for both Ferrari and Aston Martin), yet even this figure represents a massive change of fortunes for the marque – for its first four decades it produced an average of just 250 cars per year…

That production total is set to increase during 2007, but the Superleggera isn't going to contribute more than 350 units to the number, for Lamborghini wants to keep it rare and exclusive. So exclusive, in fact, that all of this year's allocation is already spoken for, despite a 20 per cent increase in price over the regular Gallardo to a very serious-sounding £150,000.

Diehard enthusiasts may feel uneasy at the hard-hearted thread of Teutonic steel that runs through the formerly chaotic but undeniably endearing Italian institution, but there's no arguing with the quality of the end product. Audi's involvement also bodes well for the future direction of Lamborghini, for although the perceived threat from the R8 shouldn't be underestimated, it's clear that the plan is to steer the mid-engined Audi towards Porsche's

mainstream 911s and push Lamborghini towards producing harder, faster and more extreme cars to tackle Stuttgart's track-bred GT3 and GT2 models and Modena's rumoured F430 Challenge Stradale. The Superleggera is the car to take Lamborghini back where it belongs.

Our launch schedule is so tight it squeaks. On arrival at Phoenix, Gus and I calculate that we'll be on US soil for just 25 hours before jumping back on the Heathrow-bound BA 747, which partly explains why we feel the need to maximise our time with the car, despite the almost total jet-lag-induced befuddlement of our brains. Lamborghini's PR team generously obliges, handing me the key to a juicy Arancio Borealis (orange to you) Superleggera.

This vibrant shot of orange bull is more effective than a gallon of the red variety. Even in the dark it looks magnificent. Squat, square-jawed and glowering with purpose and aggression, it exudes the kind of hardcore attitude you expect from a stripped and ripped version of what was already one of the most no-nonsense supercars around.

Time restrictions or not, we can't help but pause to enjoy what will clearly be a big part of the

'*Even in the dark it looks magnificent. Squat, square-jawed and glowering with purpose and aggression*'

Superleggera ownership experience: standing and staring. Everything you look at and everything you touch reveals the fanatical lengths to which Lambo head of R&D Maurizio Reggiani and his team have gone to in shaving weight from the Gallardo. Plip the key, open the door and you're confronted by gloriously glossy one-piece carbon door panels, carbon-shelled sports seats and Alcantara upholstery.

The engine cover is also made from carbon, as is the fixed rear wing, which can be had in discreet low-line spec or more obviously racerish high-rise design, complete with reversing camera. The engine cover's glass window has been replaced with transparent polycarbonate, while the rear

window is made from similarly lightweight Macrolon. Pop the engine cover release and raise it aloft and you can feel the difference, the flimsy lid flying up with minimal effort.

The engine itself develops slightly more power – 9bhp to be precise – thanks to a new ECU, the mapping of which has extracted the extra bhp at higher revs without hurting the torque output. New intake and exhaust manifolds have been developed, along with a new, reduced-back-pressure exhaust system, all of which save weight but also boost performance. Judging by the stubby tailpipes jutting from the car's rear, the happy by-product will be a blood-curdling war cry.

Carbonfibre features on the sills and the rear

diffuser too, but the exterior highlights, at least for me, are the thin-spoke 'Skorpious' rims, which are forged from magnesium for minimal unsprung weight. Proof of the fixation with weight-loss can also be found in the titanium wheel nuts, which clamp the lightweight alloy wheels to lighter but stronger wheel hubs.

The optional carbon-ceramic brakes fitted to our test car are no lighter than the standard cast iron set-up thanks to the increased size of the rotors and callipers, but they do promise to address the Gallardo's propensity to suffer brake fade in extreme use. Behind the front wheels lurk thinner driveshafts, which are lighter (of course) but have been made from stronger material to compensate

Two designs of fixed rear wing are available: a full-width, high-rise version (as fitted to the car in our studio shoot, issue 103) or, for those of a less showy disposition, a smaller, more discreet item, as fitted to this car

'You can slide the standard Gallardo too, but not with such precision'

for their more spindly design. The propshaft is also lighter.

The result is a hefty 100kg weight reduction, sucking the Gallardo's mass down to 1420kg. According to Reggiani, ditching four-wheel drive for rear-wheel drive would shed another 50kg. The very fact that he knew this figure off the top of his head suggests Lamborghini thought long and hard about the pros and cons of a two-wheel-drive Superleggera, before sticking with the brand's all-wheel-drive message.

We're not intending to drive far, just into downtown Scottsdale to find some street lights in which to bathe the Gallardo for the benefit of Gregory's Hasselblad. Short hop or long haul, the Superleggera ritual is the same: slide into the heavily bolstered seat, fiddle with the straps and buckle of the four-point harness, pull them down tight then curse as you realise you're so tightly clamped in position you can't close the door!

Twist the key, smile as the starter makes its distinctive helium chuckle, then flinch as ten cylinders pound into life, a wall of noise thundering through a free-breathing exhaust system. As the revs drop, the bypass valves slowly constrict the fanfare, and the Superleggera settles into a menacing double-time tickover. Dab the brake pedal, pull back on the right-hand paddle

and we're away, chuntering slightly as the e-gear software shuffles the clutch and engine revs, and the V10's torque fights against the all-wheel-drive viscous differentials as we peel away from our parking space.

The Gallardo has always felt and sounded tough and mechanical, with plenty of clonks and whizzes and whirrs to accompany your progress. With minimal sound-deadening, the Superleggera is even more vocal, and while the noises seem a little agricultural they're no different to the metallic rasp and chattering diff of a 911 RS. Both cars place you at the centre of it all, like you're part of the machine. However, if you're expecting the slick polish of a Ferrari 599's F1-Superfast paddleshift you're in for a disappointment (an H-pattern manual is available as a no-cost option if you don't crave paddles).

We just bimble into Scottsdale, the nuggety ride pattering across the bumps, engine barely able to clear its throat, save a furtive and raucous getaway from a set of traffic lights. Hardly the definitive test, admittedly, but confirmation that while the Superleggera is far too special to use as everyday transport, it can do humdrum stop-start urban stuff without throwing a hissy fit if needs be.

Gus sniffs out a quiet spot to work, but it's not long before the first of many visitors cruise by,

stop, turn around and come back for a closer look. Most admire it from a distance, a few summon the courage to take a closer look, but none dares to touch it, while the expression of excitement, awe even, that spreads across their faces is further proof of the Gallardo Superleggera's power. We head back to our hotel before tiredness robs us of sufficient hand-eye co-ordination to find our way, but once in my room I can't sleep. Whether it's the jet-lag or the promise of a proper drive in the Superleggera I can't decide. Whatever, morning can't come soon enough.

WHETHER THE MIDDLE of Arizona is the best place to launch the Superleggera is debatable. Even by American standards, speed limits in this blistering desert state are policed with rare zeal, and with news still filtering through the rumour-mill about Audi's repeated run-ins with the law in neighbouring Nevada during the R8 launch, it's clear the spotlight, or should that be searchlight, will be focused on Lamborghini's launch event.

Fortunately we have the Phoenix International Raceway at our disposal, which means we can cut loose without fear of a starring role in the next series of *World's Wildest Police Videos*. Sadly it also means behaving ourselves on the 40-minute drive from our hotel in the foothills of Camelback

Laps of the Phoenix
International
Raceway reveal the
Superleggera is more
suited to track work
than the standard
Gallardo. Only clumsy
brake feel lets it down

Mountain to the isolated site of the PIR.

Restrained pace or not, it takes all of a mile to appreciate how different the Superleggera feels from the full-fat Gallardo, and it comes through the rim of the steering wheel. The standard car has always felt chunky and grippy and weighty, but has lacked that last few per cent of fast-twitch response. In the Superleggera you get the muscular feel but with a new sense of urgency and responsiveness. Turn the wheel, even just a little bit, and the Gallardo responds directly. Not in a jumpy, artificial manner, but with precision and without hesitation. It certainly bodes well for our session on track.

Even by Lamborghini standards the sight that greets us at Phoenix International Raceway takes our breath away. There, arranged before us in the pit lane, are three Murciélago LP640s – one silver, one yellow and one a retina-singeing shade of Kermit green – which we're instructed to line up behind. These are to be our pace cars for the day, showing us the line around the combination of banked oval and infield squiggles.

The drivers' briefing seems to hinge around one key point: do not, under any circumstances, switch off the ESP. A fair enough request given we are the first wave of a two-week world press and dealer launch, but a rule I vow to break once I've got my eye in.

For the first few sessions we go at a brisk though hardly on-limit pace, but as the 40-degree heat sends some of the press contingent in for refreshment we stick at it, gradually goading the Lamborghini instructors into quicker and quicker laps until, with a bit of judicious sandbagging, we drop off the back of the pace car, then get a clear run through the challenging second-, third- and fourth-gear left-right-left infield complex.

It's hard to judge the gains without a standard Gallardo for back-to-back comparison, but the Superleggera feels more than convincing on track. The Pirelli P Zero Corsa tyres generate plenty of grip but also relinquish their hold in a progressive manner. Turning in to the quick third-gear right-hander under power still provokes a little understeer, though the ESP nudges us neatly back on line without killing too much forward motion, but with the system switched off the Superleggera feels far more alive and responsive to throttle play.

Tackling the same corner with a slight lift on turn-in to get the weight transfer working gets the Gallardo up on tiptoes in a way the standard model couldn't manage. Settled into a perfectly balanced neutral-to-oversteer stance, the Superleggera cuts through the corner in terrific style, changing direction with zero inertia and exiting hard on the power, all four sticky Pirellis biting into the track surface.

A tighter, opening-radius second-gear corner is made for powerslides, and once again the Superleggera delivers. A sharp lift of the throttle gets the tail moving enough to allow you to pick it up on the throttle, the all-wheel-drive system shuffling the torque around with sufficient subtlety to feel the tail settle into a more rear-wheel-drive stance before pulling itself straight as the corner opens out. You can slide the standard Gallardo too, but not with such precision.

Shame, then, that the optional carbon ceramic brakes don't have the same degree of precision. There's no arguing with their emphatic stopping power, but on the circuit, as on the road, there's not much subtlety to the way they work.

Delivering insufficient bite when you just want to gently cover the pedal, they then bite too hard when you get a little further into the pedal travel. It's a trait that's more annoying on the road than on track, but even on the circuit you sometimes want the shades of grey rather than black or white stopping power. Compared with the pedal feel you get from a Porsche or Ferrari equipped with similar brakes, the Superleggera feels clumsy.

I'd be lying if I said you can detect the additional nine horses at the command of your right foot, but what you do notice is the added ferocity with which the Gallardo's V10 locks on to the red line. The top-end of each gear is savage, the last 1500rpm or so devoured in an explosive rush and with an exhaust note that sounds like the end of the world. At first glance the claimed performance improvements are useful if hardly jaw-dropping, but then achieving a 0.2sec reduction in the 0-62mph time, to 3.8sec, and a 0.3sec advantage in the standing kilometre sprint largely by weight-loss alone is some feat. Stopping distances have also been reduced, the 62mph-0 taking a whole metre less than the standard Gallardo.

Ultimately, much like an RS Porsche, CSL BMW or CS Ferrari, the Superleggera experience is much greater than the sum of its vital statistics. More about the things you can feel than those you can measure, the Superleggera is objectively impressive and subjectively intoxicating. Meticulously constructed, magnificently aggressive and mouth-wateringly desirable, this lighter, faster Lamborghini is a compelling drivers' car in the finest Sant'Agata tradition.

SPECIFICATION

SUPERLEGGERA

■ Engine	V10
■ Location	Mid, longitudinal
■ Displacement	4961cc
■ Bore x stroke	82.5 x 92.8mm
■ Cylinder block	Aluminium alloy, dry sump lubrication
■ Cylinder head	Aluminium alloy, dohc per bank, four valves per cylinder
■ Fuel and ignition	Electronic engine management, sequential direct injection
■ Max power	522bhp @ 8000rpm
■ Max torque	376lb ft @ 4250rpm
■ Transmission	Six-speed e-gear or conventional manual, four-wheel drive, rear lsd, ESP, ASR
■ Suspension	Front and rear: double wishbones, coil springs, gas dampers, arb
■ Brakes	Ventilated discs, 365mm front, 325mm rear, ABS, EBD (carbon-ceramic brakes optional)
■ Wheels	8.5 x 19in front, 11 x 19in rear
■ Tyres	235/35 ZR19 front, 295/30 ZR19 rear, Pirelli P Zero Corsa
■ Weight (kerb)	1420kg
■ Power-to-weight	373bhp/ton
■ 0-62mph	3.8sec (claimed)
■ Top speed	196mph (claimed)
■ Basic price	£150,000 (2007)

evo RATING ★★★★★

THE WILD BUNCH

Think the Superleggera is hardcore? Then consider the '60s and '70s creations of Lamborghini test driver Bob Wallace

While the Gallardo Superleggera is undoubtedly the most focused car Lamborghini has put into production in recent memory, back in the days when Ferruccio Lamborghini was in charge, he allowed the factory's test driver, New Zealander Bob Wallace, to build a series of equally, if not even more extreme one-off 'laboratorio' cars to test his ideas and develop them for future models.

Wallace was a young man in his mid-twenties when, in 1963, he joined Lamborghini as the company's test and development driver. A race-car mechanic before he joined, he retained his passion for motorsport, but since Signor Lamborghini had always vowed that his cars wouldn't race, Wallace must have felt a certain amount of frustration.

Perhaps sensing his talented young engineer's disappointment, Lamborghini indulged Wallace with the resources to explore the potential of the latest models, though admittedly in his spare time only. The results of his passionate extra-curricula efforts remain some of the most exciting and enduringly mysterious cars ever to emerge from the Sant'Agata factory.

The most famous of these is the Miura 'Jota', so named because it referred to appendix J of the FIA's homologation rule-book of the time. Despite being an unashamed racer, the Jota never saw competition, but it did play a pivotal role in developing the changes that would ultimately transform the scary and somewhat overrated Miura into the much-improved 1971 Miura SV.

By the time Wallace had finished with the Jota the only thing it shared with the original Miura was an approximate physical similarity. Everything that could be changed was changed: most of the body was made from a lightweight aerospace alloy called Avional, as was the floor; a full-width spoiler was fitted across the nose of the car to quell the Miura's propensity for low-level flight; the pop-up headlights were junked in favour of faired-in fixed items, the side windows were made from polycarbonate instead of glass, even the dual windscreen wipers were swapped for a single upright blade. Inside, the floor-hinged pedals were changed for top-hinged items and superfluous trim was stripped out.

A new chassis was formed from a structure of box sections and square tubing, making it both lighter and more rigid than the Miura's less-than-perfect original. Meanwhile, weight distribution was improved by moving the spare wheel to the back of the engine compartment and swapping the front-mounted fuel tank for a pair of tanks built into the sills. And having completely re-worked the suspension, Wallace fitted huge Campagnolo wheels and racing tyres, behind which lurked beefier ventilated discs.

The compression ratio of the V12 engine was increased to 11.5:1, while more aggressive cam profiles were fitted along with four hungry Weber carburettors with trumpets and gauze covers in place of a conventional air filter. Instead of the original Miura's Mini-like arrangement of a wet-sump engine sharing its lubricant with the transmission, Wallace separated the two major components, giving the engine a dedicated dry-

Bob Wallace (right) completely re-engineered the Miura to create the Jota, even going as far as building a new chassis

From top: original Jota, later destroyed in an accident; 'Urraco Bob'; Wallace's Jarama

floor was fitted for improved airflow and reduced weight, while the front bulkhead was modified to allow the engine to be moved back to get the weight distribution as close to 50:50 as possible – a move that necessitated a new transmission tunnel, dashboard and instrument binnacle.

Other changes inside included jettisoning interior trim in favour of a tubular roll-cage, fitting low-back Miura seats in place of the more luxurious standard items, and removing the rear seat to make space for a custom-made alloy fuel tank. Once again the glass side windows were replaced with fixed polycarbonate panes.

Outside, the standard bonnet was swapped for one sporting huge extractor vents and the original hooded headlights were changed for low-mounted faired-in units. Wallace also fitted the centre-lock cast-magnesium Campagnolo wheels from the Miura S. The standard vented-disc brake set-up remained, albeit with improved cooling to the front brakes thanks to NACA ducts cut into the new spoiler, and adjustable Koni race suspension was fitted.

Wallace also worked his magic on the Jarama's V12 engine, fitting Weber 42 DCOE carburettors – again without air filters – along with lightened and balanced pistons, conrods and flywheel for ultimate throttle response and high revs. The result was somewhere between 380 and 400bhp, delivered at a screaming 8000rpm. In a car that weighed 1170kg – some 300kg less than standard – it must have been awesome. Also sold by the factory, the Jarama ended up in the Middle East, from where it was rescued in the late '90s and restored to its former glory.

The last of Wallace's fantastic creations was the 1973 Urraco Rallye, or 'Urraco Bob' as it was christened at the factory. Its development followed the familiar and uncompromising Wallace formula of stripping weight from the car while extracting as much power from the motor as possible and transmitting it to the tarmac through fat rubber. As the 'baby' of the then-current Lamborghini range, the Urraco Bob is perhaps closest in spirit to the Gallardo Superleggera.

Wallace dry-sumped the 3-litre V8 and extracted more power by fitting four-valve cylinder heads, which, combined with his other modifications (including a pair of megaphone exhausts), yielded a claimed 330bhp. Eventually he also swapped the standard five-speed transmission for a then-radical six-speed 'box, which was mounted in a strengthened subframe. A large rear wing was fitted to reduce lift, and broad Campagnolo rims filled the arches.

Despite Ferruccio Lamborghini's avowed dislike of racing, the Urraco did venture on track, at Misano in Italy. Although more of a 'gathering' rather than a race proper, it's said that Wallace had little difficulty in dispatching the Porsche 911 RSs present. One can only guess at the car's unfulfilled racing potential.

Like the Jota and Jarama, the Urraco Bob was eventually sold, but only after it had suffered the ignominy of being left to rot in the factory grounds. It's now fully restored and owned by the Lamborghini Owners Club of Japan.

As for Wallace, shortly after completing the Urraco he left Lamborghini to start a new life in Phoenix, Arizona. He remains there to this day, running his successful restoration and engine shop, specialising in breathing new life into old Italian exotica.

sump lubrication system and fitting a new close-ratio gearbox and ZF limited-slip differential. Four unsilenced megaphone exhausts (can you imagine the noise?) completed the extraordinary transformation.

Even today the Jota concept remains compelling, both thanks to its brutal looks and its explosive performance. All the weight-reducing measures dropped the car's mass to just 880kg (some 250 less than the Miura S) while power increased to 440bhp, giving the car an eye-watering power-to-weight ratio of around 500bhp-per-ton. According to the factory it was good for 'comfortably in excess of 185mph' and could accelerate from 0-62mph in just 3.5sec.

In 1972 the first signs of financial trouble began to show at the factory and, in what many still consider to be a brutally unsentimental move, Ferruccio Lamborghini sold the Jota, both to raise some money and to put an end to the speculation about when the company would go racing.

Despite this, the factory built a number of Jota copies, but they were more cosmetic lookalikes than true replicas, and none shared the magnificently specialised hardware of the original. Sadly these copies are all that remain of the Jota legend – shortly after being sold, the original was destroyed in an accident and subsequent fire.

Wallace must have lived and breathed Lamborghini during the early '70s, for in addition to the Miura Jota he also built two further mouth-watering one-offs: one based on the front-engined V12 Jarama and another on the smaller, mid-engined V8 Urraco.

One of Lamborghini's lesser-known models, the Jarama was still a formidable car. By the time Wallace had finished with it, the somewhat unloved Jarama was little short of sensational. Starting with a Jarama S, he discarded the original steel body and replaced it with one fabricated from glassfibre and aluminium, seam-welded for added structural rigidity. A flat aluminium

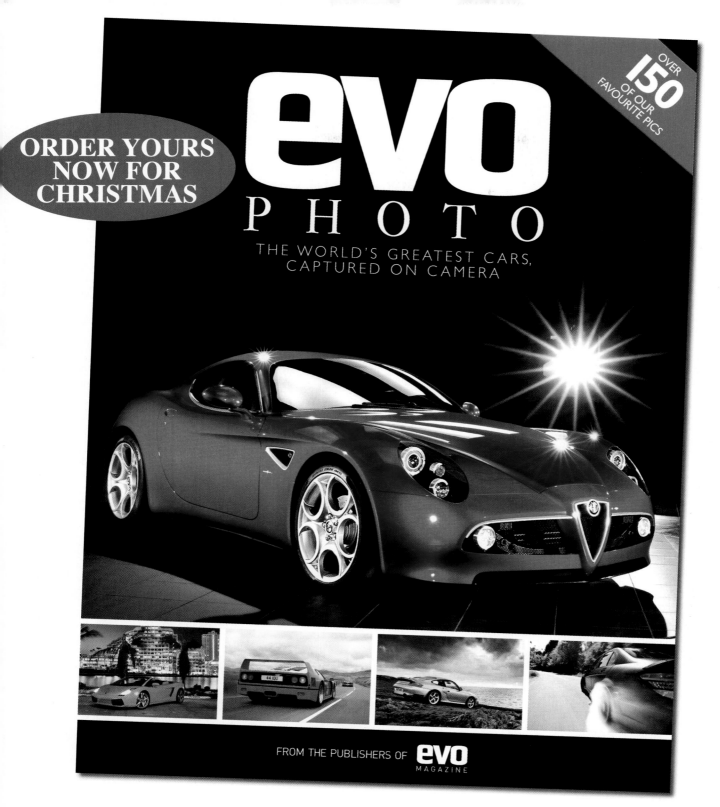

More than

It took 15 years for a British enthusiast to complete an exact replica of the long-lost Lamborghini Jota. This was its first long-distance outing, from Gstaad to Monte Carlo

a Miura

Piet Pulford is one of those people who are just naturally lucky. A couple of hours ago we set off in his recently completed Lamborghini Jota replica. The car has done virtually no road miles since it was built and we're about to drive it from Gstaad to Monaco on the Miura 40th Anniversary Tour. We'll be lucky if the fuel consumption creeps into double figures, the car has no fuel gauge and Piet has no idea how much petrol is in the tank. Shall we fill up just after the start? 'Nah, we'll be alright,' says Piet confidently.

Amazingly, we get a couple of hours'

driving under our belt before the engine stutters and its V12 roar is replaced by the quiet clicking of a fuel pump running dry. But we're drifting down a mountain pass, so the car keeps rolling. Twenty seconds later, we round a corner and there's the Swiss-French border. Complete with petrol station. And a pump selling 98-octane fuel. 'You jammy bugger!' seems the only suitable response.

But Piet deserves some good luck, having spent 15 years and a medium-sized fortune in creating a perfect replica of the one-and-only Lamborghini Jota. Built in 1970 as a personal testbed by Lamborghini

development engineer Bob Wallace, the Jota (pronounced 'Yota') was a kind of über-Miura, more race than road car. Its career was exceptionally short-lived; after being sold to Italian company Interauto in February 1972, it was heavily crashed and subsequently written off. Although a number of so-called Jota replicas were commissioned by insistent customers in the early 1970s, notably the German Lamborghini importer Hubert Hahne, these were mere pastiches of the original, civilised and tamed to make them more acceptable for road use.

No-one knows where the name Jota

'The Jota was a sort of über-Miura, more race than road car'

came from. In the 1982 book *Miura* (still available as a facsimile reprint from Mercian Manuals), co-authors Coltrin and Marchet suggest that it's because the car was built to Appendix J of the FIA regulations. Others have claimed that it's named after a Spanish dance; yet others say that it has something to do with atomic fission… One thing's for sure – given that the Italian language has no letter 'J', the UK registration that Piet Pulford has secured (see picture above) could not be bettered.

Fortunately for Piet, who has been obsessed with the Miura since he saw one during a school trip to London in the late '60s, Bob Wallace is still active. A taciturn New Zealander, who in 1960s press photos always looks as though he'd be happier working on a sheep station than mixing with flash Italians in suits and shades, Bob now lives in Arizona and fixes early Ferrari race engines in his spare time. 'I thought Piet was stark, raving mad when he first came to me,' says Bob in one of his rare bursts of emotion. 'But he's done an extremely nice job – and the workmanship is probably better than mine was on the original.'

Bob built the original Jota pretty much for his own amusement, working in tandem with chief engineer Paolo Stanzani. 'It was almost a toy,' he continues in his languid Kiwi drawl. 'Italian cars were always

overweight and I wanted something lighter to play around with. Because the Miura had become an overnight commercial success, it went into production way before any proper development could be done and it only got half-arse reasonable with the SV series. There were some major rigidity problems with the early cars, due to a lack of collaboration between ourselves and Bertone; the centre section could have been made ten times stronger. These cars weren't built by God but by mere kids like us!

'The Jota allowed me to make some major chassis revisions and try out new ideas. We had an enormously good relationship with Pirelli's R&D department and could use its private test track whenever we wanted, so the Jota was also useful for tyre development too. But my basic aim was to get weight out of the car. If you can save, say, two or three hundred kilos, you don't need massive horsepower to propel it.'

Except that, of course, the Jota did have massive horsepower. Its engine was a dry-sumped, ported and polished version of the Miura's 4-litre V12, and produced what Bob describes as '400 and change' horsepower. 'An output of 100bhp per litre was pretty good in the 1960s,' he points out. 'But we didn't do anything particularly special to the engine; just cleaned it up internally. And we strengthened the transmission housing with

Right: the monstrous, serpentine exhausts of the original Jota (left) have been faithfully replicated. There's a set of restrictors to keep the noise within reasonable limits, but they're not fitted here...

Specification

Engine	60deg V12
Location	Mid, transverse
Displacement	3929cc
Cylinder block	Aluminium alloy
Cylinder head	Aluminium alloy, dohc per bank, two valves per cylinder
Fuelling	Four triple-choke Weber 46IDL-3L carburettors
Max power	c445bhp @ 8500rpm
Max torque	n/a
Transmission	Five-speed manual gearbox, rear-wheel drive, limited slip diff
Suspension	Fr: double wishbones, coil springs & anti-roll bar. Rear: upper links and lower reversed wishbones, arb
Weight	c900kg (dry)
Power-to-weight	502bhp/ton (est)
0-60mph	5.0sec (est)
Top speed	185mph (est)
Basic price	n/a
On sale	'Fraid not

a big steel plate – otherwise the engine had a tendency to walk away from the diff casing when you applied full power.'

For the replica Jota, Bob built an engine and transmission that duplicated the original car's as closely as possible. Starting point for the project was a tired early Miura, found in the USA. The all-new bodywork and extensive chassis revisions were contracted out to Chris Lawrence of Wymondham Engineering in Norfolk – no relation to the Chris Lawrence of Deep Sanderson fame – who did a fantastic job of creating the fragile alloy nose and tail sections, which are held on by locating pins and Dzus fasteners and simply lift off rather than being hinged as on a Miura. Tragically, Chris died from cancer just a few months ago.

Final assembly was handled by another Norfolk outfit, Roger Constable of The Car Works, Ashwellthorpe. Roger is full of praise for Chris's craftsmanship but admits that getting the nose and tail to fit once the engine, dry-sump oil tank and plumbing had been installed was a trial. While the sections attach very neatly, feeding these large, cumbersome yet delicate structures over the radiator and fuel filler caps at the front, and the monster quad exhaust pipes at the back, is frustratingly fiddly.

Ah yes, the exhausts. They are the Jota's defining feature, both visually and aurally.

Piet has had a set of restrictors made up for the Bofors cannon-sized tailpipes but on this debut run down to Monaco he can't resist leaving them off. Every time one of us cranks the starter and the V12 explodes into life behind our heads I think of the opening scenes of *Le Mans*.

You sit low and casual in the Jota, legs spread as if slouched in your favourite TV-viewing easy chair. The screen sweeps

around in panoramic Stratos fashion and the broad sills, each of which contains a 60-litre fuel tank, create useful elbow room on either side. There's lots of black-painted sheet alloy, blue Dymo labels with evocative Italian descriptions, and a total absence of anything soft or forgiving.

The foot pedals are reassuringly large and well spaced, their broad metal treads looking as if they've been lifted from one

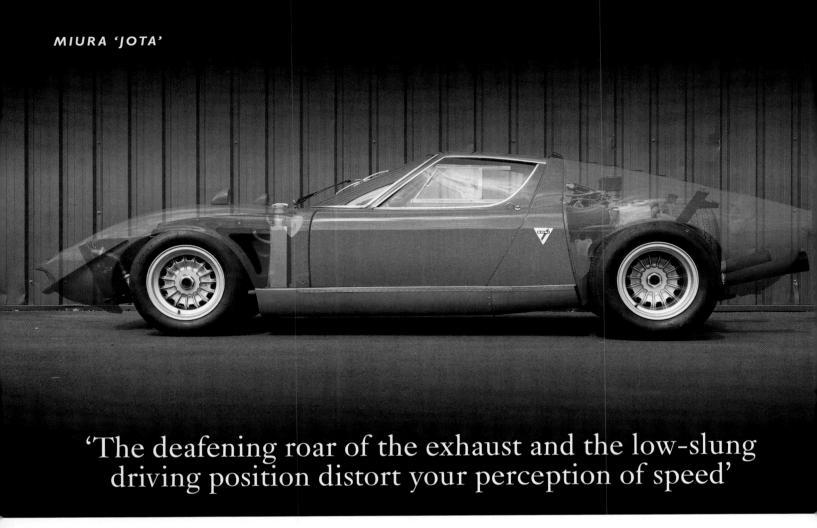

'The deafening roar of the exhaust and the low-slung driving position distort your perception of speed'

of Cavaliere Lamborghini's tractors, but it's impossible for the driver to release the handbrake without brushing an elbow against the rear bulkhead. That's a mistake you make only once: after being cooked for a couple of hours by four litres of tuned V12, that sheet of alloy gets as hot as the baking tray under your Christmas turkey.

But the clutch is surprisingly light and you can trickle the Jota away on a whiff of throttle – just as well, for the sake of the hearing of anyone standing within 40 feet. The steering is light, too, despite the 9.5-inch section front tyres (the rears measure an incredible 12.5 inches across). Rearward vision is non-existent, of course, but otherwise the Jota isn't difficult to drive.

It does make a fantastic sound. Forget all the usual niceties of induction hiss, valve-train chatter and the other nuances that journalists like to use to pep up their copy: the Jota is simply raw, animal, noise. It's loud at idle and it just gets louder as you pile on the revs. At low engine speeds it sounds as though someone is blowing a tuba straight into your ear; then at around 3000rpm the brassy blast becomes a little ragged, as though the two banks of cylinders have got out of sync; but get past that and it

sweetens into the most glorious, red-blooded howl you can imagine. Double-declutching down into third for the endless hairpins that punctuate the D900 south of Gap is one of motoring's great experiences: at each *whop! whop!* of the throttle you are, just for a moment, a proper Racing Driver, hurling a blood-red Italian supercar around an arid landscape that hasn't changed much since Bob Wallace thrashed the very first Miura down to Monaco in 1966.

With its fixed Perspex windows, zero trim, massive fuel capacity and no-compromise suspension set-up, it's not surprising that the Jota was seen by some as a potential race entry. But that was emphatically not

Top: ghosted nose and tail sections show position of engine and radiator. These shells are crafted from aluminium and can be lifted off completely, whereas a standard Miura's were hinged

the plan, says Bob. 'Ferruccio Lamborghini had nothing against racing but he had limited staff and resources, and in retrospect he was absolutely correct not to go into competition. Maybe he let me build it just to keep me happy…'

Even so, you can't escape the overwhelming impression that the Jota is a race car that's been let loose on the road. The steering wheel – perched on the end of a lengthy steel tube, itself anchored to the dash by a simple collar that looks more soapbox than supercar – is alive in your hands, constantly twitching and tugging as the road surface pulls it one way or the other; the ride, on the other hand, is

surprisingly good, doubtless because the car is some 350kg lighter than a Miura ('Still too heavy,' grumbled Bob Wallace to *Car* magazine in 1971).

While the Miura has coil-and-wishbone suspension at both ends, the Jota has a similar set-up at the front – but with fabricated rather than pressed-steel wishbones – and a unique arrangement at the rear: each upright is located at the top by a transverse and a forward-facing link, with a reversed wishbone at the bottom. This arrangement was faithfully replicated after a tip-off from Bob Wallace led Piet to uncover the original factory drawings in storage, water-damaged but intact.

But is the Jota race-car fast? Well, a standard Miura is easily capable of a 150mph cruise. The Jota, with more power and considerably less weight, should be notably faster. Trouble is, the deafening roar of the exhaust and the low-slung driving position distort your perception of speed – you think you're cracking along at a serious rate of knots but then you glance at the speedo and discover you're only doing 100mph.

Then there are the aerodynamics. The Jota gained some ankle-slicing front spoilers as a result of what Bob Wallace describes as 'some very crude aerodynamic testing, using fuel tank senders attached to the suspension to measure lift' but the Miura was notoriously light-footed at speeds above 150mph and Bob reckons the Jota wasn't much better. He suspects that front-end lift could have been the underlying cause of the 1972 crash.

Given the amount of rubber that the Jota can lay down on the road, dry-road grip (at sub-150mph speeds…) is not something you need to worry about, but it's a different matter in the rain. Appropriately enough, when we're deluged by a sudden summer storm, the Jota's single windscreen wiper

stops working – it's an Italian car, after all – and it's almost with a sense of relief that we find an excuse to shelter under a service station canopy until the downpour stops. But, considering this is the car's first proper outing since it was built, a mischievous wiper is hardly a major disaster.

It is, however, a reminder that this car is fresh out of the box and nothing's been tightened up since we left Gstaad 36 hours ago, including the wheel nuts securing those specially cast Campagnolo alloys (based on a Bizzarrini's, according to Bob). I try to put such thoughts out of my mind as Piet hurls the Jota along the autoroute towards Monte Carlo, although a tiny part of me can't help thinking rather morbidly that the phrase 'he died in a high-speed crash in a Lamborghini just outside Monte Carlo' would make a pretty stylish obituary.

Talking with Bob Wallace over the 'phone a couple of weeks later, Bob says he hopes Piet did a couple of hot laps around Casino Square, just like Bandini and Scarfiotti did with the first Miura back in '66. I reassure him that there are no worries on that score. They're probably still picking up bits of stucco outside the Hôtel de Paris even now.

In the beginning

A handful of men created the Miura and gave the world the first ever supercar. Gian Paolo Dallara, chief engineer on the project, describes its genesis

Once in a while, when my luck was really in, a school chum's cousin would collect us from school in his signal red E-type roadster. On those rare days we would be the most envied kids in the place. Then one day a terrible thing happened: a new kid rocked up at the beginning of term in a car that blew the Jag into the weeds for sheer visual impact. It was lime green and so low to the ground that even shortarse kids could look over the top of it. None of us could have spelt the words Lamborghini Miura and none of us had ever heard of the Italian company, but if Adam West had turned up at the school in the Batmobile we would hardly have been more shocked. To say that a lime-coloured Miura stood out in a car

park full of Cortinas, Morris Minors and Austin Cambridges would be a massive understatement. I can't remember the exact year but I'd guess at 1970.

Thirty years later and the Miura still shocks with its beauty. Standing next to Gian Paolo Dallara we both fall silent for a few moments as we look at this immaculate Miura SV. You might recognise this car from Lamborghini's collection as the same one that Richard Meaden drove in **evo** 38. It is immaculately restored and quite stunning. We have brought it to the small town of Varano Melegari near Parma to meet the man who played a big part in creating it.

Today Gian Paolo Dallara is best known for the world-conquering Dallara F3, Indycar and sports racing cars that are built in the modest-sized factory at Varano Melegari, but back in 1963 the then 27-year-old was taken on by Ferruccio Lamborghini and his fledgling car company to fill

the role of chief engineer. Giotto Bizzarrini, an ex-Ferrari and then freelance engineer with the 250 GTO on his CV, had a design for a quad-cam V12 in his portfolio that suited Lamborghini perfectly. This dry-sump engine went into the firm's first car, the 350GT.

But we are here to talk to Dallara about the world's first supercar, about his role in its creation and about the small team of colleagues who made a machine that shocked enthusiasts the world over as well as giving the folk up the road at

Even today, Dallara can recall the excitement of creating the Miura. Period pic (left) shows the factory in full swing with a mouthwatering line of V12s on the floor. Below left (l-to-r): Dallara talks writer Goodwin around Miura SV from Lambo museum; tight budget meant chassis had to be made up of straight steel sections welded together; engine air filter assembly was changed to fit under low roof-line of fabulous Gandini body

'Lamborghini and Bertone were going through a golden period'

Maranello a rather unwelcome surprise.

I've only driven a Miura once and that was a slightly unsatisfying experience in a poorly prepared car in the wrong place in the wrong weather. Somehow I think that the experience of poring over this Miura with the man who played such a huge part in bringing it into the world will be more pleasurable. There are several good books on the Miura but there's nothing like talking directly to someone so key to the story.

I've never read in any of the books, for example, that the Miura was inspired by the Mini. 'There have been two engineers that in my opinion were outstandingly brilliant,' says Dallara. 'One is Colin Chapman and the other is Alec Issigonis. I thought that the Mini was a masterpiece. At Lamborghini we thought about building what would have been

a mini-Miura – a small mid-engined sports car with the Mini's powertrain at the back. That wasn't to be, but it was this line of thinking that gave us the idea of fitting the existing V12 from the 350GT transversely into a new sports car using a combined gearbox and final drive just like the Mini's.'

But why transversely? Surely to fit the engine longitudinally with a conventional transaxle would have been far simpler? 'We decided upon a transverse location because it would mean that the car could be a lot shorter,' explains Dallara. 'Just look how short it is. It's barely longer than my Alfa 156.'

The Miura was created in an incredibly short period of time. The first the public saw of the car was a bare rolling chassis, complete with

powertrain, on a stand at the Turin Show in November 1965. They would have to wait until the following March and the Geneva Show before the Bertone body (designed by then-Bertone staffer Marcello Gandini) would be seen on the car. 'From start to finish that first car took us seven months,' remembers Dallara. 'It seemed at the time that both Lamborghini and Bertone were going through a sort of golden period when everything they touched was perfect. There were hardly any serious problems to be overcome, everything seemed to go very smoothly.

'We were a very young and inexperienced team and therefore didn't realise the enormity of the task. There weren't that many of us anyway. Paulo Stanzani was in charge of computing stress analysis; Achille Bevini was in charge of chassis

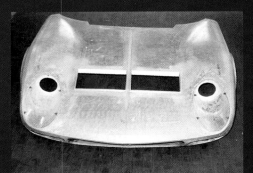

Bare Miura clamshells still things of beauty (top left); Rear of the car (top middle) clearly inspired Murciélago. Transverse engine (opposite) was trickier to engineer but made car shorter. Layout was, rather improbably, inspired by the Mini. Below right: early car out testing

'The sucking noise from the quartet of triple-choke Webers is incredible'

development; Pedrazzi [for the first and only time Dallara's memory fails him for a Christian name] developed the engine; Bob Wallace was in charge of testing the chassis; Roberto Frignani ran the engine testing programme and, finally, Gianni Malosi was responsible for the actual production of the Miura. So, you see, a pretty small team of people, nearly all of whom were only in their twenties.'

Flip up the Miura's front and rear body sections and you can see perfectly the car's construction. 'We used steel for the chassis rather than aluminium because the local Modenese craftsmen were only experienced in working with steel. If we'd been in the area of Italy that specialises in aircraft construction then the story might have been different.

'You can see also,' says Dallara pointing at the box-section chassis, 'that the chassis is constructed using straight pieces of steel without bends in them, or at most with simple bends. We didn't have a big budget and couldn't possibly afford to have any tooling or dies made, so it's all fabricated and spot- and seam-welded. The only stamping that was done was the weight-saving holes that are all over the chassis and these were done with a very cheap and simple tool.

'We tested the chassis for torsional rigidity and did get some numbers, but since we had nothing to compare them against it was pretty meaningless. Today, of course, there are dozens of benchmarks but back then we didn't know if our figures were good or bad. Ford bought an early Miura and were pretty impressed with it. They did have a transverse link break on the Belgian Pavé at their test track and rang us to let us know so that we could strengthen the piece for subsequent cars.

'Ferruccio Lamborghini was very easy to work for. He was very busy with setting up the factory and with his other businesses, but he still played a big part in the development of the Miura. He'd come in, look at something and then make a quick decision. There was no committee. Like when Bertone came in with the drawings for the Miura's body: Lamborghini liked what he saw and Bertone was sent away to produce the body.'

Surely designing a body for a chassis that already exists must be quite complicated and fraught with pitfalls? 'No,' says Dallara. 'The only changes that we had to make to the rolling chassis was to lose a little bit of height from the engine – and we did that simply by reducing the height of the aircleaner assembly.'

One thing that my only Miura experience did tell me was that its engine is a work of art. The mechanical noise and the sucking from the quartet of triple-choke downdraft Webers is incredible. Interestingly, Dallara says that one of the few

Miura SV the best of the breed, featuring wider rear tyres and vented discs that were missing from the original. Below left: holes were punched in steel structure to save weight

'I'm proud of what our small team achieved in the mid '60s'

things that he'd change on the car is the noise of the engine at low revs. 'There's a lot of vibration at low rpm,' he says. 'That is not pleasant. When we built the first few prototypes we used the V12 from the 400GT [the later, 4-litre version of the 350GT] very much as it was, apart from running it with a wet sump instead of the 400GT's dry system. Most of the gearbox internals were used from that car but obviously encased in a new housing. Mounting the engine transversely meant that we had to fit an idler gear so that the gearbox input shaft turned in the correct direction for the car to move forwards. This turned out to be a very noisy solution so instead we changed the cam timing so that the engine would run clockwise therefore making the idler gear unnecessary.'

The SV version of the Miura is the best, according to Dallara. 'We didn't think to fit the first P400 version of the car with larger rear tyres than fronts. Again, that's a result of my inexperience at the time. Thinking about it now I'm amazed that I didn't think of it at the time. Another thing that I'd do to the car now is fit it with servo assistance for the brakes. Those first cars were hopelessly underbraked; the discs weren't even

ventilated [unlike the SV's].

'Still, we are talking with the benefit of hindsight. I'm proud of what our small team achieved in the mid '60s. The car really did work very well right from the start. Bob Wallace was brilliant at sorting out problems. For example, there was a problem early on with oil surge in corners. Bob was the one who solved it. He was also very skilled at setting up the suspension.

'If I re-did the Miura now, with all the experience that I have now, I know what would happen. The result would be a car with many less mistakes but the outcome would be much more conservative. When I was young I worked so much on instinct and with passion. Today there would be too much thought, perhaps, and too much science in it.'

A few hours with Dallara is not enough. He's fabulous company and full of enthusiasm. Today his time is spent making sure that his racing car company is in fine shape for his daughters to take over from him [both are engineers and both work at Dallara Automobili da Competizione]. When that task is done he will build a museum behind the factory and buy a Miura to put in it. Also, and **evo** readers will join me in hoping that this one

day happens, he wants to build a modern version of the Lotus Seven. I'd like a fiver for every time I've heard someone say that, but somehow it means a bit more coming from the man whose F3 cars have won 63 championships and the same man who engineered the Lamborghini Miura. ∎

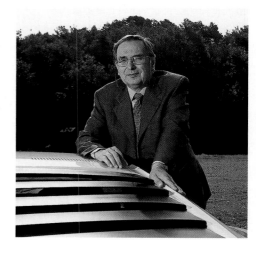

LIMITED-EDITION
evo PRINTS

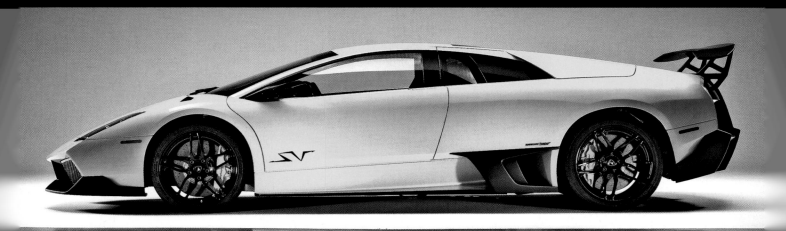

Lamborghini Murciélago LP670-4 SV Matt Vosper

BUY TWO AND GET THE THIRD FREE!

Caterham Superlight R500 Stuart Collins

Alfa Romeo 8C Competizione Gus Gregory

ALL-NEW DESIGNS ■ GIANT A2 POSTERS

HIGH-QUALITY ■ LIMITED EDITIONS

ONLY £17.99 EACH (INC. P&P)

Reach

up, grab the thick wedge of door trim and pull down firmly. *Ssssschhhh-click.* Then silence. Just the sound of your heart thumping slightly faster than usual, the smell of soft Italian leather and the sight of the world rendered into a lustrous panorama by the massive expanse of glass.

The shrill drilling of a fast-spinning starter motor cuts the silence for maybe a second, then cylinder by cylinder the big V12 wakes up with a nape-prickling, urgent bark. It's a dense, busy noise. If somebody played you a recording of it you'd know from its sheer complexity that it was a V12, but with a blip of throttle all the constituent parts meld into a tight, smooth howl. Chaos is ordered into sharp focus. This is the essence of Lamborghini. It always has been.

Well, at least it was until the short, squat Gallardo arrived in 2003. With a clean-sheet V10 instead of a development of the classic Giotto Bizzarrini-designed V12, an interior that poured solid Teutonic ergonomics into a laid-back Italian aesthetic, and (the horror!) conventionally opening doors, it forced us to reassess what a Lamborghini could be.

Of course, there had been 'small' Lamborghinis before – the Urraco, the Silhouette, the Jalpa – but, with the Gallardo, the junior Lambo grew up to such an extent that people wondered aloud if the Murciélago was effectively dead. The traditionalists mourned (a little prematurely as it turned out), but there was little doubt that the new V10 supercar had hit its target: Ferrari felt hot breath on its collar for the first time in decades and new customers flocked to a brand that had hitherto been out of reach.

Maybe the new, harder, faster, louder and downright rude Gallardo Superleggera is for those traditionalists – and I'm not just talking about the customers. This, you sense, is the Gallardo that everyone at the factory always wanted to build. It's a Gallardo shorn of weight, every sinew rippling with purpose and intent. It's a Gallardo concealing even more power and equipped like never before to unleash every scrap of it to the road. Our first taste of the Superleggera (**evo** 104) revealed that it's a true Lamborghini, maybe even the greatest ever.

Now, that sounds like a challenge…

'*You savour the moments before
you climb inside a Lamborghini*'

Miura, LP400, QV, SV, GT… we could have chosen any number of cars that equally capture the spirit, glamour and aggression that have formed the legend of Lamborghini. So why the four you see here? Well, anything with fewer than ten cylinders was out, so too anything with an engine mounted up front (even though it would have been a laugh to have brought an LM002 along). The Miura, still the most beautiful Lamborghini of all time and perhaps the most significant, was harder to dismiss. However, even the youngest is 34 years old, and although they are an intoxicating drive the cruel truth is that, in terms of sheer pace, Lamborghini's original mid-engined V12 would be easy meat for a well-driven hot hatch in 2007.

Choosing the ultimate Countach was just as contentious, but we felt that in order for it to stand toe-to-toe with the newer cars we needed the fastest, the most aggressive and the most outrageous. It had to be an Anniversary.

The Diablo dynasty is glorious, and our shortlist came down to the lightweight SV, the sensational carbonfibre GT and the immensely talented swansong, the simple VT 6.0. We would have loved to have brought together all three, but in the end it fell to the version we felt had fully realised the Diablo's previously latent potential. The 6.0 was in.

The final contender was easy. It had to be the most powerful production Lamborghini of all time, the Murciélago LP640 – all 631bhp of it. The natural successor to the crazy Countach and Diablo, the traditional Lamborghini reinvented

in the era of Enzos, Carrera GTs and Zondas.

The venue for this glorious feast of horsepower was much easier to choose. We needed fast, wide, empty roads and craggy, gnarled tarmac butted up against billiard smooth asphalt. To really test a car's consistency and depth of talent you need roads that change and challenge with every turn of the wheels. Nowhere reveals every facet of a car's character and abilities quite like the roads that sweep and loop across North Wales.

It's an epic stage, so massive that you can't escape a heavy cloak of humility when you survey the surroundings. And today God's special effects department is doing its bit to help – Wales is drenched in brilliant dazzling sunshine and a Mediterranean sky of the deepest azure drapes lazily over the spectacular scenery. Over 1000 miles from Sant'Agata, these Lamborghinis couldn't look more at home.

'COUNTACH!' LEGEND HAS IT THIS WAS Nuccio Bertone's exclamation when he first saw Marcello Gandini's new Lamborghini prototype. There's no direct translation for this wonderful piece of Piedmontese dialect, but 'Wow!' sort of sums it up. The 1970s must have been a gentler, more well mannered time, because when Jim Wiltshire's Candy Red 25th Anniversary Countach arrives in our midst the air turns blue. I guess it's a good job that John Barker, John Hayman, Henry Catchpole and I don't get to name new supercars…

Gandini's intricate wedge of metal origami shocked the world at the 1971 Geneva Auto Salon. Finished in bright yellow, the

Lamborghini Countach LP500 literally stopped the show. A Miura SV sat beside it, but nobody really noticed.

'LP' stood for 'Longitudinale Posteriore' (the position and layout of the engine, which was no longer mounted transversely as in the Miura), while the 500 was reference to the prototype's 5-litre version of the classic V12. Lamborghini claimed the new engine would produce 440bhp and propel the LP500 to 200mph…

Unfortunately the bigger engine proved fragile in testing and the LP's development was tortuous. When the production-ready Countach was finally launched in 1974, its V12's 3929cc capacity was rather less impressive. Even so it was said to produce 375bhp at 8000rpm and be capable of taking the LP400 (as it was now called) on to 180mph. Only the Ferrari Daytona could get close.

The Countach remained Lamborghini's big-hitter until 1990. By then it was a very different supercar, the lean precision of the LP400 obscured by outrageous addenda of dubious taste but unmistakable drama. The evolution began in 1978 with the LP400S, which took advantage of Pirelli's new P7 low-profile tyre. Then, in 1982, came the LP500S, which brought a capacity increase to 4.8 litres, although power remained pegged at 375bhp. Next was the LP500 QV in 1985, the increase to 5167cc and introduction of four valves per cylinder (hence 'QV', for 'quattrovalvole') taking the horsepower count to a fulsome 455bhp.

To mark Lamborghini's quarter century as a car manufacturer, the Anniversary was released

Anniversary's late '80s add-ons do little for the '70s design beneath, but the accompanying chassis tweaks make it the best Countach to drive. Left: 5.2 V12 said to have 455bhp

in September 1988. Styled by Horacio Pagani (yes, that one) and with extensive chassis development by former Italian and European rally champion Sandro Munari, the steroid-infused 5.2-litre 455bhp Anniversary may not be to everyone's taste, but it is widely regarded as the best Countach to actually drive. Which is exactly what I should be doing…

Let's not get ahead of ourselves, though. You don't just jump in and drive the door handles off a Lamborghini. You want to savour those moments before you pull the scissor door up into its arc and fall into the thinly-padded seat. With the Countach those moments tend to drag into minutes. In fact you could just look at it all day long. The Anniversary may not be conventionally pretty, but it is as big a statement as has ever been made with aluminium and four wheels. Every duct is hugely exaggerated, every sharp crease bursting with tension, and that (optional) rear wing is the final poke in the eye to sensibility. On one hand the Anniversary is a fascinating period piece, the epitome of '80s

excess, but that sells it short because even today Gandini's middle-aged wedge still shocks. Nothing draws reactions as honest and unfiltered as the Countach.

Drop backside-first into the pinched seat and pull your legs in behind you over the high sill. This car has the sport seat option, which is a relief as the plusher, electrically powered standard items make the Countach a nightmare for anyone over about 5ft 10in. So I can sit up straight, but the pronounced side bolsters make the seat so narrow that my frame only just squashes itself down onto the seat cushion. Broader drivers might find themselves clasped into place but suspended a few centimetres above the seat base.

To your left, mounted on the narrow transmission tunnel, is an open-gated gearshifter – dogleg first, metal surround finished in matt black. Ahead there's a plain three-spoke steering wheel, beyond that a rectangular instrument binnacle that looks like it could have been made out of an old shoebox. Despite the wheel's tiny diameter you get a good view of the speedo and the rev counter. Note the markings – up to 320kph (199mph) on the former, the first red marking at 7500rpm on the latter.

Push the flimsy key into the ignition barrel on the left-hand side of the steering column, gently squeeze the accelerator three times to engorge the six carbs and then twist towards you. The dentist's drill of a starter-motor spins and then

the big V12 catches cleanly. You won't be able to resist a quick blip and you won't regret the indulgence; the 12 cylinders spin up in a flash and the quad exhausts emit a pure, trebly howl.

The gearbox action is heavy, almost like it's lacking oil, and the clutch is pretty beefy too. Worse, the throttle feels solid for the first millimetre or so of its travel and then frees-up instantly, making pulling away a fraught juggling act between bogging down and potentially stalling or sounding like you're trying to extract a 0-60 time (apparently this is a trait of all right-hand-drive examples). So far the legend of the truculent Countach is spot-on.

Then there's the steering. It's massively heavy at manoeuvring pace and remains unusually weighty even as you slot deliberately into second and then third. However, it's immediately apparent that there's a rich stream of information flowing back through the tiny wheel, and the Countach rides with a finesse that's at odds with its low-speed awkwardness. Meanwhile the engine's willingness to rev and the response it elicits in terms of acceleration shed any remaining doubts that the Countach will be a ham-fisted irrelevance.

In fact, with the V12 ripping up to 7000rpm (we stopped revving at the yellow line) and the fat 225/50 ZR15 P Zeros guiding the shovel nose into each apex, the Countach feels genuinely quick. The searing, wailing cacophony, a mixture of hungry induction and exhaust yowl, adds to

the sense of speed, and you're so focused on trying to get gearshift and throttle inputs to fuse smoothly that the fearsome soundtrack edges you towards sensory overload. It takes a good few miles to actually think clearly and feel what the Countach is all about, to break down the experience and analyse its behaviour. Initially it's just noise and heat and power.

Take a few deep breaths, relax a little, and you start to appreciate that under the shock-and-awe tactics there's a talented chassis. Body roll is contained well and the engine never feels like a threatening mass ready to come around on you if you so much as dare to brake into a turn. You sense its mid-engined configuration from the gently writhing front end and the stupendous traction rather than from an uncomfortable roll-oversteer balance. The Countach corners flat and very securely and the simply enormous 345/35 ZR15 rear rubber feels absolutely keyed-in on dry roads.

There are limiting factors, of course. Chief amongst these is the brakes – acceptable 20 years ago but pretty hopeless in modern terms. The steering, too, hinders your commitment. It's so heavy when loaded in a turn that the thought of having to find a quick and accurate correction knocks mph from your entry speed. This is a car you relax into and enjoy within its limits. And then there's the engine, very much the star attraction, but producing 455bhp? Well, at least 100 of those seem to be spent making noise

rather than turning the rear wheels…

Click-ssssscchhhh… I emerge from the Countach with a huge grin. Barker has already sampled this immaculate Anniversary and he seems to have enjoyed it as much as I just have. 'The V12 doesn't feel like it's giving over 450bhp,' he agrees, 'but it certainly sounds like it. The mid-range is a multi-voiced cacophony and from there it just gets stronger – it spins so sweetly to 7000rpm. It prefers smooth, quick roads but I can't imagine really attacking at ten-tenths in it. I suppose you don't need to in order to become totally absorbed in the experience, anyway…'

Long time Lamborghini zealot John Hayman, meanwhile, has been reacquainting himself with an old friend, the Diablo VT 6.0. Owner Jenny Rothwell has only just bought this gorgeous Pearl Orange example and out of respect for her and the car Mr Hayman has been driving it flat-out for the last 15 miles or so. Quite right. His thoughts? 'I always look back fondly on these – it was my favourite at eCoty 2000 – and I thought maybe it'd be a case of rose-tinted spectacles. But not a bit of it. The 6.0 still has the magic.'

I've never driven the last-of-the-line Diablo. Sounds like I should put that right as soon as possible. Still slightly flushed from my Countach experience, the very generous Ms Rothwell virtually drags me over to the Diablo and thrusts the key into my hand. 'See what you think,' she says. 'Erm, well if you insist…'

'Wow.' That's all I can think when I'm locked into position, steering wheel pulled close, dazzling orange bodywork filling the widescreen mirrors, cool alloy gearstick resting in my left hand. One of the all-time great **evo** photographs must be the one of a similarly hued Diablo 6.0 back in issue 022. A low-down rear chasing shot, empty road stretching into the distance, rich blue cloudless Italian sky picking out every delicious curve on the car's body. Gus Gregory captured that perfect moment back in 2000, and now I feel like I've dived into that shot and muscled the driver out of the way to take that frame and stretch it out into an unforgettable sequence.

Everything feels more exaggerated in here than the smaller Countach. The speedo now reads in mph, all the way to 220; the yellow zone on the rev counter now begins at 7200rpm. The steering wheel – with carbon trim – is still quite small, but you can get it much closer to you, allowing a Grönholm-style driving position. And all around there's masses of bodywork. You feel even closer to the pointy end, like your legs reach beyond the front axle, and that mighty 6-litre V12 feels a long way behind. Glance in the rear-view mirror and you see buttresses that funnel back for what seems like miles, finally stopping in the shadow of the vast spoiler. This is a big, intimidating car.

A dozen years on from the Anniversary, this Diablo was the first Lambo developed under the watchful eye of Audi. And it shows. Quality is unrecognisable from the wonderfully hotchpotch Countach, switchgear now borrowed from Ingolstadt instead of Turin, and everything feels more substantial and more thoughtfully designed. Have no fear, though. At its heart the final Diablo is still rooted in Sant'Agata. The 6-litre V12 produces 550bhp at 7100rpm and 457lb ft at 5500rpm, enough to punch its clean profile through the air at over 200mph (without the wing) and to launch it to 60mph from rest in under four seconds.

Despite the added weight burden of its four-wheel-drive system (the VT in its name stands for 'viscous traction'), the use of carbonfibre for everything bar the aluminium roof and doors means that, at 1625kg, the 6.0 is just 57kg heavier than the shorter, narrower and lower Anniversary. You'd swear it was lighter still. The steering is perfectly weighted and quick enough to make the big Diablo feel genuinely nimble. It's alive with feedback too, proving that power-assistance doesn't have to rob you of feel. Meanwhile, the gearbox (still a five-speed with a dogleg), clutch and throttle are all much more manageable. Maybe not Golf light, but certainly requiring no more effort than something like, say, a TVR. The 6.0 is light on its toes, too. Softer in its vertical absorption than the Countach, making for a very supple, fluid gait, but also more controlled when you start to string a few corners together. Where the Anniversary's damping might run out of ideas, sending the wheels skipping across the surface, the 6.0 simply glides serenely.

The gearbox is a peach, requiring precision timing and some physical effort, but rewarding with a fast, mechanical action and a delicious *clack!* as it slots home. Not that you seem to change very often – the Diablo has an epic stride, with second gear stretching beyond 90mph and third pushing deep into three figures. To be honest, this does dull the expected viciousness of

'Most of the time the Diablo feels like a friendly old beast'

its 550bhp, but the payback is enjoying the huge engine's mighty and ever-changing delivery without any punctuation, and this approach suits the polished, poised, unhurried chassis.

Like the Countach there's a bit of understeer to nudge up against, but it's harder to find on the road as grip levels are much higher. The four-wheel drive allows you to jump on the power as soon as the nose has dug-in without any fear of power oversteer. You certainly feel liberated to work its massive tyres harder than you might the Countach's. However, unlike the older car, the Diablo, perhaps because of its supple suspension, feels more conspicuously mid-engined when you really start to push hard. Hit a big bump mid-corner and the front doesn't budge, but the rear becomes unsettled, floating momentarily and threatening to slip wide. It rarely does, but the harder you push, the more you have to be aware

Diablo was extensively reworked for the VT 6.0, launched in 2000. Interior (left) benefited particularly from new owner Audi's input, while the bodywork was now mostly carbonfibre

SWEATY PALMS

I've only ever suffered from sweaty palms on two occasions. The first was when landing at Luton airport a few years ago, when the pilot overshot the runway and had to go round again. The second was when Bovingdon piloted the LP640 along a deserted stretch of Welsh B-road with yours truly in the co-pilot's seat.

Despite the LP640's huge dimensions it's surprisingly agile, while the reworked 6.5-litre V12 possesses noticeably more punch across the whole range than the previous 6.2. This Murciélago also seems a little more predictable in the handling department, its levels of grip appearing so alarmingly endless that I found myself wondering what my obituary might read like. I'm glad Lamborghini retained the passenger grab-handle on the left of the transmission tunnel. It came in useful.

Impressive though the LP640 was, the 6-litre Diablo was without doubt my favourite of the bunch. Purists would argue that it's still an 'Audified' Lamborghini, and indeed it was the first of the Italian company's creations to be influenced by its new German parent, but it's hardly what you'd call compromised. Its aggressive stance, its roar, even its smell (believe it or not), are all a kick in the teeth to those who believe the first of the more modern Lambos are watered-down versions of their ancestors. It manages to rid itself of almost all the nasties of earlier models while retaining all the good bits.

None of these supercars suffers fools, and what gladdens the heart is that Lamborghini continues this tradition even today, despite all the electronic wizardry now routinely added to the competition. But then that's what makes this marque so special.

Simon George

of that massive V12 pendulum.

Which isn't to suggest the Diablo is untrustworthy. In fact, through smooth corners it feels totally hooked-up. It's just that when you're asking the car to slow down, change direction and contain its rear-biased mass on a cresting corner, or one that drops away sharply, physics start to take over. Most of the time the VT feels like a friendly old beast, though, and it's a fantastic sensation as it squats down under acceleration out of a corner and the steering lightens in your hands. Even Catchpole, who was full of trepidation before stepping into the 6.0, is won over. 'It's like a big scary bouncer that lives

with his nan,' he says. 'Remarkably friendly.'

Disappointingly the brakes don't feel like they've benefited from 12 years' worth of development. On a flat bit of road, and if you haven't been working them consistently hard, they work pretty well. Throw in a few bumps, though, and the ABS triggers even with fairly light pressure on the middle pedal – odd considering there's plenty of front grip. If you've been exercising that V12 for the last few miles the pedal-feel goes west, too, and a soft, long pedal that pulses furiously on the way into a bend is not something you expect when the rest of the package feels so well sorted. It is perhaps

Just seven years on from the Diablo 6.0 (left), the Murciélago LP640 (above) represents a massive leap forward for the V12 Lamborghini line. Additional 81bhp helps, but it's the way it deploys it that really amazes

the Diablo's only real weak link.

Such is the speed of development of supercars since the turn of the millennium that both Countach and Diablo are almost pensionable, but the old-timers have put on a phenomenal show. OK, so the Anniversary doesn't feel like it could ever reach 295kph (183mph), not unless it was pushed out the back of a Hercules at 35,000 feet, and even the Diablo doesn't feel as manic or aggressive as you might expect, but both still tick all of the supercar boxes. They ooze charisma, fill driver and bystanders alike with that childlike glee that only an impractical mid-engined car with scissor doors can, and, at

sane speeds, deal with these incredibly tough roads with a casual shrug. The progeny of the Countach and Diablo have a lot to live up to.

IT SEEMS FITTING TO SCRIBE A NEAT line from Countach to Murciélago, so with the 6.0 still tinkling and clicking as it sheds some of the enormous heat that a 550bhp V12 generates, I grab the chunky key to the LP640. In contrast to the older cars, I've spent a lot of time with various Murciélagos since the model's launch in 2001, but familiarity doesn't dim the big Lamborghini's incredible presence. It's a beautiful shape. So beautiful that even in military green you ache to own it.

Barker has already driven the LP640 and the Superleggera. He doesn't want to give too much away but muses on the low-key colour schemes of both the LP640 and the undercoat-spec Gallardo: 'The subtle, weapons-like hues of the pair reflect the shift in attitude at Lamborghini. More than ever before these are serious drivers' tools.' Hmm… intriguing.

Same ritual to get in, same sense that you're in a big, old-school supercar. Starter motor drills that same high-pitched tune, too. But milliseconds after you turn the key, the LP640 experience deviates from that of its ancestors. The engine doesn't catch cylinder-by-cylinder, noise building layer-upon-layer, it just explodes with an intense whoop of revs and then settles to a rock-steady, digitally programmed idle. Blip the throttle and the needle flicks around the rev counter with seemingly no inertia. It's not quite Carrera GT-responsive (little bar an F1 car is),

but, incredibly, the 6.5-litre development of the Bizzarrini V12 feels cutting-edge.

No gated 'shifter here, no need to juggle a heavy clutch with a sticky throttle. Just flick the right-hand sculpted alloy paddle to select first, ease off the brake pedal (noting how its action is short and very, very firm) and the 631bhp V12 sets the sticky Pirelli P Zero Corsa tyres rolling. The gorgeous suede-rimmed steering wheel immediately gives the LP640 an edge; subconsciously you know it's there to soak up moisture from your palms. The steering itself is heavier than that of the Diablo, but that only adds to the sense that this Murciélago is a tougher, more serious piece of kit.

The LP640 has a tight brief. It's almost as though Lamborghini knows that all the peripheral supercar stuff – the drama, the charisma – is taken care of simply by that shape and that engine, so instead it has focused on the thing that matters when the scissor door has been pulled shut: the way it drives. The LP640 is all about clenched-fist dynamics, about getting from one place to another in the minimum timeframe. It's angry – with you, with the road, with anything that might slow it down, and you'd better be up to it. A supercar tamed by Audi's cool influence? Right now it feels about ten times as scary as the Countach or Diablo…

We're running in convoy over my favourite section of the **evo** Triangle. The LP640 is in 'Sport', quickening the gearshift, adding a superfluous extra burst of revs on downshifts and allowing the V12 to spin up to 8000rpm (without Sport engaged it hits a very abrupt limiter at

7500rpm). The structure feels rock-solid, the damping is tight – the ride is much firmer than the Diablo's and everything you touch exacts a measured, consistent reaction. It's so stable, so composed through direction changes that you can *feel* that the engine is mounted 5cm lower than in the Diablo. The gearshift is quick and smooth, better than earlier e-gear examples we've tried; the carbon ceramic brakes feel simply mighty.

That sixth ratio allows the LP640's lower gears to be stacked tighter, but the 6.5-litre engine hardly needs that advantage. Quite simply it blows the Diablo 6.0 into the weeds. The acceleration is effortless at low revs, then at around 4500rpm the thumping torque starts to give way to manic horsepower. Such is the noise and the ferocity of the delivery that by 6000rpm you're instinctively pawing for the upshift

paddle, but you must fight the urge, because it's beyond that where the LP640 truly rams home its advantage. It kicks hard, the noise focusing down into a single piercing howl as 8000rpm approaches. This here, right now, is progress. This is what a supercar feels like in 2007.

Of course, it's no surprise that the LP640 charges harder than its predecessors, but by how much you wouldn't quite believe. And it's the way it controls its mass, the way the body never gets out of phase with the wheels and the road, that is truly spectacular. I've driven down this hallowed piece of hellish road in Ferrari 360 Challenge Stradale, Noble M400 and various 911s, but nothing has been so immune to its wicked compressions as the LP640. There's one particular braking zone that you arrive at after a stomach-churning crest, the car light and unsettled. As you hit the middle pedal the road is still falling away from you, but as the brakes start to bite it begins to climb rapidly. The suspension has to deal with the weight of the car settling back down after the crest and heavy braking and the gradient of the road simultaneously. The Stradale bottomed out so alarmingly here that we actually stopped to make such its venturis hadn't been sheared off, the 996 GT3 RS thumped its bumpstops and skittered unnervingly; even the Enzo couldn't keep its belly off the road. But the LP640 simply checks its body movement, zips through the compression and then attacks the following

'The Countach is much better than received wisdom would lead us to believe'

right-hander quicker than I've ever been through it before. Total composure.

By now the Countach and Diablo are nowhere to be seen. In fact when I pull over I can hear them coming for a good minute before they actually appear on the horizon, first the 6.0, then the Anniversary. John Hayman clambers out of the Countach and it seems he's unconcerned that he's just been dropped like a diesel Corsa: 'Proper drop-dead looks, proper soundtrack, proper old-school supercar – not perfect, for sure – but it's really tugging my heartstrings. You have to make some allowances for its age, the brakes particularly, but in terms of steering feel it's right up there with the Diablo for me, and you can still hustle it along at a fair old lick.'

He's right, of course. It's just that 'a fair old lick' and what the LP640 can achieve are two very different things. Speed isn't everything, though, and Barker is falling back in love with the Diablo: 'The 6.0 is a car that really flows and feels connected. Yes, you know you're in charge of a big mid-engined car, but the poise that the damping delivers and the precision of the steering give huge confidence. In some ways it makes the LP640 seem a bit edgy. Oh, and it's a manual – a weighty, deliberate shift – but that doesn't date the car, it just gives you another ingredient to reap reward from. I love it.'

Me too, but I'm struggling to see past the LP640's pace, control and sheer energy, which it serves up with a lush cinematic flavour that's pure Lamborghini.

THE SUNSHINE IS EBBING AWAY AND the clear sky slowly drawing in with rain-heavy clouds when I finally get to sample the Superleggera. It's a bulldog of a car, broad and muscular and bunched-up, a ball of aggression. The grey finish camouflages the carbon details (sill extensions, engine bay surround), but, as Barker suggested, it's a clear statement of intent. This is not some frivolous trinket, it's a weapon.

Swing open the door – no effort required (the lacquered carbon trim sees to that), no look-at-me special effects – and fall into the seat: carbon again, and much more upright than those fitted to the V12s. They're Countach-tight and fitted with four-point harnesses. Glossy carbonfibre adorns the centre console and even the lower quadrant of the flat-bottomed steering wheel. Everywhere else there's black Alcantara. It seems only right and proper that instead of a conventional stick there are two paddles peeping out from behind the wheel. For sense of occasion it's got the Lamborghini act down to perfection.

The Gallardo feels tiny after the LP640, all wheelbase and ruthlessly cut-off extremities.

Concentrated supercar. Supercar deconstructed and then reformed with no waste, nothing surplus to requirements, just a bucketload of serious hardware and a super-sized side order of attitude. The V10's flat blare fits the sinister stance perfectly, and the deep, ugly noise that builds with every rev only heightens the sense that you're piloting a different sort of Lamborghini.

The ride is hard. Every bump is felt through the grip of the carbonfibre seat, and yet the Superleggera doesn't tramline or hop and skip when the surface deteriorates. The wheels are always firmly in touch with the ground, and although there's not a great deal of steering feel you know there's plenty of grip to lean on from the way the front tyres lock instantly onto line. Nail the throttle and it responds with the same snap. There's so much torque you'd be forgiven for thinking it was turbocharged.

A full day on these roads means I'm fully dialled-in and quickly up to speed. Immediately it's obvious that the Superleggera is right up there with the LP640 in terms of sheer pace. Shorter geared and with rippling torque and less weight to carry, the 5-litre V10 gets working from tickover and never really lets up. The initial punch is too much for the LP to live with, but it doesn't quite have the crazy top-end kick of the

'The Superleggera is not some frivolous trinket, it's a weapon'

Superleggera's cornering ability (above) is nothing short of phenomenal – it feels like it's on slicks. Magnesium wheels (right) part of the car's weight-saving measures, as is the widespread use of carbonfibre both inside and out

Murciélago. Even so you'd swear it had more than a 9bhp advantage over a 'standard' Gallardo.

But that's only half the story, because it's the Superleggera's chassis that really stuns. I've mentioned the control – of the wheels and the body – which is boundless and easily appreciated even at seven-tenths. Push harder, though, and you slowly uncover the Gallardo's almost supernatural levels of grip. It's on P Zero Corsas, just like the LP640, so you expect a faithful front-end, but this is something else. You turn, it responds, so next time you try harder. No change, just grip and instant response. Harder still, not even a whiff of understeer.

OK, time for a big commitment. The front tyres turn and bite simultaneously, there's no body roll to speak of and certainly no slip at the front. The rear tyres follow, but now you sense them just edging a few degrees wide. Not really sliding, just taking up a bit of attitude to glue those sticky front tyres to the apex. Incredible.

Try again, this time through a fast left-right combination, and it's better still. It manages to tear chunks out of the road and yet still feel on tiptoes, flicking from one direction to the next with total security yet a fluid, effortless poise.

Such is the Superleggera's composure and raw speed that it throws any tiny weakness into sharp focus, and there are two glaring holes in its armour. The first is the e-gear 'box. It should be as smooth as the LP640's but it isn't. It thumps changes through with no finesse and there's no pay-off in terms of shift speed. The Gallardo's downshifts, too, are pretty clumsy, and made all the more disconcerting by the other problem area: the brakes. Oh, they stop the car all right, as you'd expect with massive 365mm

carbon ceramic discs and eight-pot callipers up front, but you don't have enough say in exactly when and where. Pedal feel is awful. On light applications it's mushy and inaccurate, making the Superleggera very tricky to drive smoothly. Up the pace and it's worse. You go for the brakes and get nothing but dead travel, then in a mild panic you push the pedal a bit harder. Suddenly the brakes bite – really bite – and you shed too much speed and wreck your approach to the corner. On the road, where you often need subtlety rather than brick-wall power, it's almost impossible to drive around the problem. Maybe the brakes work better on track, but out here they really slow you down. On reflection, maybe that's a good thing…

Later I follow Barker – him in the Superleggera, me in the LP. He's just climbed out of the Countach so I know I've got a good couple of miles before he gets his head back into maximum attack mode. The LP easily keeps him in reach as the road winds up a hillside and then plateaus across a vast plain raggedly slashed by this perfect bit of tarmac. The Gallardo's exhausts spit an angry stab of V10 on downshifts, a warning shot to the LP maybe. The pace escalates, but the Murciélago responds, losing a little ground into corners but shrinking the gap in mighty lunges of acceleration on anything vaguely resembling a straight.

Now the road is kicking and turning like a rollercoaster and the Gallardo is in full flight. I'm using every last one of those 631bhp and calling on all the braking power the LP can summon. The traction control is off (it's a hyper-sensitive system that is best switched off in dry

weather), but the Murciélago stays composed, remarkably so – just a bit of understeer here, a little twist of correction needed there. What a feeling! And what a sight. The Superleggera looks like a slot-car, such is the speed with which it changes direction, and as the tyres hook into the surface a shower of shale is thrown up behind it. Finally, through a series of demanding left-right flicks, the Superleggera steals a meaningful lead that the LP640 can't recover. The baby supercar is all grown up, and there's the proof.

I'm stunned. Both by the LP640's incredible engine and awesome control, and by the Superleggera's mind-boggling point-to-point speed. The Countach and Diablo, in every rational sense, are out of their depth. And yet when I ask anyone to rank the four cars, they look at their shoes and mumble something about them all being wonderful.

I'm not surprised. Throw a Lamborghini into any group test and choosing a winner becomes an emotive, soul-searching dilemma. With four of them it's like some sort of group therapy session. Sorting out a clear finishing order is almost impossible. Barker, Hayman, Catchpole and I all have different lists – in fact Barker has two: 'I want a Lamborghini' and 'I want a Lamborghini to drive fast' – but one car emerges as everyone's number one.

'The engine is the core reason that I feel so passionately about it. Not just the thrust, but the noise and the feel of it climbing its power curve. And the chassis – so forgiving but still easy to impose yourself on – is simply brilliant.' That's Hayman, and Catchpole echoes the sentiment: 'It's truly remarkable. It feels really, really light. The engine is everything a Lambo engine should

'Sorting out a clear finishing order is almost impossible…'

Above from top: Diablo chases Murciélago; Superleggera's speedo; LP640's carbon-clad V12; European Anniversary's rear view restricted by bulge housing carbs (US cars had fuel injection)

DANCES WITH THE DEVIL

In early 1992 the original Diablo came my way for three whole days, so I decided to give it a workout. I plotted a 1500-mile route that took in the south coast and Scotland, not realising that it was me that was going to get the workout...

After the sharp-creased Countach, the fatter, softer-edged Diablo looked like its panels had been cut from pastry. It was no softy, though. Its V12 crackled and boomed like a thunderstorm and delivered torque like a tidal wave, but its clutch was so stiff it felt like the brake pedal, and its unassisted steering was so heavy it felt like the 5.7-litre engine and 335/35 section tyres were at the front. During the trip, I made the mistake of leaving the M6 to head across country for Edinburgh. Every corner was a wrestling match. At least I was in the passenger seat on the way back when we hit a stop-start jam near Birmingham. Ever tried doing step aerobics on one leg?

A Diablo that you could enjoy between the straights came along a couple of years later. The four-wheel-drive VT was a massive leap forward in Diablo driveability, yet it wasn't the all-wheel drive that was truly significant but the addition of power steering. It transformed the Diablo.

Two very memorable models that we could have included in this test used the simpler rear-drive layout: the lightweight SV of '96 and the last of the pre-Audi Diablos, the GT of '98.

The Sport Veloce was lighter thanks to having had most of its cockpit trim removed, along with the bulk of its sound deadening. Imagine the echo in a room without carpets or curtains. Now put a dirty great V12 in it, just behind the armchair where you're sitting, and rev the bollocks off it. I loved it. The noise and vibration probably made it feel even faster and more ferocious than it was, but with 510bhp the SV *was* a little more powerful. It also

had the shortest gearing option (pegging top speed to a mere 186mph) and a sharper chassis, all of which helped make it more agile and responsive. Hell, given a smooth, second-gear corner you could powerslide it. And gather it up too, something the non-power-steered original would never have allowed. (Confession: the shot of the original Diablo smoking around a corner that appeared on the cover of *Performance Car* was achieved by positioning the car to *look* like it was on opposite lock, then doing a wheelspin start.) Even if the SV was conceived to boost sales by lowering the entry-level price for a Lambo (at £125K it was £23K cheaper than the 'regular' leather-lined Diablo) it resulted in a raw, thrilling and hugely desirable supercar.

Influenced by the GTR racer, the GT was a riot of sculpted add-ons, but unlike the Anniversary Countach's they were all functional. The bodywork was mostly carbonfibre, only the doors and roof being metal, and the front arches were neatly extended to accommodate the 110mm wider front track. Its 567bhp 6-litre brimmed with heavyweight V12 character, as you'd expect, but at 5000rpm it kicked so hard that it was like triple-strength VTEC. It felt as if the GT had been cut free from a milk-float it had been towing up to that point. Like the SV, the GT had a feelsome chassis that allowed grip to be precisely exploited, though the physics of a big, mid-mounted engine seemed more obvious with such a vigorous delivery, especially as there was no traction or stability control...

Just 80 of these highly specialised, £195K Diablos were built, and while the Audi-influenced 6.0 VT that followed was the more rounded, more brilliantly polished road car, the GT was the wildest ride of all, a last hurrah for the rear-drive Lambo supercar.

It's incredible that, since the GT, the long-serving V12 has been enlarged by another half-litre and gained another 64bhp. Mind, the power-to-weight ratio of the Murciélago LP640 is no better than the GT's. Wonder if Audi would sanction a rear-drive LP640 Superleggera...

John Barker

Top: the last pre-Audi Lamborghini, the outrageous 567bhp, rear-wheel-drive Diablo GT. Left: earlier SV was a more affordable lightweight

Superleggera (above left) quickest point-to-point, but it has its flaws; Countach (left) wonderful within its limits; Diablo 6.0 (below left) everything you hope it will be; LP640 (right) combines the best bits of all of them

be – the immense reach, the noise. And even when it started to rain I found you could drive it faster than you'd believe possible. Everything feels so right, I'll never ever forget that drive.'

Need more clues? OK, well it isn't the Countach Anniversary. The oldest car here is much, much better than received wisdom (obviously from people who've never driven one) would lead you to believe, an enthralling drive and a solid-gold investment, but things have moved on to such as extent that we simply can't call it the ultimate Lamborghini. You need only to look to the frighteningly fast Superleggera

to see that. But that car also misses out in this company. For me the brakes are inexcusable and the gearbox is a major annoyance. For others it's that it's just too unemotional, too bloody good.

'How can they get the brake feel so wrong?' asks Hayman. 'That aside, it's mind-blowingly capable, and just *so* fast around the corners. The scary thing is how big the crash would be when you finally breached the limits...' Quite. But don't think for a minute that the Superleggera is just a Gallardo with a few overwrought embellishments. It's a stunning achievement. Barker, fresh from a bit of LP640-slaying, is unequivocal: 'I pedalled it moderately fast for the first mile or two and it felt very grippy, very poised. The weight feels evenly distributed, the nose well tied down. Then I summoned up the courage to find the throttle stop and the Superleggera raised its game. No scuffing of underbody, no hint of understeer, it just pummels the road into submission. Turn more, later and

harder, get on the power earlier, and it just grips like it's got slicks and downforce. Gobsmacking.' Doesn't sound like a loser, does it?

The Diablo VT 6.0 has a magnetism about it, more than any of the others. It's the shape that pops into our heads when somebody says 'supercar'. And I'm pleased to report that it fills the brief brilliantly. Not only does it look simply stunning, but its 550bhp V12 is a true supercar hammer of an engine, long-legged but with a savage edge, and its chassis is grippy and faithful but still holds a sharp blade over your head should you step out of line. You could drive a 6.0 every day but it would still deliver a big hit of adrenalin whenever you went looking for it. It's a great Lamborghini. But it's not our winner...

I knew it. Within maybe a couple of miles I knew the LP640 was too much for the Anniversary and VT 6.0. It does everything they do and about a million things they can't. It looks like a Lamborghini should, its V12 is smoother and more venomous than ever and its chassis is simply sublime. It's a car shot through with passion and attention to detail. It's an incredible mix of old-school charm and new-wave tech. It's overwhelmingly faster than the old heroes and yet it provides all of their tactile joy. The only possible match for it could have been the Superleggera, yet while the smaller, lighter V10 car feels more aggressive and has the LP licked for pace (just), this test was always going to be about more than raw speed, and in many of the crucial areas the Superleggera lags behind its big brother. It lacks the steering and brake feel, it lacks the V12 soundtrack that's so core to the Lamborghini experience. Simply put, it doesn't involve and exhilarate like the LP640.

They thought the Gallardo would make the V12 Lambo redundant. They were wrong. For now at least, in the form of the LP640, the Murciélago is still very much at the top of the Lamborghini food chain.

A big thank you to David Price at Lamborghini Club UK, Mike Pullen at Carrera Sports, Simon George, Jenny Rothwell and Jim Wiltshire.

	COUNTACH	DIABLO VT 6.0	LP640	SUPERLEGGERA
■ Engine	V12	V12	V12	V10
■ Location	Mid, longitudinal	Mid, longitudinal	Mid, longitudinal	Mid, longitudinal
■ Displacement	5167cc	5991cc	6496cc	4961cc
■ Bore x stroke	85.5 x 75mm	87 x 84mm	99 x 82.8mm	82.5 x 92.8mm
■ Cylinder block	Aluminium alloy	Aluminium alloy, dry sump	Aluminium alloy, dry sump	Aluminium alloy, dry sump
■ Cylinder head	Aluminium alloy, dohc per bank, 4v per cyl	Aluminium alloy, dohc per bank, 4v per cyl, variable valve timing	Aluminium alloy, dohc per bank, 4v per cyl, variable valve timing	Aluminium alloy, dohc per bank, 4v per cyl, variable valve timing
■ Fuel and ignition	Six Weber carburettors, electronic ignition	Electronic engine management, sequential fuel injection	Electronic engine management, sequential direct injection	Electronic engine management, sequential direct injection
■ Max power	455bhp @ 7000rpm	550bhp @ 7100rpm	631bhp @ 8000rpm	522bhp @ 8000rpm
■ Max torque	369lb ft @ 5200rpm	457lb ft @ 5500rpm	487lb ft @ 6000rpm	376lb ft @ 4250rpm
■ Transmission	Five-speed manual, rear-wheel drive, lsd	Five-speed manual, four-wheel drive, front and rear lsd	Six-speed e-gear, four-wheel drive, front and rear lsd, ESP, ASR	Six-speed e-gear, four-wheel drive, rear lsd, ESP, ASR
■ Front suspension	Double wishbones, coil springs, gas dampers, anti-roll bar	Double wishbones, coil springs, gas dampers, anti-roll bar	Double wishbones, coil springs, gas dampers, anti-roll bar	Double wishbones, coil springs, gas dampers, anti-roll bar
■ Rear suspension	Multi-link, coil springs, gas dampers, anti-roll bar	Double wishbones, coil springs, gas dampers, anti-roll bar	Double wishbones, coil springs, gas dampers, anti-roll bar	Double wishbones, coil springs, gas dampers, anti-roll bar
■ Brakes	Vented discs, 300mm front, 284mm rear	Drilled and vented discs, 365mm front, 335mm rear, ABS	Vented carbon ceramic discs, 380mm front and rear, ABS, EBD	Vented carbon ceramic discs, 365mm fr, 325mm rr, ABS, ABD
■ Weight (kerb)	1568kg	1625kg	1665kg	1420kg
■ Power-to-weight	295bhp/ton	344bhp/ton	385bhp/ton	373hp/ton
■ 0-62mph	5.0sec (claimed)	3.9sec (claimed)	3.4sec (claimed)	3.8sec (claimed)
■ Max speed	183mph (claimed)	200mph+ (claimed)	211mph (claimed)	196mph (claimed)
■ Basic price	c£70,000 (1988)	£155,000 (2000)	£192,000 (2007)	£150,000 (2007)
evo RATING	★★★★★	★★★★★	★★★★★	★★★★⯪

'The LP640 is a car shot through with passion and attention to detail'

CLAIM 3 ISSUES OF

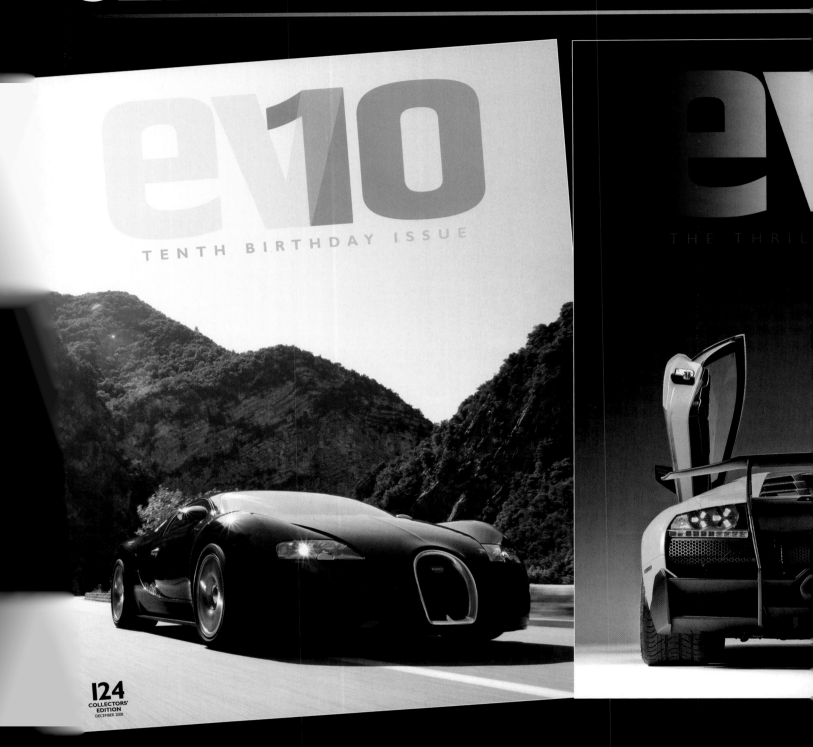

eV10

TENTH BIRTHDAY ISSUE

THE THRIL

124
COLLECTORS'
EDITION
DECEMBER 2008

If **evo** is for you, your subscription will continue at the low rate of just **£21.30** every 6 issues by Direct Debit, saving you 19% on the shop price. If you decide not to continue receiving your monthly issue delivered direct to your door, simply cancel within your trial period and you'll pay no more than the £1 already debited.

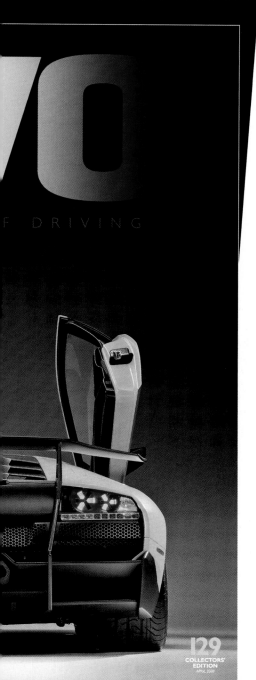

TOP GUN

With an all-new body inspired by a jet fighter, in 2007 the LP640-based Reventón was Lambo's most extreme – and expensive – supercar ever

It may be an LP640
underneath, but every
body panel is new. The
redesign isn't subtle,
either, with the jet
fighter influences hard
to miss. Centre right:
even the instruments
get an aeronautical feel

How do you turn a Lamborghini Murciélago LP640 into something more extreme? The temptingly glib answer is you can't. Or possibly a counter-question: why would you want to? After all, you might think, the Murciélago wrote the book on 'extreme'. It has one of the most dramatic shapes in supercar history. And, ramming home the point, it's a well-known fact that old women and children still hobble/run away or faint when they see one coming towards them.

But is the Murciélago really that extreme, or is it just stunningly beautiful? I'd go with the latter. Yes, it has presence. And yes, its size and shape generate plenty of drama, but it's actually a remarkably restrained piece of work, unsullied by any stick-on bits that might be calculated to top up its already ample testosterone levels.

You might remember that, many years ago, the same 'clean 'n' simple' descriptions were applied to the original Countach and Diablo. But there's a grand tradition at Lamborghini – and one that owner Audi is clearly keen to keep alive – that once a design reaches a certain age, its aesthetic envelope gets pushed. Hard. But never quite this hard.

Called the Reventón, this new variation on the Murciélago takes its name, in the Lamborghini tradition, from a fighting bull (and one with a reputation, having killed the famed Mexican bullfighter Felix Guzman in 1943). It is being billed as the company's most expensive and extreme supercar ever, and for the 20 'friends and collectors' who've placed deposits on the entire limited production run, life with a Murciélago will never be the same again.

Or maybe it will. According to Manfred Fitzgerald, marketing manager at Lamborghini for the past nine years, now head of design, and the man directly responsible for the million-euro (plus taxes) Reventón, the decision to makeover a Murciélago was entirely design-led. So despite the identical price, it's not a Veyron chaser. It hasn't been made to set a new land speed record either, and it won't accelerate any quicker than the standard LP640 or go round corners any faster.

Not intentionally, anyway, though the liberal use of carbonfibre composites and

'Each V12 will be blueprinted, guaranteeing 641bhp'

the fact that each one of the 6.5-litre V12 engines will be blueprinted (liberating a minimum 10 extra bhp, bringing the total to a guaranteed 641bhp at 8000rpm) may exert subtle influences in these areas. Still, you could argue that the LP640 is fast enough already…

Tempting as it might be to dream, this most certainly isn't the Murciélago equivalent of the Gallardo Superleggera. No, Lamborghini describes the Reventón as 'haute couture', 'a symbol of extreme exclusivity', which is refreshingly candid at least. A bigger clue to the thinking behind it is given by Stephan Winkelmann, Lamborghini's chairman and CEO, who explains, 'Our designers at the Lamborghini Style Centre based in Sant'Agata took the technical base of the Murciélago LP640 and compressed and intensified its DNA, its genetic code.'

But only after a trip to the local American airbase to introduce a degree of stealth fighter loading to their collective inspiration. The dispenser of shock and awe that really caught their eye, relates Fitzgerald, was the F-22 Raptor, with its simple, angular shape, sharp edges and distinctive nose-forward canopy.

Exported to the four-wheeled realm, this translates into a more technical and edgy-looking Murciélago with interrupted lines and contorted surfaces to create a more dynamic play of light across its surfaces. The aerospace overtones account for the paint finish as well; also called Reventón, the new hue is described as a mid-opaque green/grey 'without the usual shine'. Very *Top Gun*.

As with the LP640, the Reventón's exterior is carbonfibre, glued and riveted to a carbon and steel structure. The overall dimensions and proportions remain similar to the Murciélago's but, panel for panel, the bodywork is all new.

Above, centre: carbonfibre fins on the wheel spokes improve brake cooling. Above: rear LEDs are of a special heatproof design. Far left: interior has the air of a cockpit

Below: even the upper air intakes have been restyled, becoming more angular. Right: exhaust hasn't got any smaller…

The heavily revised, pointed nose section features gaping jet-fighter-like ducts that cool the carbon brake discs and six-pot callipers. Further back, the doors still scissor upwards, just as on the regular Murciélago (and the Diablo and Countach before that), but the sill spoilers beneath them are functionally asymmetric – the one on the driver's side is larger to allow an increased flow of air to the radiator; on the other side the spoiler is flat as it only has to contain the airflow below the floor.

The downforce-generating flat underbody now terminates with a highly visible rear diffuser, which, along with the adjustable rear wing, enhances stability when approaching the car's claimed top speed of 'over 340kph' – that's 211mph, unchanged from the LP640.

The airflow and section of the variable-geometry air intakes for the engine have also been modified, while the engine cover is made of glass laminate (with open ventilation slits) – all the better to show off the V12 beneath. And for lovers of tactile petrol caps, the Reventón's is nothing short

of a work of art, being milled from a solid aluminium block.

Perhaps unsurprisingly, the lighting jewellery seen on the latest Audis gets an outing here, too, with the restyled bi-xenon headlight units gaining sparkling LED daytime running lights and indicators. There are LEDs at the back for the tail-lights, brake lights and indicators, too, arranged in three arrowhead shapes to mimic the theme seen throughout the rest of the new design. Being located near the exhaust and just above the engine cooling ducts, these LEDs have been specially developed to be heatproof.

Completing the external makeover is a striking new wheel design that sees a carbonfibre fin screwed to each aluminium spoke. The fins aren't there just for show, either, they're there to create a turbine effect to further aid the cooling of the massive 380mm brake discs.

Inside, Lamborghini's favoured blend of Alcantara, carbon, aluminium and leather is stunningly resolved and, massaging the cutting-edge strike-fighter theme, the

dash has no dials, only three TFT liquid crystal displays set in a housing milled from solid aluminium billet and shrouded in a carbonfibre casing. The driver can choose from three vehicle information settings and, at the press of a button, switch from a digital to a quasi-analogical display with classic circular instruments. There's even a g-force meter that represents dynamic driving forces by the movement of a sphere on a 3D grid, depending on the direction and intensity of the acceleration. An instrument along the same lines can be found in high-performance aeroplanes, and Formula 1 teams also use a similar device to analyse dynamic forces.

At over a million euros, it would be hard to say who might be tempted to buy the Reventón – if they hadn't already all been sold. As ever, 'extreme exclusivity' is a sought-after commodity. It's something of a collectors' item. But you'll be glad to hear that orders have been spread fairly evenly around the globe, with only a slight clumping in the USA. One is even destined for the UK. A very rare Lambo indeed.

Specification

Engine	V12
Location	Mid, longitudinal
Displacement	6496cc
Cylinder block	Aluminium alloy
Cylinder head	Aluminium alloy, dohc per bank, 4v per cylinder, variable valve timing
Fuel and ignition	Lamborghini LIE ignition and fuel injection, variable intake geometry
Max power	641bhp @ 8000rpm
Max torque	487lb ft @ 6000rpm
Transmission	Six-speed e-gear paddleshift gearbox, four-wheel drive
Suspension	Double wishbones, coil springs, gas dampers, anti-roll bar front and rear
Weight	1665kg (est)
Power-to-weight	391bhp/ton (est)
0-62mph	3.4sec (claimed)
Top speed	211mph+ (claimed)
Basic price	c£795,000 (2007)
On sale	2007 only

'There's even a g-force meter, as used by Formula 1 teams'

GALLARDO LP560-4

IN 2008, THE V10 LAMBO GOT A VISUAL MAKEOVER AND EVEN MORE POWER

A n 18 per cent reduction in CO2 output. Did that opening sentence grab your attention? Lamborghini hopes so. 'Lamborghini takes its social responsibility very seriously,' says communications supremo Dominik Hoberg. Yes, and Tazio Nuvolari was my father's uncle.

So seriously is this social responsibility being taken that the new Gallardo LP560-4 comes with a new, pedestrian-friendly front end and, for this first drive of the car, a heartfelt exhortation from its creators not to exceed the local Las Vegas roads' hyper-nannying speed limits – limits based on the abilities of a 20-year-old Chrysler Voyager with bald tyres, dead dampers and no brakes rather than those of a four-wheel-drive supercar retarded, optionally, by carbon-ceramic brakes.

Luckily there's the Las Vegas Motor Speedway. Here we can discover what the LP560-4 is mostly about, and chiefly the LP560-4 is about a brand new engine, which, says engineering chief Maurizio Reggiani, has no commonality with any 90-degree V10 that Audi might make apart

from the odd pump (it has no fewer than three scavenge pumps for its dry sump) or sensor. Its capacity is up from 4961cc to 5204, taking power up by 39bhp to 552bhp (or 560 PS – hence the model name) at 8000rpm, while torque climbs from 376lb ft to 398 at the 6500rpm peak of a flatter torque curve.

All that and CO2 down from 400g/km to 327. How? Mainly thanks to direct fuel injection with stratified charge (it sounds better if you say *iniezione diretta stratificata*), and the 12.5:1 compression ratio it allows because squirting the fuel directly into the cylinder has the effect of cooling the air that has been heated by compression. No production direct-injection engine has revved higher: its limit is 8500rpm.

The bigger capacity comes partly from bigger bores, for which there was no room in the old engine, so there's a new block with more widely spaced bore centres. That called for a longer crankshaft, for which Reggiani had doubts about the strength of the old engine's split-crankpin design, so the new engine's opposing cylinders

share a common, unsplit crankpin and to hell with even firing intervals. To add further sonic mystery, each bank has a three-into-one and a two-into-one manifold, each 'one' then joining downstream.

Also new is the way the optional e-gear sequential gearbox selects its ratios, now by rotating cam instead of a pair of hydraulic rams. The result is shifts as quick as 120 milliseconds from torque cut to torque reinstatement (that is the whole shift, not just the gear engagement), down from 200ms. The new mechanism saves 13kg, too. Then there's the revised suspension with an extra toe-control link at the rear, plus lighter brakes with better ventilation. Indeed the whole car is lighter by 20kg, despite the engine weighing 10kg more.

Sonic mystery… Lambo CEO Stephan Winkelmann, whose name suggests Germanicness but whose looks and speech are decidedly Italian (he grew up there), walks along the long dinner table to tell us of the Gallardo's new attributes. Then he is replaced by dancing girls with attitude, who take care to avoid the many wine glasses, while LP560-4s snarl past the windows, radio microphones by their exhaust pipes. Sound is central to this car. It's a hard, dirty, savage sound, an explosion of energy, an automotive Tourette's, yet somehow it gets past drive-by noise regulations.

Day two and we're at the Speedway, about to chase a Murciélago driven by a Lamborghini test driver. Even a throttle blip in the pit lane turns each cylinder into a firecracker. Yet this newest Gallardo doesn't look as menacing as it sounds. The satin-black one on radial-spoke

Above left: new, slightly larger V10 has an extra 39bhp and a harder sound to go with it. Right: restyled nose is pedestrian-friendly

Superleggera wheels looks the moodiest, the white ones with gloss-black wheels look the purest. Some have new polished-aluminium lattice-spoke wheels, which are much too Ripspeed for my taste.

That new nose is longer, more chiselled, more Reventón. Slimmer headlights, with optional LED running lights, make it look sterner. There are more LEDs, fashioned in a repeat of Y-shapes, in the narrow tail-lights, which no longer flow up into the rear deck. Designer Manfred Fitzgerald says the idea is to make the Gallardo look wider and flatter, because Lamborghinis should be wide and flat. He also thinks LEDs can be over-used and has tried to keep these discreet. Helped by a new rear diffuser, the revised body shape gives 32 per cent more downforce to give a total of 20kg on the front wheels and 50kg on the rears at full chat.

Inside, things look much as before apart from glitzy knurled switches above the centre console and clearer instrument graphics. And, in this e-gear car (as they all are here, like 90 per cent of customer cars) there's a new 'Corsa' button, which activates the fastest gearshifts and the standing-back-with-arms-folded ESP mode.

'SOUND IS CENTRAL TO THIS CAR. IT'S A HARD, DIRTY, SAVAGE SOUND'

It gets pressed, but we'll save killing the ESP completely for later.

Onto the banking, down into the infield. Yes, the low-end torque is plentiful, but then it wasn't exactly lacking in the previous car. But around 4000rpm – a significant point in the variable valve timing's modus operandi – the note changes from something boomy and gruffly V8-like to a hard-edged barrage of sound waves in which the former neat, tidy, 10-cylinder half-octave harmonic has been ousted by something much more complex.

If I don't ease the throttle slightly the upshift has a savagery to match, but the downshift is perfect. Reggiani says the problem with a twin-clutch transmission is that customers prefer a gearchange to have a definite jerk when they're trying hard (I don't agree, and I expect you don't either), and the e-gear provides this. It's also lighter. Anyway, e-gear does give a scope for honing your skills in a way a twin-clutch system wouldn't, and that is a good thing.

This Gallardo has a suede-and-carbonfibre steering wheel, preferable to the standard leather version whose flattened, plastic base feels as cheap as the similar one did in the

Audi RS4. Via it I feel initial understeer as I aim through the infield corners, but the now quicker-acting viscous coupling sends energy decisively rearwards as I apply power, making the understeer evaporate.

In Corsa mode the LP560 becomes deliciously steerable on the throttle, helped by the limited-slip differential at the rear, but the oversteer decays before it gets out of hand. It's the worry-free mode; ESP off, by comparison, brings on a tetchy tail that could be bad news in the wet.

Sport mode? That's a notch down from Corsa, and the trade-off for smoother full-bore upshifts is the need to apply power later in the corner, otherwise the nose is pushed wide. And normal mode is pointless on the track, as you'd imagine.

The new, low-rolling-resistance Pirelli P Zeros seemingly sacrifice no grip to their CO2-friendly rotation, but I'm unimpressed with the carbon brakes, whose pedal action is worryingly soggy on the track. Out on the road, meanwhile, they feel springy, snatchy and ill-defined, so I'd suggest specifying your LP560 with the regular stoppers. There's not much you can do about the hard-edged ride, though, which is unforgiving of broken road surfaces and a fly in the ointment

for this faster, madder Gallardo.

And if you want to find out just how mad the LP560-4 is there's a 'thrust' control in the e-gear system, used when in automatic mode with Sport or Corsa in play. It's like Ferrari's launch control and it's how you get the 0-62mph time down to 3.7sec and the 0-124mph to 11.8sec. Not that you ever would in a socially responsible Lamborghini, of course.

John Simister

Specification

Engine	V10, 5204cc
Max power	552bhp @ 8000rpm
Max torque	398lb ft @6500rpm
Top speed	202mph (claimed)
0-62mph	3.7sec (claimed)
Price	£147,330
On sale	2008-present

EVO RATING ★★★★☆

+ Great car gets quicker and cleaner
− Rocky ride and mushy carbon brakes

WEALTH FIGHTER

All 20 examples of the extraordinary Lamborghini Reventón were snapped up by super-rich collectors. So what did they get for their £900,000? We found out

Below: bodywork is more aerodynamic than the standard LP640's. Carbon fins on the wheel-spokes aid brake cooling

ntil I actually 'locked horns' with the Lamborghini Reventón, I was pretty sure that there was little of any real significance in this special edition Murciélago LP640. What was of note here had little to do with the product per se and more to do with the status of Lamborghini and its new ability to cash in on its successful image-building campaign. How wrong can you be…

Cast your mind back to the car's public unveiling at the Frankfurt motor show last September. The Reventón just sort of sat there under the unflattering lights of the show hall. With its flat, dark grey paintwork, the new bodywork looked contrived, almost forced upon the chassis. I left feeling a little sorry for Automobili Lamborghini and slightly cheated considering the price tag of 1 million euros (plus local taxes). I honestly came close to cancelling this test drive a week prior to driving over to Sant'Agata. Fortunately a wiser friend convinced me to keep my appointment.

In the north-central Italian flatlands and Apennine foothills, under the low, hard sun of early Italian spring, so much changes. The 'Grey Barra' paint finish (also being called 'Reventón Grey' as it appears nowhere else but here and is the only colour the car can wear from the factory) reveals metallic flakes that subtly give off all the colours of the spectrum. Suddenly the forced feeling of the stealth fighter-inspired carbonfibre body panels is gone. The Reventón looks great. But still the price of the car keeps getting in the way. How in hell can this re-skinned LP640 be worth nearly *five times* the price of the car on which it is based? Regardless of whether I like it or not, my prejudice towards Lamborghini customers continues. Surely they have more money than sense.

Prior to this Reventón experiment there have been a number of rather less interesting 'limited edition' Lambos, models like the LP640 Murciélago Versace, the Gallardo Nera and the personalised 'Privilegio' models. Closer in spirit to what the Reventón is about were the 2005 Concept S Gallardo and 2006's overly retro Miura concept. Manfred Fitzgerald, Lamborghini's director of brand and design, explains the lead-up to Reventón: 'When we showed the Concept S two-and-a-half years ago, we [the Lamborghini brand] were not yet established well enough image-wise to give that car the go-ahead. Gradually, cars like the Versace and Nera have shown that our image was consistently gaining authority with customers willing to invest.'

Lamborghini executives made the decision to go ahead with the Reventón during the Paris motor show in September 2006 and design and development got under way in Sant'Agata in spring 2007. 'After a couple of visits to the NATO base at Ghedi near Verona,' adds Fitzgerald, 'we all agreed that the most inspiring look was of the F-22A Raptor stealth fighter.'

To give you an indication of how ready Lamborghini's super-rich fans now were to spend big money, with just a one-quarter scale static model shown to prospective clients at Audi's design studio in Santa Monica, California, all 20 Reventóns were sold before the car's Frankfurt debut.

'Our original thought,' says Fitzgerald, 'was to sell just one car to a devoted client. Then we said maybe three, then five, then seven. Before we knew it we had to cap production at 20 cars in order to promise these customers the exclusivity they seek, but we have a waiting list of 20 more people in case someone ever pulls out of their order.' Deliveries began in January this year and should be finished by October: one to the UK, one each to Switzerland, Germany, Italy, France, Canada, Dubai, Austria and Japan, then 12 to customers in the United States.

With the arrival of the Reventón you can kiss goodbye to any notions of ever seeing a Lambo that looks anything like the 2006 Miura concept.

'Under the Italian sun, the forced feeling
of the stealth fighter-inspired body is gone.
The Reventón looks great'

According to sources within the company, all future additions to the product line-up (i.e. beyond the LP560-4 Gallardo driven in this issue) will be bolder and edgier-looking, taking the Reventón as inspiration and steering clear of any sentimentality for the past. Furthermore, with Lamborghini at last paying all of its own bills and reinvesting all of its own profits, all such projects can get the go-ahead and final approval without any intervention from owner Audi or its design centres. So despite all the Audis sitting in the car park at Sant'Agata, Lamborghini is in charge of its own destiny for the first time since the end of the '60s.

The Reventón is a Murciélago, true, but that's hardly a bad thing. Talk to any lifetime employee of Lamborghini in Italy and, away from the German owners' ears, they will tell you that, for them, the LP640 is the only true Lamborghini in the current line-up, while the Gallardo is seen as pure VW/Audi material. It's

important that the people building a car feel a spiritual connection with it, especially in this market, and especially if the car is Italian.

So the striking carbonfibre bodywork is produced almost wholly on-site from the Lamborghini autoclaves. Get up close and you can see the glorious, dry-sump 6.5-litre V12 clearly visible through a louvred glass-laminate cover cut in the arrow shape that reappears all over the car. And from there you'll notice the new fuel cap bored from aluminium billet. People behind you are entertained by the (again) arrow-shaped and heat-resistant (think of the engine's proximity) LED brake lights.

Most engaging of all these touches is the digital display that greets you when you've settled into the radically reclined bucket seat, covered in green and grey Alcantara. This screen can be switched between a traditional dial scheme and a jet fighter-inspired display that shows revs and gearshifts with such flair

that it can be distracting. Then there's the G-Force Meter, which reveals forward, rearward and lateral g-forces, the latter reaching brief peaks of 1.3*g* during our drive in this pre-production car, limited, sadly, to just 140kph (87mph).

Torso gripped by the sturdy-feeling seat, the Reventón – no surprise here – drives almost entirely like an LP640 Murciélago. Physically, it remains one of the true heavyweights of the supercar world, yet despite its heaviness and feeling of utter massiveness out on any road, I have always liked the Murciélago's way of handling its power and torque. And the Reventón feels every bit as good.

Every bit as accelerative too. As with the donor car, acceleration to 62mph is estimated to be 3.4sec with a top speed of 211mph-plus, although Lamborghini's test drivers admit that during testing at both Nardo in southern Italy and Volkswagen's test track at Ehra-Lessien,

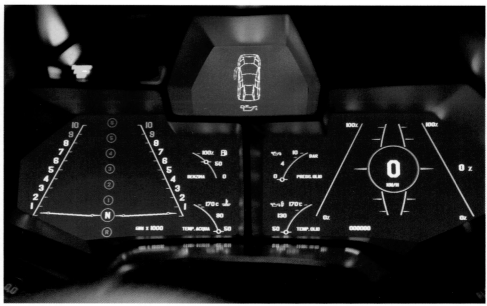

'There's no doubt that this is an uncompromised supercar in the finest tradition'

Top right: aeronautics-inspired instruments were developed entirely in-house and consist of three liquid crystal screens offering a choice of two display modes. Far right: output of the 6.5-litre V12 is up 10bhp to 641bhp

Germany, the Reventón hit 62mph in 3.2sec and touched 213mph. Only the 'e-gear' automated version of the six-speed manual gearbox is being offered (word is that the conventional manual 'box will soon be completely eliminated from Lamborghini's offerings), and the shifts, executed via new carbonfibre paddles, are definitely at their best in the quicker Sport mode.

Wind-tunnel testing has resulted in improved air-flow through the openings all over the new bodywork and a drag coefficient down to 0.27 from the original 0.30, while front and rear downforces at high speed increase for greater stability at the far end of the speedometer. Better air supply is partially responsible for the ten additional horsepower for the Reventón, bringing the total to 641bhp at 8000rpm, with the rev-limiter still set at 8200rpm. The sweet-spot for the best mix of torque and power really doesn't come until above 5000rpm, when the

baffles open and the engine begins to bellow to nape-prickling effect.

As standard, the Reventón comes equipped with the stickier Pirelli P Zero Nero tyres – 245/35 ZR18 front, 335/30 ZR18 rear – and big ceramic-composite brake discs that are both optional on the LP640. Lateral grip is simply huge, and matched by serious stopping power, allowing you to brake late into turns.

At the end of my all-to-brief drive I'm in no doubt that the Reventón is an uncompromised supercar in the finest tradition, and, of course, a major event just to be around. Yes, ultimately it is primarily a piece of collector self-expression. And I still can't look past the price. But, as Manfred Fitzgerald says, 'Many people around the world require a practical justification for buying such a car, but buyers in this league are more willing to indulge life. It's not a question here of straightforward product benefits, but of a work of art. We're selling dreams.' ∎

Specification

Engine	V12
Location	Mid, longitudinal
Displacement	6496cc
Cylinder block	Aluminium alloy
Cylinder head	Aluminium alloy, dohc per bank, 4v per cylinder, variable valve timing
Fuel and ignition	Lamborghini LIE ignition and fuel injection, variable intake geometry
Max power	641bhp @ 8000rpm
Max torque	487lb ft @ 6000rpm
Transmission	Six-speed e-gear paddleshift gearbox, four-wheel drive
Suspension	Double wishbones, coil springs, gas dampers, anti-roll bar front and rear
Weight	1665kg (est)
Power-to-weight	391bhp/ton (est)
0–62mph	3.4sec (claimed)
Top speed	211mph+ (claimed)
Basic price	c£795,000 (2007)
On sale	2007 only

RAGING BULL

In 2009, Lamborghini revealed the lightest, fastest and most powerful Murciélago to date, the 661bhp, 212mph LP670-4 SV. Prepare to have your frames of reference rearranged…

f all the senses that get shattered when you drive a truly fast, loud and visceral supercar flat out, the one that's hardest to put back together is a sense of perspective. The intensity/insanity of the act obliterates normally reliable frames of reference embedded in a world of largely benign forces and sounds. To an F22 Raptor pilot or Lewis Hamilton, it might not seem extraordinary; they'd probably award the experience no-big-deal out of ten. For the rest of us, the hit is pure, mind-scrambling, off-the-scale exhilaration. There are advantages to being merely human.

So a few words of warning to anyone thinking of buying a Ferrari 599 GTB Fiorano in the belief that it will feel shockingly fast and as perspective-warping as the good bit of the Oblivion ride at Alton Towers. It will. Especially if you order it with the HGTE chassis upgrade pack which will allow you to brake later and turn harder. It will be a thing of beauty, dynamic grace and a joy forever, too. But if you want it to turn your sensible world coordinates to sushi, whatever you do don't be tempted to sample – either just before or after – the one car on earth that will put the fiercest Ferrari into perfectly focused perspective: the Lamborghini Murciélago LP670-4 SV.

I'd driven a 599 HGTE a few days before returning to Italy to try the Super Veloce. The thrill generated by the Enzo-engined GT still hadn't worn off, especially the hot laps around Fiorano. Sir Stirling Moss, making the most of a rare visit to Maranello by chalking up his Fiorano debut with a dozen or so laps in a 250 GT SWB, was later treated to a few more laps in the passenger seat of the 599 and was rendered almost speechless by the experience, later registering his shock at the cornering and braking forces. It's that sort of car. You get out of it thinking, 'Well, bring it on. What can possibly deliver more pukka Italian V12 supercar violence than this?'

When Lamborghini released official details of the car that just might – the lighter, more powerful, granite-knuckled swansong version of Lambo's scissor-doored, mid-engined Murciélago LP640 flagship – I counted myself among the ranks of the slightly dubious. I'd hoped it would have still less weight, more power and rear- rather than four-wheel drive. And surely a nice round 700bhp wouldn't

have been that hard to extract from 6.5 litres and 12 cylinders. A stripped-down, rear-drive Murciélago with 700 horsepower: the definitive Italian exoticar statement.

But Lamborghini boss Stephan Winkelmann argued that at minus 100 kilos, plus 30bhp (making 661, or 670 PS) and with a bodyshell, aerodynamics and suspension extensively reworked to generate more grip, not only would the Murciélago SV offer 'an utterly unparalleled driving experience', but it would actually *need* its four-wheel drive to exploit the extra potential. The claimed headline performance figures – 0-62mph in 3.2sec, the ton in under seven and a top speed of 212mph (or 209mph with the optional larger 'Aeropack Wing', as fitted to our dazzling metallic orange example) – certainly help distance the SV from the LP640 and Ferrari 599 by the requisite fractions of a second and handful of mph on paper.

It wouldn't really matter which you'd just stepped from, though. However much you felt you'd synched with the visuals, sonics and heavy-duty manipulation of g-force, what the SV serves up is altogether more extraordinary, relentless and all-consuming.

Truth is, attacking an empty stretch of mountain road in the SV hammers so much immediacy and raw excitement into the usual supercar mix, your heart nearly leaps out of your chest. The noise, the bite, the response, the grip and braking power – all require rapid mental recalibration to make much sense of. Not because they in any way defy the physics of what's possible given the basic hardware but because they're delivered with such unfiltered honesty and intensity. Both against the clock and subjectively, the SV is a savagely, intimidatingly fast car.

Although the shift speed of its e-gear transmission is less slovenly than before, it's still very far from seamless. Yet, in a strange way that seems entirely in keeping with the SV's physical, bull-necked character – a double-clutcher would be altogether too smooth and suave for this car, though there's little doubt the optional (but heavier) six-speed manual gearbox would suit it best of all.

Below 4700 revs the engine is merely brutal, from there to the 8500rpm red line it's insane – an electrifying ball of energy that screams the hairs off the back of your neck and thumps the lightened LP to three-figure speeds quicker than you can decide if that's where you really want to

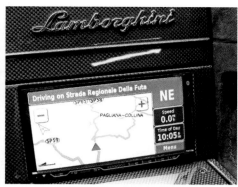

Left: despite 100kg having been shed from the Murciélago's weight, the SV's cabin isn't without its modern conveniences – a radio/satnav system comes as standard, although it can be deleted as an option. Below: that massive LP tailpipe isn't all that it seems…

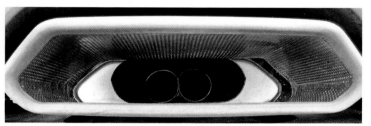

'The noise, the bite, the response, the grip, the braking power – all require mental recalibration'

Below: seat belts have Lamborghini badges stitched onto them, while the instrument panel (opposite page) gains SV logos. Bottom: black detailing clearly distinguishes the SV from lesser Murciélagos

go. If it isn't, the enormous carbon-ceramic discs can wipe off the speed even more rapidly.

But not today. Gus Gregory hasn't found us a photo location so much as a tarmac rally stage, and what's more, we seem to be the only people up here. But even now I feel under-prepared for the onslaught of sensations I know I should moderate but, for the life on me, simply can't seem to: not least the way the SV grabs tarmac and hurls it backwards. Again, it isn't just the accelerative lunge for the horizon that momentarily makes me forget to breathe but the way it builds to a shattering crescendo gear after gear. In summary, this thing goes like hell.

And corners do little to blunt its charge. What's perhaps most remarkable about the SV's chassis is its eagerness to translate even the most fleeting and subtle helm input into meaningful action. You can nuance a cornering line with steering or throttle. And with so much width to place on the road, it's a revelation that it can be done so accurately. This is the other side to the SV's character – it feels focused and intimate. The colossal output from the engine is met without contrivance or nerves from the chassis.

Just grip, conviction and precision.

The ride is remarkable, too: ultra firm and biased heavily towards body control over comfort, but it still manages to round-off edges without jinking or jarring. It's completely oblivious to mid-bend bumps as well. Power oversteer? With the torque split rear-biased it isn't off the agenda, especially if you stay on the brakes while turning in, but you'd better be quick with the opposite lock. Let it get too out of shape and there's no way back.

In some respects, though, the Murciélago SV misses the mark. When you first see it, it looks incredibly dramatic. With familiarity that palls and you realise that the beauty of the plain Murciélago has been corrupted by the fussy black SV modifications. And, for me at least, the carbon-shelled race seats are almost excruciatingly uncomfortable, providing zilch in the way of lumbar support. In these respects, a Ferrari 599 HGTE has it well and truly beaten. The Fezza is also miles ahead as an all-round, everyday supercar. But when it comes to sheer, epic supercar sensation, the Murciélago SV might well be the best there's ever been.

'The lunge for the horizon builds to a shattering

Specification

Engine	V12
Location	Mid, longitudinal
Displacement	6496cc
Max power	661bhp @ 8000rpm
Max torque	487lb ft @ 6500rpm
Transmission	e-gear paddle-shift gearbox (six-speed manual optional), four-wheel drive, front and rear limited-slip diffs
Front suspension	Double wishbones, coil springs, gas dampers, anti-roll bar
Rear suspension	Double wishbones, coil springs, gas dampers, anti-roll bar
Brakes	Vented carbon-ceramic discs, 380mm front and rear, EBD, ABS, TC
Wheels	8.5 x 18in front, 13 x 18in rear, aluminium alloy
Tyres	245/35 ZR18 front, 335/30 ZR18 rear, Pirelli P Zero Corsa
Weight (kerb)	1565kg
Power to weight	429bhp/ton
0-62mph	3.2sec (claimed)
Top speed	212mph (claimed)
Basic price	£221,335
On sale	Summer 2009

evo RATING ★★★★★

crescendo gear after gear. This thing goes like hell'

ALONG CAME A
SPYDER...

In early 2009, Lamborghini took the roof off its 552bhp Gallardo to create the LP560-4 Spyder. It's just as stunning to look at, but is it still as good to drive?

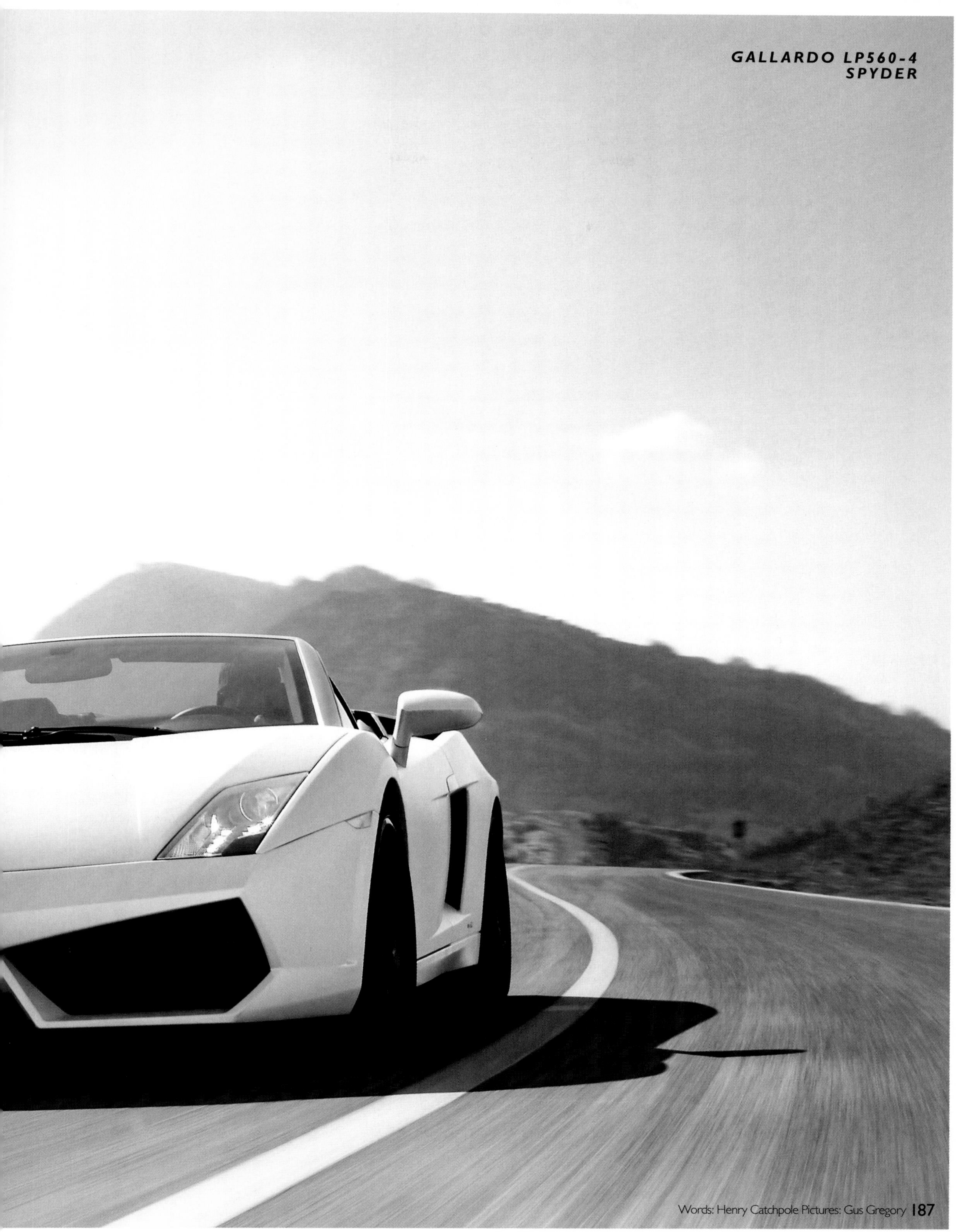

Words: Henry Catchpole Pictures: Gus Gregory

Spyder takes 4.0sec to complete the 0-62mph dash – 0.3sec longer than the coupe – but its top speed is down just one mph, to 201mph

R oof down, air temperature hovering around five degrees, a thin layer of mist gently dispersing into the bluing sky and, most importantly, the heated seat turned up to six. We're skimming low across the flat, open countryside heading south from Sant'Agata. There's something comforting about the sensation of warmth seeping through to your back and hamstrings in a convertible; it's like sitting on one of those big old-fashioned radiators you used to find in cold classrooms and draughty church halls.

The LP560-4 has been turned from a wedge to a sliver of Italian automotive sculpture. It looks absolutely stunning, of that there is no question. But de-roofing divides people. Some hate it because they see it as emasculating a wonderful car. They say it's a process that reduces rigidity, then adds weight trying to get that rigidity back. They see something like a Gallardo Spyder as a compromise, a shadow of what the car was designed to be.

And then there are those who love cars like this. They, I suspect, fall into two categories. The first lot want to pose and be looked at. They want to bathe conspicuously in the reflected glory that the car gathers around it (failing to realise that people are interested in the car, not the person driving it. Plus you only really look

Right: electrically operated canvas hood stows neatly beneath the carbonfibre rear deck, resulting in what must be one of the best convertible profiles (above)

cool in a convertible if you live in a country with a climate that complements it). The second reason for buying a drop-top is because you want to be that little bit closer to the world you're driving through. You want to hear the changes in the tarmac you're covering, feel the reverberating exhaust note, catch the smell of the brakes as you haul off speed into a hairpin. But if that's why you want a convertible then you'll want one that hasn't been compromised, hasn't been produced purely for people in the first category. So what is the LP560-4 Spyder? Drivers' car or poseurs' carriage?

Well, whether you want to or not, you'll attract attention. We slow down to 50kph and the almost impossibly exotic bodywork of the Gallardo glides through a village. I might be

tucked up behind the collar of my coat and the shallow rake of the windscreen, but I can feel every gaze that falls on the car. Stop at traffic lights and the people walking along the pavement might as well be in the passenger seat fiddling with the toggle switches. Exposed by the lack of roof you suddenly seem to be that much more accountable too, you feel more compelled to let people out of side turnings, and it seems like a personal affront if you get cut up on a roundabout.

Hold second gear on the long, curling slip-road away from the toll booth. A white dotted line appears to the left as the road straightens. Check the wing-mirror for a gap then slam forward onto the autostrada, engine note ricocheting off the side of a lorry. With the roof down but the windows up (including the rear one, which acts like a wind deflector when the hood's down), buffeting is minimal, but there is a cold stream eddying its way down to the handbrake and gently freezing my right hip.

It could be distracting, but frankly I'm more concerned with making the most of the multiple tunnels we're going through. The last time I was out this way I was able to wind the windows down on a Scuderia, which was pretty spectacular, but having a Lamborghini V10 behind and an uninhibited view of the barrelled stone ceiling above makes for nothing less than orchestral ecstasy. The noise seems to spill from the exhaust, bounce off the tunnel walls and

'Having a Lamborghini V10 behind
and no roof above makes for nothing
less than orchestral ecstasy'

Above: suspension is slightly softer than the coupe's but the limits of grip are every bit as high. Below: multi-function computer displays chosen e-gear mode and the currently selected gear

then tumble all around you so that you feel as if you're actually inside the sound. It's like standing where the conductor does at a concert rather than perching in row M, seat 11.

Soon our exit appears and we turn onto smaller and altogether less smooth roads. In places the tarmac looks as though it has melted and then suddenly re-hardened, leaving a surface as rough as any I've seen, yet the Spyder remains resolute, the scuttle never shimmying and the damping soaking up the choppy tarmac with aplomb.

We're climbing now, well above any remaining mist hanging about in the valley below. It seems to get brighter and brighter as the road twists ever skywards, the road and countryside looking almost bleached in the glare of the sun, the pearlescence of the Gallardo sparkling as the rays dance on its surface. Then virtual darkness.

The arrival of big, brooding evergreens on either side is like the point in a film when a hero suddenly becomes outnumbered by his nemesis's henchmen closing in around. The road changes character too, straightening and allowing the Gallardo to stretch its legs, sweeping into corners without the need for even a lift of the throttle. Look up and there's still a narrow strip of blue high above, but there's a sense that you want to press on with speed until that strip blossoms into an overarching dome once more.

The Gallardo always feels like a dense car to drive (unlike the Murciélago, strangely) and seems to be constantly exerting pressure on your body. You accelerate and there's an instant and heavy shove from behind, then you change direction and the weight of the steering requires effort from your forearms, while the immense lateral grip from the chassis and P Zero Corsas makes the seat's side bolsters lean weightily on your torso. As we burst out of the trees there's a section of seemingly endless left-rights that need short stabs of acceleration, then dabs of brake. Combined with the constant direction changes, the occasional positive camber that

pushes you down into your seat and the bark of ten cylinders, it's a very physical experience.

You might have guessed by now where we've been heading. The Futa and Raticosa were the last mountain passes in the Mille Miglia before the final charge over the plains of the Emilia-Romagna to Brescia. They've been used many times in **evo** shoots, but *I've* never been here before and it's a huge thrill to be driving these historic bends. It's midweek and there's only the occasional car to get in the way. We have a chat with two smiling policemen in a Bravo who conform to type with the 'Shall we swap cars?' joke before leaving us alone up on the ridge.

Whilst I'm daydreaming about the Mille Miglia, something crosses my mind (not a long journey). We tend to think that sports cars without roofs should be small and light and that the biggest engine you should shoehorn in is a six-cylinder. But some of the greatest and most desirable sports cars of all time, cars like the Moss/Jenks Mercedes Benz SLR of '55 and the Collins/Klemantaski Ferrari 335 S of '57, were relatively big cars with hulking great engines. And how much more romantic and exciting were they for exposing their pilots to the elements as they roared over these passes? In many ways, something like the Gallardo Spyder could be their the modern equivalent.

Then again, with four-wheel drive (split 30:70 front-to-rear by a viscous coupling) and a mechanical limited-slip differential on the rear axle, it's hard to imagine the driver of an LP560 working at the wheel like those heroes of old. Surely it's all maximum grip and no slip? Well, not entirely. The suspension on the Spyder feels just slightly softer than the coupe's and when it's loaded up in a corner you have to balance all the inputs neatly to avoid upsetting it. Change gear when the chassis is working hard on the exit of a long corner, for example, and you can feel the car shift underneath you, squirming as the transmission loads and unloads. Turn into a bend hard on the brakes and you'd better be careful what your next move is, because the V10

'The surface is as rough as any I've seen, yet the Spyder remains resolute, the scuttle never shimmying'

Leather and Alcantara trim is standard, but the 'Ad Personam' programme allows buyers to 'think the impossible' inside and out. You can even have matt brown paint…

behind you won't hesitate to snap out of line if you provoke its momentum too much. There is ESP, of course, but it loosens appropriately depending on which shift mode you choose for the e-gear transmission (Normal, Sport or Corsa), and nevertheless the LP560 can feel intimidating for a while because although there's masses of reassuring grip, this means the limits will be high if and when you breach them.

But work with the grip, subtly use little lifts of the throttle to tighten the line in the first part of the corner, then get on the power early and use the four-wheel drive to pull you towards the exit and the Gallardo is mesmerising. The 552bhp feels as strong and intoxicating as you'd imagine, simply hurling you up the road until your head feels light. All out, Lamborghini claims it will hit 201mph. I can well believe it.

In Corsa mode each e-gear change has a suitable amount of theatre about it, downchanges being executed with particularly decadent acoustic flourishes. Photographer Gus Gregory says that in these seemingly deserted mountains you can hear the Gallardo approaching from miles away, starting off as a

'The 552bhp feels as intoxicating as you'd imagine,

small, intermittent cacophony as it dives in and out of corners and disappears momentarily behind hillsides, then gradually building to a crescendo as it howls up the road directly towards him and fills his camera's viewfinder in a sudden rush.

I play for a couple of blissful hours, but all too soon our time on the Raticosa is up and we have to descend and return. Behind the new, optional black 'Cordelia' wheels of this car are the standard steel brake discs, the front ones clamped by eight-piston calipers. These brakes are much better than the optional carbon-ceramic items we've had on most of the Gallardos we've tried (and which, strangely, only have six-pot calipers on the front). They give more feel through the pedal – although it's still not perfect — and don't show any signs of wilting in a long and tight descent. As we wind our way back down the narrow and more populous roads towards the autostrada, I am also aware of just how easy it feels to place the Gallardo on the road, something that I'm sure is helped by the added spatial awareness afforded by the lack of roof.

As we roll back through the gates of Automobili Lamborghini and park up (half an hour late, but I don't think the Italians can really give lectures on punctuality), I suddenly realise that I haven't tested the roof. Hold the beautiful chromed toggle switch on the transmission tunnel and the whole carbonfibre rear deck slides up and back before a small black canvas tent unfurls and descends on you, attaching itself to the top of the windscreen with a whirr of electric motors. It's very neat, much better than the Murciélago's, but I quickly put it down again because being in a convertible supercar with the roof up feels about as awkward as answering the door in a shower cap.

And so to the car or carriage question. Well, the LP560-4 Spyder is slightly softer than the hard top, something I suspect you'd notice more on a trackday. But it is also still an unequivocally ruthless drivers' car, plus you get all the theatre of feeling, seeing, smelling and hearing the world you're travelling through, which I love. And if you're worried about appearing to be a poseur, grow a beard, wear a hat and drive it on a mountain where no one can see you.

Specification

Engine	V10
Location	Mid, longitudinal
Displacement	5204cc
Cylinder block	Aluminium alloy, dry sumped
Cylinder head	Aluminium alloy, dohc per bank, 4 valves per cyl, variable valve timing
Max power	552bhp @ 5800rpm
Max torque	398lb ft @ 6500rpm
Transmission	Automated sequential manual (option), four-wheel drive, rear limited-slip differential, ESP
Suspension	Double wishbones, coil springs, dampers, anti-roll bar front and rear
Brakes	Ventilated discs, 365mm front, 356mm rear, ABS, ABD
Wheels	8.5 x 19in front, 11 x 19in rear, aluminium alloy
Tyres	235/35 ZR19 front, 295/30 ZR19 rear, Pirelli P Zero
Weight (kerb)	1550kg
Power-to-weight	362bhp/ton
0-62mph	4.0sec (claimed)
Top speed	201mph (claimed)
Basic price	£149,500

EVO RATING ★★★★½

hurling you up the road until your head feels light'

BOLOGNA 45
PIANCALDOLI 10

GLAM SHOCK

With their odd styling and costly habits, Espadas have long been the neglected members of the Lamborghini family. So it's quite a surprise to drive a good one

Words: David Lillywhite Photography: Matthew Howell

You could love this or hate it. On paper, there's everything to love and only fuel consumption, a reputation for corrosion and hefty parts prices to hate. But, in the metal, an Espada divides opinion like nothing else.

This car represents the culmination of a life-long dream for its owner, who first came across one in 1973 and lusted after it from that day on. It's apparently a common affliction, for we've been inundated with enquiries about this feature ever since we first revealed our plans for it three months back. But other readers have sent vehement hate mail on the Espada, outraged that we should consider publishing even the smallest picture of such a 'monstrosity'.

There's no right or wrong to it. How could there be? But the Espada, with virtually the same engine as a Miura, is overlooked and under-valued, with decent examples going for around £16,000 in the UK and $25,000 in the US. Not a minor amount, but relatively small outlay for a 150mph four-seater supercar.

So here we are with one of the UK's best Espadas, and I have to admit something from the start; that I'm afflicted with the great British love of the underdog, a bit of sympathy for the devil, and for me the Espada joins the ranks of cars that I quietly admire, even though I know I shouldn't. That's Ferrari 308 GT4, Porsche 914, Maserati Khamsin, Aston DBS…

Like the 308 GT4 and the Khamsin, the Espada was a product of the Bertone design house. Marcello Gandini, then a young, rising star at Bertone, had already worked closely with Lamborghini engineer Giampaolo Dallara on the Miura, but soiled his reputation with the Marzal prototype, a radical interpretation of how a four-seater GT Lamborghini should look.

With gullwing doors, a rear-mounted six-cylinder engine and stretched Miura chassis, the Marzal looked odd and handled badly. There was no way it could replace the idiosyncratic but stylish 400GT that occupied the company's four-seater slot at that time. Instead, Ferruccio Lamborghini chose a less radical reworking of the 400GT – the Islero – by Mario Marazzi.

But Carrosserie Bertone couldn't sit back and lose such a lucrative contract, so Gandini was instructed to rethink his

'Gandini was instructed to rethink his four-seater GT ideas, and emerged with a new front-engined design. But to Lamborghini's disapproval, this new V12 still made use of gullwing doors… Gandini returned to the drawing board'

Above: the upright rear glass was decorated with vertical slats on the Series I (this is a Series III). The slots behind the front wheelarches are to let out hot air from the engine bay. Left: no-nonsense front end looks much better with these stainless bumpers than US cars' impact absorbers. NACA ducts in bonnet feed the cabin, not the carburettors

four-seater GT ideas, and emerged with a new front-engined design. To Ferruccio's disapproval, this new V12 still made use of gullwing doors, to allow easier access to the rear seats. Ferruccio's preferred conventional doors and folding front seats, and Gandini returned to the drawing board.

He quickly came back with a revised design, doing little more than swapping the gullwing doors for front-hinged equivalents. This is the design that became the Espada, named after a matador's dagger – a further play on Lamborghini's fighting bull logo. The small badges on the front wings depict a dagger.

The Espada was completed in time to be shown off at the 1968 Geneva motor show. It was powered by Lamborghini's usual 3929cc, twin-overhead camshaft, 60-degree V12, seated four in comfort and, with 325bhp, was capable of 155mph and a 0-60mph acceleration of under eight seconds. Over

the following ten years, 1217 Espadas were produced in Series I, II and III designations, making it one of Lamborghini's most successful models. In contrast the Islero, initially sold alongside the Espada, sold just 125.

The car you see here is a Series III, generally thought of as the best version of the Espada. At the risk of appearing to be an Espada bore, let me quickly tell you that the Series I, or 400GT, built from March 1968 to November 1969, is known for its hexagonal instrument console shape (similar to the ill-fated Marzal's), vertical slats on the lower rear window and centre-lock Miura wheels. The Series II (400GTE, December 1969 to November 1972) lost the oddball dash, gained extra ventilation for the rear passengers, five-bolt wheels, ventilated disc brakes all round and optional power steering, as well as receiving a boost from 325 to 350bhp.

So then we get into the Series III (built until 1978) and why not use the car here as an example? The first impression is of size, its 1.86m (6ft 1in) width swallowing up all available road space. And the shape… well, it's bizarre of course, an odd mixture of muscular curves (like over the rear

wheelarches) and incredibly large, flat panels, while the narrow front snout and long, tapering rear overhang suggest a little clumsiness from some angles. But – and this is a cliché I know – it does look better in the metal than in pictures. It's deeply imposing, aggressive from the front and surprisingly delicate at the rear.

Compared with a Series I or II, its appearance differs in the detail only. The front grille treatment is a little neater and the rear lights more rectangular, incorporating reverse lights rather than having them hang under the bumper. US models were fitted with larger 'impact' bumpers, which became standard equipment on all Espadas after 1976, but this car still has the slim bumpers. They're beautifully formed in stainless steel, with perfect sharp creases and deep shine.

Inside, there's an all-new dash that wraps around the driver. It curves round from the centre console, lessening the flight deck effect of the earlier cars' central panel and edging far enough away from the driver to make it feel a long way off. That's no bad thing, it just adds to the general feel of airiness in the cabin, with its masses of glass, thin pillars and low door-tops, widely spaced

Clockwise from top left: Wrap-around dash is a Series III characteristic; controls are chunky; engine features six Webers and original equipment air horns; superb rear seating.

'Only after several miles does it become obvious that the best way to drive this machine

seats and, of course, all that space behind you – there really is a lot of room for back seat passengers and plenty of luggage behind them.

I could loll around in those lovely leather seats, click-clack the chunky rocker switches on and off over and over again, and just stretch out in the charismatic space. But I want to know how the famous Lamborghini V12 will sound in the Espada, having experienced it bellowing behind my head in a Miura.

It starts after a powerful-sounding second-long churn on the starter. It catches, revs to the tune of a deep, smooth roar then settles down to a perfect idle. At no point can the sound of an individual cylinder be heard.

The clutch is heavy and the gearlever needs a long, firm movement to engage first. Through the gearknob I can feel the synchromesh working, unfussed, doing its own thing at its own speed (this is not a gearchange to be rushed). I'm expecting waves of torque from the 4-litre engine but, although the car pulls away without needing much in the way of revs, it would clearly benefit from a heavier right foot to make the

most of its 365bhp (up from 350bhp for the Series III).

There's a little hesitation, roughness even, as it moves off, which is simply the six individual Weber carburettors taking it in turns to move off their idle jets and onto throttle control, which they should do in synchronicity – but keeping six Webers perfectly synchronised really isn't possible for long.

What follows next is this: the Espada moves off at a reasonable speed accompanied by an unreasonable (albeit enjoyable) amount of noise. With electric windows up, the soundtrack is dominated by a deep, bellowing intake roar but wind down a window and the twin exhausts take over, to great effect. On every gearchange the car dips up and down slightly, like a boat over gentle waves, while the speed builds up to 70mph and way beyond. Only after several miles does it become obvious that the best way to drive this machine is to forget its Grand Touring tag and rev it harder, pushing it a long way past 4000rpm, at which point the engine takes a harder, more aggressive note and the car heads for the

horizon at a noticeably more rapid rate.

The steering, although power-assisted as standard on the Series III, is heavy at low speeds but evens out to give a decent feel once on the move, before it goes light at 100mph-plus when the 1970s aerodynamics come into play, and the car begins to shows its aspirations towards manned flight – 150mph might be scary. At least the brakes are strong.

Unsurprisingly, this big, heavy machine needs some hustling through the bends, but it handles well despite the tall tyres, which you can feel flexing when you're pushing hard. Through competent design and a much heftier build quality than you might expect, the Espada manages to give a comfortable ride and reasonably composed, flat cornering. With a few days to learn its limits, I reckon an Espada could be hustled cross-country at seriously high speeds.

Certainly this car's owner doesn't hang about. Phil James is a man who likes his cars fast and stylish, and the Espada had been top of his list for most of his life.

'It's the ultimate '70s plutocrat chic,' says Phil. 'It's such a buzz having one, I've

is to forget its Grand Touring tag and rev it harder, pushing it a long way past 4000rpm'

waited 30 years to own one; I never wanted something so much in my life.'

Phil first came across an Espada when his step-father's brother, Gregory, turned up in one in 1973. Gregory was employed as Alistair McLean's chauffeur and regularly arrived in Rolls-Royce Silver Shadows, but the Espada was something very different. 'It looked like a spaceship', says Phil, who was seven at the time. 'I'd wanted one ever since. A few years back I nearly bid for the Shah of Iran's Espada but thought I wouldn't be able to afford it. I looked at a few for sale after that, but they weren't what I was after.

'Then I was in a car storage warehouse and I recognised an Espada under its cover. I peeled back the cover – it was an SIII, the only one to have, in dark blue with tan leather, which was just perfect. I contacted the owner and told him that if it ever came up for sale, I wanted it.

'Not long after, he contacted me and I just had to have it. In the boom [late-1980s] it had been bought by a group of investors, who'd had the shell completely rebuilt, without any filler. A Lamborghini specialist did the drivetrain, and all new seals and bits

and pieces were shipped in from Sant'Agata. Then the market crashed and the car was sold on.

'My real horror was that it would drive like a truck, but I just had to have it and I didn't test-drive it. Turns out it drives properly and feels really tight. I don't burble around in it worrying about oil pressure, because these cars were properly built. Its natural cruising speed is 110mph – it's turning at about 4000rpm at that speed – and the fastest I've had is 130mph. It's run much better since then; it's smoother and it starts more quickly.

'Lamborghini really got the driveline right – it shouldn't give any problems [Phil is MD of Zeroshift, manufacturers of a revolutionary gearbox, so he understands the engineering behind the Espada]. You can see it's built by craftsmen. Some parts are expensive – you could lose your shirt buying an original exhaust but I had one made in stainless steel – and you can find other parts really cheaply. I paid £500 for a set of clocks but picked up lights for £40.

'But what I really like is the reaction of other motorists. They seem to like seeing it driven as it's meant to be driven.'

Specification

Engine	V12
Location	Front, longitudinal
Displacement	3929cc
Cylinder block	Aluminium alloy
Cylinder head	Aluminium alloy, dohc per bank, two valves per cylinder
Fuel and ignition	Six twin-choke Weber 40 DCOE carburettors
Max power	365bhp @ 7500rpm
Max torque	290lb ft @ 5500rpm
Transmission	Five-speed manual gearbox, rear-wheel drive
Suspension	Double wishbones, coil springs, gas dampers and anti-roll bar front and rear
Brakes	Ventilated discs front and rear
Weight	1635kg
Power-to-weight	227bhp/ton
0-60mph	7.5sec (claimed)
Top speed	155mph (claimed)
Value	c£20,000

And with that, Phil floors the accelerator. The Espada squats down, bellows and roars and disappears down the road in a haze of unburnt petrol and '70s nostalgia. Sure, it's just used another gallon of fuel, and will struggle to top 20mpg all day. Sure, it's kind of odd looking. But it does have a certain style.

EVOLUTION OF

THE SUPERCAR

Miura and Murciélago neatly bookend the story of the supercar. Henry Catchpole drives them in ultimate SV form, while we chart the evolution of the breed over four decades

Above: honeycomb grille in the Miura SV's tail is echoed in the rear deck and rump of the Murciélago LP670-4, seen here (below) arriving for our meeting of the SV generations

The world's first supercar looks breathtakingly, spine-tinglingly gorgeous from any angle. Any. But the best angle, the perfect height from which to catch its curves, is from the seat of another Lamborghini. And, perhaps surprisingly, the best place to hear the world's newest supercar, a car with possibly the best exhaust note ever, is not from the driver's seat but from another car, with the window down. So as the Gulf-coloured convoy heads into a tunnel on the way to Wales in a scene spookily reminiscent of the opening frames of *The Italian Job*, life for both drivers is pretty tremendous.

Check the Murciélago's hugely elongated black door-mirror and shuffle out to the right-hand lane. Then pause, holding station at 50mph, drinking in the view ahead down the offside flank of the Miura, honeycomb grille tucked under the tail, long bonnet leading the way, tyres and wheels perfectly filling the swollen arches. There has never been a better-looking, sexier car. Pull the carbon paddle twice

with your left index finger, listening to the *click click* electrically firing the 'box down two gears to second, and then open the throttle wide. A thump of acceleration appears to land square in my sternum, making me recoil into the seat, momentarily stunned before the revs climb past 4800rpm, the floodgates open and the darkness of the tunnel is filled with an utterly wild yowl. As the bright orange cacophony goes catapulting past the older car, heading for the light, I hope the Miura's windows are down. On days like these…

With these two cars we have the yellow and violet of the supercar spectrum, the origin of the species and the latest of the breed, and the aim of today's trip into the Brecon Beacons is to try to get to the heart of what makes a supercar. The term had been applied to a few monster vehicles in the 1920s, and evidence can still be seen in old advertisements, but it's legendary motoring scribe LJK Setright who is credited with using the term as we now understand it, bringing it back into circulation when he labelled the Miura a supercar in the late '60s.

'The aim of today's trip into the Brecon Beacons is to get to the heart of what makes a supercar'

Right: Murciélago is slathered in carbonfibre, a material that was in its infancy in the late '60s. Miura's body is aluminium, and arguably the most beautiful shape ever wrapped round four wheels

It's all very well saying it of course, but what do we actually understand by the word? What are the qualities that made Setright single out and elevate the Miura above other cars of its generation? Harry Metcalfe, who is quite old, recalls seeing a Miura for the first time: 'It was pulled over in a lay-by, a lime green car if my elderly memory serves me. It was so wide and low – there might as well have been a UFO hovering there. It really was that extraordinary.'

Marcello Gandini (at the time working for Bertone) had created something beyond exotic, and there I think we have the first common thread visible in both these Lamborghinis: they look out of this world. This last of the Murciélagos might be an almost familiar shape by now and its scissor doors can trace their roots back 25 years to the birth of the Countach. But drive past or park up and swing a door skywards and it still stops onlookers dead in their tracks.

The honeycomb-shaped rear grille, and what looks like a water feature running down over the engine bay, both pay obvious homage to the

Miura, as does the Arancia paint. The Miura was famous for being available in colours that would have had most manufacturers spluttering but the Azzuro Cielo of this car is very subtle. It's an original colour and possibly my favourite of all, as it looks so bright, clean and different, yet doesn't dominate the shape.

What the designers of the Miura wouldn't recognise is the plethora of carbonfibre on the Murci. Even the struts supporting the huge carbon rear wing are made of the black weave – whether it's overkill or not will depend on personal taste, but like the gold leaf in the McLaren F1's engine bay there's something perfectly excessive about it.

The second essential supercar ingredient that the Miura has is a glorious, many-cylindered, mid-mounted engine. But it nearly didn't. When three men in their early twenties, Giampaolo Dallara, Paolo Stanzani (both poached from Ferrari, no doubt to Ferruccio Lamborghini's delight) and Bob Wallace (legendary New Zealand test driver), started creating the Miura outside of office hours they

Miura was a miracle of
of packaging, siting its
4-litre V12 transversely,
with the engine and
gearbox as one casting.
Here, in ultimate P400
SV form, it produced
a claimed 380bhp

envisaged a small, lightweight car inspired by their love of motor racing. But Ferruccio did not love motor racing (he thought Ferrari was too obsessed with it) and so when the idea for the P400 was tentatively presented he insisted that they use the now legendary V12.

To tell the story of that engine is really to tell the story of Lamborghini. When Ferruccio turned away from tractors (Lamborghini Tractori) and air conditioning units (Lamborghini Bruciatori) to concentrate on building cars that could outstrip Enzo's machines he knew he wanted to utilise the engineering talent of Giotto Bizzarrini. Having already worked on Alfa's V12 and the iconic Ferrari 250 GTO, Bizzarrini was recognised as a huge talent. He had also designed a 1.5-litre V12 Formula 1 engine, which at Lamborghini's request he set about enlarging and refining into a road car engine. There is a theory that the engine was actually created by Honda, but as it's an argument that emanated from that man Setright (an absolute Honda devotee) and is almost entirely based on the position of the inlet ports, it seems unlikely. Anyway, the

'An essential ingredient is a many-cylindered mid-mounted engine…'

engine that was eventually placed into the first Lamborghini, the 350 GT, was a 3.5-litre V12 with four overhead camshafts. The block was aluminium with steel liners and an internal angle of 60 degrees was thought to give perfect balance and keep vibrations to a minimum. The engine was enlarged to 3929cc by Dallara and was producing 350bhp by the time it was dropped transversely into the middle of the Miura's box-section chassis. Incredibly, the same basic architecture of that original Bizzarrini design has been a constant thread from Miura, through Countach, Diablo and all the way to this 6496cc, 661bhp incarnation of the V12 in today's Murciélago SV.

The third and final stipulation for inclusion in the supercar club is price. A supercar should definitely, sadly, be in the unobtainable, lottery winner, shop-at-Waitrose category. In its day the Miura went on sale at just under £11,000, which was over four times the price of a Jaguar E-type and £2000 more than a Ferrari Daytona. At £220,000, the Murciélago SV looks almost good value in 2009.

So, extreme engine, exorbitant price and extraordinary looks. They are, I think, the

The Miura had first appeared in 1966, but it wasn't until the '70s that the supercar really gained momentum. Driven by the competitive instincts of the early supercar pioneers, the concept was distilled and refined, given shape and meaning and a sense of geographical place.

Italy made all the early running as Ferrari, Maserati and De Tomaso responded to the Miura. Up until now Enzo Ferrari had refused to develop a mid-engined road car, believing his customers would find it too challenging to drive. His engineers managed to convince him otherwise, but it was not until 1973 that the 365 GT4 BB (above) went on sale, with a longitudinal 344bhp 4.4-litre flat-12 and a claimed top speed of 188mph.

Rivals used longitudinal V8s – a 310bhp 4.7 for the 1971 Maserati Bora and a 330bhp Ford 5.8 (351 cubic inch) for the 1971 De Tomaso Pantera. The trouble for all these marques was that Lamborghini was one step ahead. While they responded to the Miura, the 1971 Geneva show witnessed the unveiling of perhaps the most influential and charismatic supercar of them all – the Countach.

It mattered not a jot that it took three more years for production versions to be ready, nor that the world was then in the grip of an oil crisis – the Gandini-styled Countach (below) was wild, outlandish and extravagant. The supercar kingdom had its first real champion, the '70s had its pin-up and boys everywhere learned to say 'Coon-tash'.

Big claims were made for the LP400, but the

375bhp 4-litre V12 of the early cars was largely carried over from the Miura and performance was of the same order – 0-60mph in 5.6secs and 175mph all-out. The template was there, though: mid-mounted longitudinal engine driving the rear wheels, a feast of cylinders, two-seat cabin and captivating bodywork.

Unless of course, you're Porsche. On the northern side of the Alps they were building sweet, delicate sports cars, but by 1974 Porsche was keen to prove its worth against the Italians, so it turbocharged the rear-mounted air-cooled 3-litre flat-six. Even back then 256bhp was not a supercar output, but a 1140kg kerbweight gave it the necessary acceleration (0-60mph in 5.5 seconds) and a star was born.

Outside Europe the supercar wasn't even on the automotive radar. The Japanese car industry was where the Chinese are now – just starting to look beyond its own borders, while America was under

'Geneva witnessed the unveiling of perhaps the most influential supercar of all'

the muscle-car spell and the nearest they had to a supercar was the 1971 Corvette C3 Stingray, which did the numbers (454cu in, 425bhp, 0-60mph in 5.3secs) but was blue collar through and through when the Italian template was pure exotic.

British engineering was flying high in 1976 – Concorde started flying commercially and Colin Chapman gave us the first Esprit. With 160bhp. Not really a supercar. Aston Martin tried too, with the 432bhp, 170mph Vantage – but with the engine in the front it lacked the necessary glamour.

The '70s: the decade in which Italy nailed the supercar concept and everyone else just gawped. **OM**

Miura's dash looks like the flight deck of a 1960s light aeroplane. Has Murciélago easily licked for charm, if not for ergonomics

essential tangible supercar ingredients, because, from these, all other elements such as performance and sensationalism extend. But there's also something else, something more subjective. It has to do with driving them, but it's not the *actual* driving, more the anticipation.

Think back to the first time you saw a supercar. You probably had the same sense of excitement, awe and wonder that I felt when the wide low orange wedge was being backed off the transporter first thing this morning. Clearly I've been jammy enough to drive quite a few supercars, but the excitement is still always tempered by a slightly uncomfortable sense that you are about to get into an unwieldy, perhaps uncontrollable machine. A supercar is monstrous yet precious and will make you nervous just thinking about driving it. And if you are one of those rare people who have supreme confidence and don't know what I'm talking about, then try driving a Lambo between two rows of parked cars in a cramped town centre, with no rear vision but a good grasp of the fact that the entire population is

standing or leaning out of windows to see if you'll make it through without a scratch…

Once we emerge from Llareggub (thankfully with all layers of paint intact) we head towards the wider roads of the Beacons. Wider but not smoother, and they reveal a depth to the LP670 that I hadn't expected. Despite the much firmer control of the SV's suspension compared with the standard car, the horribly churned tarmac is simply soaked up. Relatively dinky 18in rims probably help, but it still seems spooky the way this hardcore car is gliding across the troubled asphalt. The SV is demonstrably, demonically different to the standard car in other ways too, the steering heavier and meatier, the grip more insistent but edgier and the engine so nuts that as John Barker says, 'beyond 6000rpm it seems to have broken free of its shackles and about to rev itself to oblivion'.

After a while we stop so that Matt Howell can get a few photos onto his memory cards. Then half an hour later he signals that it's time to roll out again and Ian Tandy, the owner of the Miura, asks if I'd like to drive his car. Gulp.

'A supercar is monstrous yet precious, and will make you nervous just thinking about driving it'

After a restoration that redefines the word meticulous, his car actually looks like it rolled out of the Sant'Agata gates more recently than the Murciélago. In fact this SV (one of only 150 in total and fewer than ten right-hand drive) was originally owned by Tony Iommi, bassist in Black Sabbath. Mr Iommi ordered chassis number 4814 in 1971 in the most desirable spec available, with air conditioning and a split sump. Since then it's belonged to, amongst others, a Scottish potato farmer (records are unclear as to whether he thought he was buying a tractor) and collectors Sir Anthony Bamford and Simon Draper. It even appeared back in issue 50 of **evo** as the world's sexiest car.

The driving position is a sort of one-size-fits-

all, with the emphasis on the driver instead of the car making the adjustments. Fixed seat, fixed steering column, fixed pedal box. My arms seem to be stretched out, while my legs are bunched up and splayed akimbo round the wheel, with my knees definitely nearer my ears than is natural. It's not unlike the position you'd adopt if, after one too many sherbets, you thought it would be fun to try to get into and then operate a child's pedal car. The simple key is down on the transmission tunnel and the switches for various illuminations, fans and heaters are up in the roof near the rear view mirror, so starting the Miura feels a bit like running through pre-flight checks. The fact that the throttle (which I'll come back to in a

second) needs pumping vigorously while you turn the key and wait and wait for the engine to catch only adds to the similarities with getting a light aircraft going. The handbrake is iffy, the gearbox won't go into first and we're on an upslope, but with my heart ticking over considerably faster than the engine we miraculously get away first time.

There is no rushing the gearbox and it needs a calm but firm hand, feeling delicate because of the wand-like gearstick but chunky because of the mechanicals below. You slide it out of one heavy, oiled cog, sense the lightness through neutral and then push with smooth pressure to slot into the next gear. The accelerator pedal is beyond sticky. As John says, 'opening 12 throttle

The V12 in the
LP670-4 can trace
its basic architecture
right back to the
Miura. It's grown a bit
though – to 6.5 litres
– and peak power has
swollen to 661bhp

butterflies with a cable that loops and twists from the throttle pedal to somewhere over your shoulder isn't going to give precision control', but even so it's hard to recalibrate a mind used to featherlight electronic or even recent cable-operated throttle pedals. If you stomped on the Murciélago's accelerator with the force that is required in the Miura then you would probably snap your own neck.

John's up ahead in the Murci and indicating right. Bit of traffic coming so he rolls to a halt. Brake. Oh dear Lord where's the brake pedal? I mean literally where is it? My contorted foot has hit fresh air where it anticipated a middle pedal and now my generous braking distance is shrinking as quickly as my panic is rising. Come on, come on. Don't miscue and go back to throttle. Where is it? There it is! And the brakes are actually alright too, thank God. Unthinkable million pound disaster averted, we wind our way out across more open countryside and gradually I start to relax again. Third and fourth are all you need out here and there's plenty of torque. The ride gives you confidence, the Miura feeling settled over the

'To tell the story of this V12 engine is really to tell the story of Lamborghini'

bumps and cambers, the 275/55 R15 Avons (they don't make the original Pirelli Cinturatos any more) tracking smoothly underneath you. Although there's nothing really over the front end, it's still a surprise that the steering is relatively light given the relative weight of the other controls. It's communicative too, the unasssisted rim weighting and unweighting in your hands as you guide the nose accurately into a corner before metering out the throttle travel in jerky chunks as you use the power to drive through and down the next straight. A firework of small explosions crackles from the exhaust as I back off to give a wandering sheep a wide berth. A glance in the rear-view mirror (no wing mirrors) is like looking at the Welsh landscape through a Venetian blind. Sheep have become zebras.

A couple more miles. We pull over and I start breathing again (whilst blipping the throttle to keep the engine going). It is an absolute privilege and a thrill to be allowed to drive a Miura SV, particularly one as immaculate as this. But it is also a huge responsibility, and in the same way that you want to meet your heroes long enough to say 'hello', you don't

Money ruled the '80s and the supercar brands made hay while Wall Street shone. As international trade opened up, so did new markets – particularly in America and the Middle East. This led to a shift in the image of the supercar driver: no longer was he a titled European playboy, now he was Gordon Gekko.

The cars changed to suit these new buyers. Still mostly mid-engined, vastly powerful and rear-wheel drive, but now with a different, more boulevard vibe. They lost focus, catering not to wannabe racers, but a more middle-aged clientele. Step forward the Ferrari Testarossa (right) and, once again, the Lambo Countach. Be-winged and be-slatted, they suited the big-hair-and-shoulder-pads generation to a tee. Miami Vice was the new creed.

But underneath the yuppie fluff, the 1984 Testarossa was a damn good car with a 4.9-litre 390bhp flat-12. The 180mph barrier was now being breeched with increasing regularity. Previously, aerodynamic advances had lagged well behind engine development, with many early supercars most notable for becoming highly unstable above 150mph (step forward, Miura), their claimed top speeds speculative at best.

The Countach, a decade old when the Testarossa arrived, soldiered on through the '80s, becoming ever more ludicrous. The culmination was the 1988 25th anniversary model, with the 5.2-litre V12 now developing 425bhp for a 183mph maximum.

Ferrari became the dominant force in supercardom, largely because of Lamborghini's parlous financial state (it had gone bust in 1978 and was in Swiss hands until Chrysler took over in 1987). But the Prancing Horse wasn't without competition – a turning point had been reached and the result was a schism in the supercar world.

Almost as a reaction to the softness that had crept in, and mindful that racing can improve the breed, two new heroes emerged in the mid-80s. Forged by a new sense of purpose, they were champions of hardcore: the Ferrari F40 and Porsche 959. Hailed as the most technologically advanced supercar ever, the 4wd 959 finally arrived in 1987 and rewrote the acceleration rulebook. 0-60mph took 3.6sec, 100mph just 8.3sec and it knocked on the 200mph door, too.

But the F40 was the first to break through. It followed on from the 288 GTO which had been built to satisfy Group B racing regulations and used a slightly larger 2.9-litre twin-turbo V8. Its 478bhp trumped the 959's 450bhp and the last car that Enzo commissioned was also the first to officially top 200mph.

'Two new heroes emerged in the mid-80s, the Ferrari F40 and Porsche 959'

The '80s were too good to last and the year that brought us the 959 and F40 also gave us Black Wednesday, which put paid to the ambitions of other firms to join the supercar party. There had been tantalising glimpses of potential contenders throughout the decade: the Aston Martin Bulldog, the Vector W2, Ruf's CTR, but they were intermittent and rarely amounted to anything; until in 1988 Jaguar showed us the shape of things to come: a 6.2-litre 500bhp V12 with 4wd named the XJ220. But that's another story. **OM**

'With these two
cars we have the
origin of the species
and the latest of
the breed'

Miura's beauty continues on the inside but it would benefit from an adjustable steering wheel. And an adjustable seat, for that matter. The driving position is a challenge, particularly for the tall

want to go much further for fear that one of you will say something so disappointing or embarrassing that it spoils the moment forever. In all honesty the Miura has more in common with a car built 40 years before it than it does with a car built 40 years later, so I'd rather just look at it for the rest of the day. I know I won't be disappointed doing that.

Look at the Miura and drive the LP670. In truth, although some might reminisce through rose-tinted glasses and claim that cars were better when it was all purely mechanical, 21st century supercars are capable of delivering driving highs that the older generation simply can't match. Many of the old generation of supercars claimed extraordinary numbers and may even potentially have had the performance to live up to their looks. But the chances of actually getting near the limits and the numbers that smacked your gob (and made you desire the car so much) were miniscule unless you had plums the size of cantaloupes and the skill of Ricardo Patrese. Now, thanks to tyre and suspension technology, aerodynamic modelling, carbonfibre and, probably most of

'My legs are bunched up and splayed akimbo around the wheel'

all, the microprocessor (40 years ago just one megabyte cost approximately $1million; today it costs a fraction of a dollar) supercars are more exciting and driveable than ever.

Would I want to drive an early Diablo up the side of this Welsh mountain? Yes. Of course I would. But would I, could I, hustle one relentlessly, corner after corner, pushing grip limits in the way that I've just done in the brilliant LP670? No. Don't think that driving the Murciélago is as simple as driving a Mondeo because it's not. You feel your concentration spike every time you drop down into the seat (which actually needs a bit more lateral support) and turn the key. The forces that it exerts on you under acceleration, or when you hit the huge carbon brakes (they still need more progression, but they're much better than in the Gallardo) or when you lean on the Pirelli P Zero Corsas are massive and intimidating. To keep your foot pinned on a valley road, accelerating unremittingly as you flick each gear at the limiter and watch the strip of tarmac in the windscreen narrow relentlessly around the car as the speed builds, is to be immersed in an unforgettable supercar

If the '80s made us comfortable with the idea of the 200mph supercar, the '90s was the decade that rolled it up into a little ball and batted it straight out of the park. There were a number of great supercars in what some were already beginning to call the last golden era of motoring: thundering supercharged V12 Astons, a particularly rich seam in the evolution of the Porsche 911 GT2 and GT3, a slew of sensational Ferraris including the underrated F50 and even a Japanese entry-level Ferrari rival in the never-quite-right shape of the Honda NS-X. But one car overshadowed them all and, for good measure, supercars from every other decade, too. The McLaren F1.

The idea that 200mph was quite fast enough and would probably only be improved on in small increments had already been dealt a shattering blow by the Jaguar XJ220, launched in 1992. Itself built as a definitive response to '80s heroes the Ferrari F40 and Porsche 959, the beautiful but vast Jag immediately raised the bar to a barely believable 217mph (sans cats) with acceleration to match, hitting 60mph in 3.6sec and dipping under eight to the ton. For various reasons – not least its size and the fact it was powered by the engine from the Metro 6R4 rally car and not the promised V12 – it

was a commercial fiasco, but surely its position as king of the supercar hill would be safe for a good long time while the rest of the world caught up. That's if it even felt like trying.

But the XJ220's reign lasted just one solitary year. In 1993, the F1 made its move. The brainchild of Formula 1 designer Gordon Murray and styled by Peter Stevens, the McLaren wasn't just the fastest and most expensive supercar the world had ever seen, it was nothing less than mind blowing. Built around a carbon monocoque with a central driver's seat forward of the two flanking passenger seats, it was powered by a naturally aspirated 6-litre V12 supplied by BMW developing 627bhp at 7400rpm and 480lb ft at 5600rpm. But it weighed just 1140kg and therefore had a power-to-weight ratio of 559bhp-per-ton, hitherto the preserve of the fastest superbikes.

It did to the XJ220's performance stats what the Jag had done to those of the world's previous fastest supercars. It destroyed them. It touched

'The XJ220's reign lasted just one solitary year. In 1993 the F1 made its move'

240mph at the VW test track, it accelerated to 100mph in 6.3sec and, above 150mph, it was quicker than a Formula 1 car. It may have cost £635,000 when it was new but it became an instant legend and good examples now fetch twice that.

The '90s may have been the decade Geri Halliwell left the Spice Girls, the first cloned sheep was christened Dolly and Pepsi briefly thought clear cola was a neat idea but, in the world of supercars, only one story really mattered. **DV**

XJ220 was the world's fastest car. Briefly. Its 217mph top speed was eclipsed just one year later by the 240mph McLaren F1 (above)

'A firework of small explosions crackles from the exhaust as I back off'

Above: profile shows the genius of Gandini's design to perfection. Miura SV rides well on these roads, while its steering is nicely communicative, but it's unsurprisingly blown away in terms of straight-line and cornering speed

experience. But I like the fact that it still feels planted at 170mph, not flighty and lethal. It makes me want to go back to 170mph and experience it again, push further.

And in the corners it is even more noticeable. On entry you can brake so late you're weightless in the seat belt. Turn in and you can adjust the balance through the corner. Because it corners flatter and there's more edge to the grip, the nose of the LP670 actually pushes more obviously than the LP640. As a result you need to play sensitively with the throttle and steering through a long corner, leaning into the invisible lateral G but feeling the fluctuations in load as you adjust your inputs. Bumps are soaked up and telegraphed by the SV's suspension in a way you can compensate for. You don't jump on the throttle early in the corner because the big rear tyres will push the nose wider still, so you wait until you're past the apex, then you begin straightening the wheel and feeding in the power, using the traction of the rear-biased four-wheel drive to ride the furiously ignited torque. You can't turn the ESP to Corsa mode and take ham-fisted liberties – there's still a huge V12 slung behind you. But even on the road you can dig right into the Murci's handling repertoire and enjoy it – not just nibble nervously at the edges.

Above: Miura rides on 15in alloys, the rears shod with 275/55 Avon radials (Pirellis originally). Murciélago's 18in rims are wrapped in Pirelli P Zero Corsa rubber

THE RISE OF THE SUPERCAR

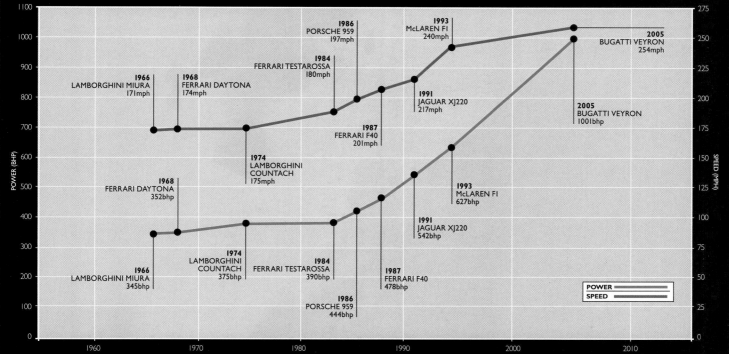

1966
LAMBORGHINI MIURA
171mph

1968
FERRARI DAYTONA
174mph

1986
PORSCHE 959
197mph

1984
FERRARI TESTAROSSA
180mph

1993
McLAREN F1
240mph

2005
BUGATTI VEYRON
254mph

1987
FERRARI F40
201mph

1974
LAMBORGHINI
COUNTACH
175mph

1991
JAGUAR XJ220
217mph

2005
BUGATTI VEYRON
1001bhp

1968
FERRARI DAYTONA
352bhp

1993
McLAREN F1
627bhp

1966
LAMBORGHINI MIURA
345bhp

1974
LAMBORGHINI
COUNTACH
375bhp

1984
FERRARI TESTAROSSA
390bhp

1987
FERRARI F40
478bhp

1991
JAGUAR XJ220
542bhp

1986
PORSCHE 959
444bhp

POWER (BHP)

SPEED (MPH)

POWER
SPEED

Murciélago SV's bucket seats look the business but they could actually do with a bit more lateral support, though that might be something to do with the huge cornering forces…

The Brecon Beacons echo to the sound of two V12s for the rest of the day.

The Brecon Beacons echo to the sound of two V12s for the rest of the day. People stop and stare. Three men in a Transit held together with faith and copies of the *Daily Star* stop and chuckle that they wouldn't get much in scrap for the Murciélago's carbonfibre. Eventually we drag Matt Howell away from the Miura and, as darkness falls, we bid farewell to Ian Tandy, taking one last long look at the powder blue shape slinking away before heading East and home, stopping only to fuel up the LP670-4 ready for its big day tomorrow.

Millbrook's mile straight is slightly damp when we arrive and, although dry patches emerge, the conditions are far from ideal. And yet the SV is stunning. It is one of the most fun cars I've ever figured, partly because it feels mechanically happy repeating full-bore standing starts time after time and partly because of the dramatic way it gets off the line. To launch it you need to have Corsa mode engaged and TCS (Traction Control System) turned completely off. Then you simply engage first gear and stamp on the throttle. At this point the car twigs what's going on, selects

'You feel your concentration spike every time you drop into the seat'

appropriate revs and dumps the clutch. All four wheels spin up, the car snaps sideways off the line, you apply half a turn of lock, ease the revs whilst keeping the wheels spinning all the way through first gear then time the flick of the right-hand paddle just before snagging the limiter at 8000rpm (no automatic upchange) and from then on it's easy, just watch the rev-counter, keep changing up and bingo you've got your figures!

The Miura recorded 6.0sec to 60mph in the early 1970s. After a couple of runs at 3.4sec in the Murciélago, we nail a couple more at 3.2sec. That, as I'm sure I don't need to tell you, is McLaren F1 fast. Indeed the Lambo's only a second behind the Macca at 100mph, yet it's carrying 500kg more. Phenomenal. (Alright, so the big VW was even more phenomenal six days later, see page 91, but it didn't oversteer on the way there, or sound like an '80s F1 car).

Round the lap the SV was like the standard Murciélago, only more. There was understeer, particularly through the Palmer Curves, which needed quelling with a little lift on turn-in, but the rear was absolutely hooked up except out of Bank. The man with the fastest name ever, Max

So the '90s gave us by far the fastest car the world had ever seen (F1), comfortably the second fastest (XJ220) and a whole raft of tarmac-skimming missiles that could approach, do or exceed 200mph. It was the out-of-reach itch finally scratched, Chuck Yeager breaking the sound barrier, the supercar living up to its name. Ferrari consolidated its membership of the double-ton club into the next decade with its fastest-ever road car, the Enzo, though it faced tough competition from the Porsche Carrera GT and new kid on the supercar block, the Pagani Zonda C12S. Interestingly, the carbon-bodied Zonda claimed to be the McLaren's spiritual successor and, in design philosophy, the parallels were clear.

But the F1's influence on the cars that would follow it turned out to be more far-reaching than that. It acted as a catalyst, igniting a let's-shoot-for-the-moon initiative bold enough to fill the vacuum left by NASA. The F1, prematurely hailed as a once-in-a-lifetime phenomenon in the previous decade, was merely the starting point in this one.

It set projects rolling in two directions. One, to exceed the F1's phenomenal top speed and general accelerative prowess, however much power and technology it took. And two, perhaps more realistically, to apply the lightness and efficiency principles at the core of the McLaren in pursuit of speed without excess. The former approach found its ultimate expression in the Bugatti Veyron, the £1m, 16-cylinder, quad-turbo, four-wheel-drive, 1000bhp hypercar that effectively did to the McLaren what the McLaren had done to the XJ220 by smashing its top speed and acceleration records out of sight and, once and for all, drawing that line in the sand for ultimate supercar performance.

Except that, as we head towards the end of the

'The Bugatti has become just another target to shoot at'

new millennium's first decade, the Bugatti, far from being regarded as the absolute summit of supercar endeavour, has become just another target to shoot at. The 9ff GT9-R, Ultimate Aero SSC and Koenigsegg CCXR all claim to best the Veyron's 252mph top speed and, beyond a certain speed, once the Veyron's off-the-line all-wheel-drive advantage has ebbed away, accelerate harder, too.

At the same time, ultra-lightweight minimalism is forging new extremes for what is almost certain to become the enforced supercar playground of the future: the track. Step forward the Caparo T1 and Ariel Atom 500. One thousand horsepower-per-ton is the new 200mph.

The first black president of the United States, a programme to fly men back to the moon, an iPhone that can send picture texts, and 0-100mph in 5sec. Things could be worse. **DV**

Koenigsegg CCXR is just one of the supercars that picked up the gauntlet thrown down by Bugatti. 9ff GT9-R (above) is another

Huge thanks to
Miura owner Ian
Tandy for allowing
us to drive and
photograph his
wonderful car, and
thanks also to Simon
Kidston (www.
kidston.com) for
putting us in touch

Venturi (Lambo's test driver) wasn't surprised that the SV was almost 4sec quicker than the standard car but the 1.21.3 lap is even more impressive when you consider the only cars ahead of it are the Gumpert Apollo (effectively a race car) and the super-lightweights.

John Barker and I agree that the standard Murci is enough really (and actually looks better), but also that that's not really the point. Thoughts of sufficiency aren't really applicable to a supercar and the LP670-4 takes everything gloriously to extremes.

It also marks the Bizzarrini engine's swansong and you have to wonder how many manufacturers will be willing or able to make such a gloriously politically incorrect engine in the future. Ferrari claims to be going lightweight, and Lamborghini is talking about green issues (and not lime green issues either). Which only makes the latest SV even more special. As John says, 'it's the fastest, hardest, maddest, baddest Murciélago, a car that deserves the SV badge as much as any car that has gone before'. And when the back catalogue of initialled cars includes a car as iconic as the Miura, that's some accolade.

	MIURA SV	LP670-4 SV
Engine	60deg V12	60deg V12
Location	Mid, transverse	Mid, longitudinal
Displacement	3929cc	6496cc
Bore x stroke	82 x 62mm	88 x 89mm
Cylinder block	Aluminium alloy	Aluminium alloy
Cylinder head	Aluminium alloy, dohc per bank, two valves per cylinder	Aluminium alloy, dohc per bank, four valves per cylinder
Fuelling	Four Weber carburettors	Multipoint fuel injection
Max power	380bhp @ 7700rpm	661bhp @ 8000rpm
Max torque	286lb ft @ 5500rpm	487lb ft @ 6500rpm
Transmission	Five-speed manual, rear-wheel drive, limited-slip differential	Six-speed e-gear paddle-shift, four-wheel drive, front and rear limited slip differentials
Suspension	Double wishbones, coil springs, anti-roll bars front and rear	Double wishbones, coil springs, anti-roll bars front and rear
Brakes	Steel discs front and rear	Vented carbon-ceramic discs front and rear, ABS, EBD, TC
Wheels	7 x 15in front, 9 x 15in rear, cast magnesium	8.5 x 18in front, 13 x 18in rear aluminium alloy
Tyres	215/70 R15 front, 275/55 R15 rear, Avon radial	245/35 ZR18 front, 335/30 ZR18 rear, Pirelli P Zero Corsa
Weight (kerb)	1306kg	1565kg
Power-to-weight	295bhp/ton	429bhp/ton
0-60mph	6.0sec	3.2sec
0-100mph	13.4sec	7.3sec
Top speed	168mph	212mph (claimed)
Basic price	c£11,000 (1972)	£270,038 (2009)

Miura performance figures from Motor magazine

LP670-4

0-30	1.6
0-40	2.2
0-50	2.6
0-60	3.2
0-70	4.2
0-80	5.0
0-90	5.8
0-100	7.3
0-110	8.4
0-120	9.6
0-130	11.5
0-140	13.2
0-150	15.4
0-160	18.2
0-170	21.2

1/4 MILE

sec	11.4
mph	129

IN-GEAR TIMES (2nd)

20-40	2.3
30-50	2.1
40-60	1.9
50-70	1.8
60-80	1.7
70-90	1.6

IN-GEAR TIMES (3rd)

30-50	2.9
40-60	2.8
50-70	2.8
60-80	2.7
70-90	2.4
80-100	2.3
90-110	2.3
100-120	2.5

IN-GEAR TIMES (4th)

70-90	3.8
80-100	3.7
90-110	3.3
100-120	3.1
110-130	3.2
120-140	3.4
130-150	3.8

IN-GEAR TIMES (5th)

70-90	4.6
80-100	4.7
90-110	4.9
100-120	4.6
110-130	4.2
120-140	4.3

BRAKING

100-0	4.2
dist. ft	286.9
0-100-0	12.0

Conditions: slightly damp

'The only cars ahead of the SV are the Gumpert Apollo and the super-lightweights'

Far left: LP670-4 passes the Bedford Autodrome noise test (just), then it's on with VBOX timing gear and out onto the West Circuit for some truly memorable lapping

WEST CIRCUIT
Bedford Autodrome,
1.8 miles

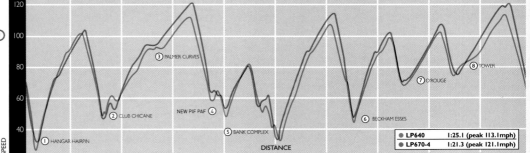

● LP640	1:25.1 (peak 113.1mph)
● LP670-4	1:21.3 (peak 121.1mph)

▲ LP670-4 almost four seconds quicker round the West Circuit than 'regular' Murciélago LP640. It accelerates much harder and therefore reaches higher peak speeds on the straights, but it also generates greater lateral grip, particularly noticeable in the slower corners like Hangar Hairpin. Still needs a lift through Palmer Curves though

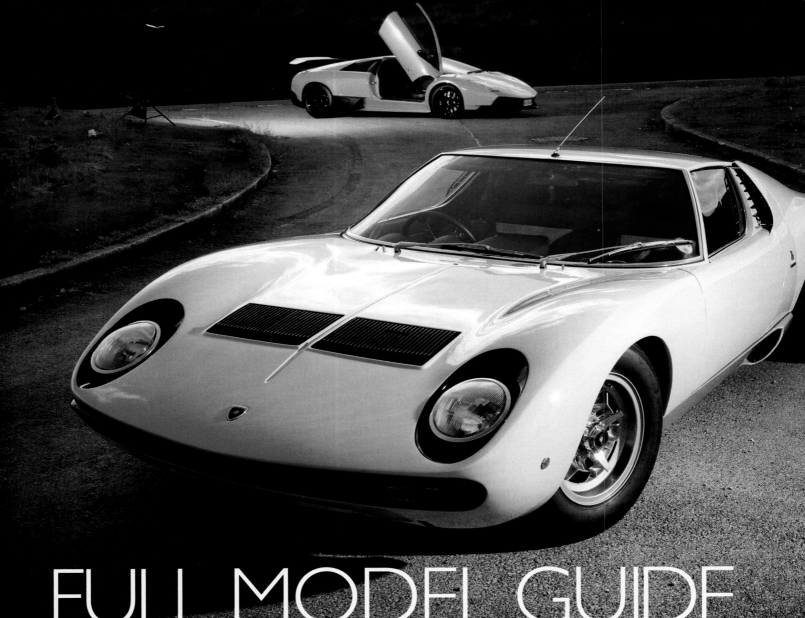

FULL MODEL GUIDE

Here's the lowdown on every Lamborghini production model since the original 350 GT

350 GT 1964-66
The pretty 350 GT was Lamborghini's first ever production car, and gave it the foothold in the sports car market its boss craved. While the 350's performance figures are matched or bettered by much of today's hot hatch class, the architecture of its V12 has graced every one of the manufacturer's 12-cylinder cars, right up to the Murciélago.

Total produced 120 **Layout** Front engine/rear-wheel drive **Engine** V12 3.5-litre **Power** 320bhp/7000rpm **Top speed** 155mph

400 GT 1966-68
The 400 GT was an evolution of the 350 GT rather than a new model: the V12 engine grew in size but not peak power, while a longer chassis and roomier interior were hidden underneath a largely similar exterior. That extra space enabled the 400 to be sold as a 2+2, though there were also 23 350 GT-based two-seaters produced.

Total produced 273 **Layout** Front-engine/rear-wheel drive **Engine** V12 3.9-litre **Power** 320bhp/6500rpm **Top speed** 155mph

MIURA P400 1966-1971
Lamborghini broke new ground with the Miura, which was the first major sports car to use a mid-mounted engine, and in turn create the 'supercar' as we know it. It looks stunning, and was the first Lambo to take its name from a fighting bull. 1968 saw the launch of the P400S, which boasted an extra 20bhp and a higher 177mph top speed.

Total produced 614 **Layout** Mid-engine, rear-wheel drive **Engine** V12 3.9-litre **Power** 350bhp/7000rpm **Top speed** 174mph

ISLERO 1968-1970

One of the lesser-spotted Lamborghinis, the Islero struggled for attention alongside the more radical Miura. It's essentially a rebodied 400GT 2+2, with more modern styling, although it's arguably the plainest car the company has made. Nevertheless, it was good enough for Ferruccio Lamborghini, who drove one himself.

Total produced 225 **Layout** Front-engine, rear-wheel drive **Engine** V12 3.9-litre **Power** 350bhp/7700rpm **Top speed** 162mph

JARAMA 1970-1976

The Islero was replaced by the Jarama. The new car was based on a shortened Espada platform, and the design came from Bertone's Marcello Gandini, the man behind the Miura. An improved 365bhp Jarama S appeared in 1972, but sales never really took off. Pictured is the extensively tuned and modified Jarama developed by test driver Bob Wallace.

Total produced 227 **Layout** Front-engine, rear-wheel drive **Engine** V12 3.9-litre **Power** 350bhp/7500rpm **Top speed** 162mph

ESPADA 1968-1978

The Espada (sword in Spanish, if you're wondering) introduced unprecedented levels of production to Lamborghini, hitting four figures in its ten-year life. Its space-age styling hid the company's first proper four-seater too, while options such as power steering and an auto gearbox were offered.

Total produced 1217 **Layout** Front-engine, rear-wheel drive **Engine** V12 3.9-litre **Power** 350bhp/7500rpm **Top speed** 155mph

MIURA SV 1971-72

The new and improved Miura saw the debut of Lamborghini's SV badge. The Miura SV was slightly more powerful again, while suspension tweaks and wider rear wheels made the Miura handle like it always should have. There was one final Miura model, the SV/J, which featured further upgrades to the engine and chassis.

Total produced 150 **Layout** Mid-engine, rear-wheel drive **Engine** V12 3.9-litre **Power** 385bhp/7850rpm **Top speed** 186mph

URRACO 1972-1979

The 2+2 Urraco rivalled the Ferrari 308 Dino and Porsche 911. It was Lambo's first car to eschew the brand's V12 engine, and while the 2.5-litre V8's output looks modest, it was ahead of the competition. A 250bhp 3-litre joined the range later on, alongside an Italy-only 2-litre version to dodge high taxes on big engines.

Total produced 776 **Layout** Mid-engine, rear-wheel drive **Engine** V8 2.5-litre **Power** 220bhp/7850rpm **Top speed** 149mph

COUNTACH 1974-1985

One of the all-time great supercar pin-ups, the Countach oozes madness from every pore and was the first Lamborghini with scissor doors, a feature now intrinsically linked with the brand. The now familiar 3.9-litre V12 increased in size to 4.8 litres for the Countach LP500S of 1982, which got closer to Lamborghini's extravagant performance claims...

Total produced 710 **Layout** Mid-engine, rear-wheel drive **Engine** V12 3.9-litre **Power** 375bhp/8000rpm **Top speed** 186mph

SILHOUETTE 1976-1979

The Urraco had failed to hit sales targets, and the beefed-up Silhouette was something of a rush replacement. The 3-litre engine remained, with the biggest changes being the loss of the rear seats and the introduction of a targa roof. The Urraco ancestry is obvious, though, and the Silhouette struggled to sell.

Total produced 55 **Layout** Mid-engine, rear-wheel drive **Engine** V8 3-litre **Power** 250bhp/7500rpm **Top speed** 162mph

JALPA 1981-1988

An evolution of the Silhouette, the Jalpa is the last Lamborghini to have used an eight-cylinder engine. The unit itself expanded to 3.5 litres, but power is nearly identical to its forebear. The Jalpa, though, is a much better drive and consequently sold in much higher numbers than the car it replaced, despite largely similar styling.

Total produced 421 **Layout** Mid-engine, rear-wheel drive **Engine** V8 3.5-litre **Power** 255bhp/7000rpm **Top speed** 154mph

COUNTACH QV/ ANNIVERSARY 1985-1990

The Quattrovalvole saw Countach sales really take off, with the V12 now 5.2 litres in size and boasting 455bhp: more than Ferrari's contemporary Testarossa and 288 GTO. The QV's bewinged body was further embellished for the Countach 25th Anniversary, introduced in 1988.

Total produced 1275 **Layout** Mid-engine, rear-wheel drive **Engine** V12 5.2-litre **Power** 455bhp/7000rpm **Top speed** 184mph

LM002 1986-1992

The all-terrain LM002 stands out like a sore thumb in Lamborghini's model history, with styling that shouts loudly about the car's military origins. With the 5.2-litre engine from the Countach QV, 0-60mph takes a reasonably sprightly 7.7sec. It cost over three times as much as a Range Rover in its day, making it a rare beast now.

Total produced 301 **Layout** Front-engine, four-wheel drive **Engine** V12 5.2-litre **Power** 450bhp/6800rpm **Top speed** 130mph

DIABLO 1990-1998

As the '80s came to a close, the Countach was replaced by another iconic Gandini-designed supercar, the Diablo. A number of variations of the standard car were available over the years, with coupe and roadster body styles, the limited-run 520bhp SE30, and the VT, which introduced four-wheel drive to Lamborghini's supercar range.

Total produced 2332 **Layout** Mid-engine, rear/four-wheel drive **Engine** V12 5.7-litre **Power** 492bhp/6800rpm **Top speed** 183mph+

DIABLO SV 1995-1999

The SV (Super Veloce) badge returned in the mid-'90s, paring back the Diablo's weight considerably over the VT and returning it to rear-wheel drive. There was a three-way adjustable rear spoiler as well as a small hike in horsepower for its 5.7-litre V12. A handful of race-ready 540bhp SVR versions were also produced.

Total produced 234 inc. SVR **Layout** Mid-engine, rear-wheel drive **Engine** V12 5.7-litre **Power** 500bhp/7000rpm **Top speed** 186mph

DIABLO GT
1999-2000

Even more hardcore than the SV, the Diablo GT boasted extreme body mods and carbonfibre panels. The bigger capacity V12 was particularly potent too, with 575bhp on tap and the potential to hit 210mph depending on the gear ratios and rear wing configuration. The last all-Lamborghini Lambo before the Audified Diablo 6.0.

Total produced 113 **Layout** Mid-engine, rear-wheel drive **Engine** V12 6-litre **Power** 575bhp/7300rpm **Top speed** 210mph

DIABLO 6.0 VT 2000-2001
Audi took over Lamborghini in 1998 and,
keen to keep the Diablo fighting-fit while a
replacement was developed, gave the ageing
supercar a major overhaul for 2000. There
were styling changes inside and out as well as
a 550bhp iteration of the GT's 6-litre engine,
with a host of refinements to keep it on terms
with Ferrari's sophisticated 550 Maranello.

Total produced 383 **Layout** Mid-engine,
four-wheel drive **Engine** V12 6-litre **Power**
550bhp/7100rpm **Top speed** 205mph

MURCIÉLAGO 2001-2006

As another decade began, the Diablo made way for the Murciélago, the first all-new Lamborghini produced under Audi ownership. The more subdued but still unmistakably Lambo styling was the work of Luc Donckerwolke, and the Murciélago signalled a new, accessible side to the Fighting Bull without losing the raw excitement of the legendary V12. A Roadster version came along in 2004.

Total produced 1500 (approx) **Layout** Mid-engine, four-wheel drive **Engine** V12 6.2-litre
Power 570bhp/7500rpm **Top speed** 205mph

GALLARDO 2003-2008

The spiritual successor to the Urraco, the Gallardo's design brief was simple: take on the Ferrari F430 and Porsche 911 Turbo and win. It's an impressive package – a surefooted four-wheel-drive chassis mated to a screaming V10 engine. There were some complaints about its relative conventionality, though – it even has normal doors!

Total produced 7500 (approx) **Layout** Mid-engine, four-wheel drive **Engine** V10 4.7-litre
Power 513bhp/8000rpm **Top speed** 196mph

MURCIÉLAGO LP640
2006-present

Both coupe and convertible Murcies were given an overhaul in 2006, with an increasingly packed supercar marketplace forcing Lamborghini to raise its game. An engine upgrade, from 6.2 to 6.5 litres, ensured a nicely potent 631bhp. The Roadster offers full access to the gorgeous V12 soundtrack.

Total produced Still in prod. **Layout** Mid-engine, four-wheel drive **Engine** V12 6.5-litre **Power** 631bhp/8000rpm **Top speed** 211mph

GALLARDO SUPERLEGGERA
2007-2008

Meaning 'Super light', the Superleggera does exactly what it says on the tin, being a lighter, more hardcore Gallardo. Grip levels are phenomenal and it's a real weapon with which to attack roads, but it's flawed by its grabby carbon ceramic brakes and the clunky e-gear transmission.

Total produced 618 **Layout** Mid-engine, four-wheel drive **Engine** V10 4.7-litre **Power** 522bhp/8000rpm **Top speed** 196mph

REVENTÓN 2008

A refreshing moment of insanity from Lamborghini: a slightly more powerful Murciélago that costs five times as much as its donor car (a cool £1million). Yet somehow the Reventón gets away with it, being a supremely collectable supercar for those rich enough to afford one and perfect schoolboy poster material for those who can't.

Total produced 20 **Layout** Mid-engine, four-wheel drive **Engine** V12 6.5-litre **Power** 641bhp/8000rpm **Top speed** 211mph

GALLARDO LP560-4
2008-present

A mid-life update for the Gallardo, with more power and styling tweaks that make it a truly great looking car. The 200mph barrier was breached and the driving experience improved further, while the upgrade for the Gallardo Spyder – introduced in 2009 – is as close to perfect as its hard-top sibling.

Total produced Still in prod. **Layout** Mid-engine, four-wheel drive **Engine** V10 5.2-litre **Power** 552bhp/8000rpm **Top speed** 202mph

MURCIÉLAGO LP670-4 SV
2009-present

The swansong for both the Murciélago and
Lamborghini's classic V12 engine that, in one form
or another, has put in over 40 years of service.
It's an entirely fitting send-off. While it remains
all-wheel drive, the modern-day SV still manages to
be utterly mad both in looks and sheer speed, with
extra power and less weight.

Total produced 350 **Layout** Mid-engine,
four-wheel drive **Engine** V12 6.5-litre **Power**
661bhp/8000rpm **Top speed** 212mph

GALLARDO
LP550-2
2009

The special edition Gallardo
LP550-2 Valentino Balboni,
built to commemorate the
retirement of the brand's
legendary test driver, marked
a welcome return for the
rear-drive Lamborghini. It
injected a dose of extra
excitement into the brand's
baby supercar to make this
the best iteration yet.

Total produced 250 **Layout**
Mid-engine, rear-wheel drive
Engine V10 5.2-litre **Power**
542bhp/8000rpm
Top speed 199mph

The very latest version of the seemingly immortal Lamborghini V12, now up to 6.5 litres and 661bhp, pictured in the carbonfibre engine bay of the 2009 Reventón Roadster